The State You're In

UNIVERSITY PRESS OF FLORIDA

Florida A&M University, Tallahassee
Florida Atlantic University, Boca Raton
Florida Gulf Coast University, Ft. Myers
Florida International University, Miami
Florida State University, Tallahassee
New College of Florida, Sarasota
University of Central Florida, Orlando
University of Florida, Gainesville
University of North Florida, Jacksonville
University of South Florida, Tampa
University of West Florida, Pensacola

THE STATE

FLORIDA MEN,

FLORIDA WOMEN,

AND OTHER WILDLIFE

CRAIG PITTMAN

YOU'RE IN

University Press of Florida

Gainesville · Tallahassee · Tampa · Boca Raton

Pensacola · Orlando · Miami · Jacksonville · Ft. Myers · Sarasota

The following articles were originally published in *Sarasota Magazine*: "Last Look" (July 2010), "Loved to Death" (April 2013), and "Unintelligible at Any Speed" (August 2017). Reprinted with permission of *Sarasota Magazine* and SagaCity Media, Inc. All rights reserved.

Illustrations on pages ii–iii by Andy Marlette

First cloth printing, 2021
First paperback printing, 2022

27 26 25 24 23 22   6 5 4 3 2 1

ISBN 978-0-8130-6695-0 (cloth) | ISBN 978-0-8130-6886-2 (pbk.)
Library of Congress Control Number: 2021930601

The University Press of Florida is the scholarly publishing agency for the State University System of Florida, comprising Florida A&M University, Florida Atlantic University, Florida Gulf Coast University, Florida International University, Florida State University, New College of Florida, University of Central Florida, University of Florida, University of North Florida, University of South Florida, and University of West Florida.

University Press of Florida
2046 NE Waldo Road
Suite 2100
Gainesville, FL 32609
http://upress.ufl.edu

To all the Florida storytellers who came before me, with thanks for all their efforts at educating us about the Most Interesting State. As for the ones who come after me, I hope this helps you understand what we were thinking.

CONTENTS

Introduction   1

PART I. FLORIDA MEN AND FLORIDA WOMEN

1. Working for Scale   7
2. A Florida Love Story (with Tattoos)   11
3. Of Nudists and Their Packages   13
4. Panacea amid a Pandemic   15
5. The Ketchup Murder   18
6. The House of Turtles   25
7. The Ballad of Alligator Ron   29
8. Oh, Snapp!   33
9. Gambling on Nature   37
10. Thankful for the Turkey Lady   40
11. One Foot in Front of the Other   43
12. Elvis and the Florida Man   48

PART II. CRIME DOES NOT PAY (ENOUGH)

13. "The Phoniest Sumbitch That Walks"   53
14. Encyclopedia Brown and the Case of the Mysterious Author   59
15. Mug Shots   65
16. "An Alias Name"   68
17. The Bard of Boca Raton   74
18. Unintelligible at Any Speed   82
19. Mission of a Lifetime   86
20. Double Trouble   91
21. "The Morning from Hell"   96
22. Bradys on a Train   104

23. Killing Time on Death Row   106

24. A Flash of Green   115

25. Fifty-Five Seconds   120

26. The Wonderful World of Willeford   129

PART III. WILD, WILD LIFE

27. The Fastest Gopher in Florida   141

28. A Nasty Bathroom Surprise   143

29. Swamp Thing   147

30. Cukes for Couples   151

31. Monkeys Amok   154

32. We're Going on a Bear Hunt   157

33. Loved to Death   161

34. Where the Buffalo Roam   168

35. Last Look   171

36. Cat Fight in the Lap of Luxury   174

37. So Long, Snooty   179

38. Snakes Alive!   183

PART IV. THE STATE YOU'RE IN

39. Don't Okahumpka My Wewahitchka!   193

40. Farewell to Some Classic Florida Kitsch   195

41. Haunted Highway   198

42. Statues We'd Salute   200

43. The Bridge to Nowhere   203

44. The Last Bookstore   207

45. Let Us Now Praise Florida Lovebugs   210

46. Dying Every Night at the Rodeo   213

47. Hurricane Central   223

48. Andrew, Plus 10   226

49. Springs of Love   233

50. My Florida Bucket List   237

51. Uncle Carlyle Knew the Way   240

Acknowledgments   243

INTRODUCTION

On a beautiful spring morning in 2020, I was sitting in the waiting room at a car repair place in St. Petersburg when I got a text from my boss's boss. She asked: Did I have a minute to chat on the phone? Yes, I said, dreading what came next.

Sure enough, one four-minute phone call later, I had joined the ranks of America's rapidly growing multitudes of laid-off newspaper journalists. That's all it took to end 40 years of writing words to fill a daily product made out of dead trees, 30 of them at the same paper, the one that billed itself as Florida's best. I couldn't complain—I had had a great run. I had lasted longer than some other people whom I knew were far more important to the newspaper's continued smooth operation.

But as I sat there in that waiting room, newly unemployed, it occurred to me that this was not the way I had intended my career to play out.

Four decades ago, when I was snoozing through an 8 a.m. "Introduction to Journalism" class at what was then called Troy State University in Alabama, I was not one of those idealists who heard a heavenly call to a long-term career of writing newspaper stories.

As courtly old Dean James W. Hall attempted to drum into our thick freshman skulls his lessons about the inverted pyramid lede, AP style and what he called "the POW-aaahhh of the PRAY-uss," I dozed on, secure in the belief that whatever I was missing was not, in the long run, all that important. For me, a journalism degree was just a stepping-stone toward my real goal: writing the Great American Novel.

My plan, I thought, was pure genius: Work for five years as a newspaper reporter, starting in my hometown of Pensacola and then moving on to some place more cosmopolitan, like New York or Los Angeles. I would use that time to hone my writing skills. Learn about the world. Gather ideas. Then I would use everything I had learned and gathered and honed to write my novel, which I was sure would be a huge bestseller. After that I would retire on the proceeds from the movie sale and do something *really* worthwhile—maybe travel around doing good deeds and righting wrongs like Kwai Chang Caine from the TV show *Kung Fu*. What could go wrong?

I have actually written a couple of novels since then, neither of them great—in fact, neither of them publishable and thus of zero interest to Hollywood. In the meantime, I just kept on slogging along in the news biz, learning little by little about how to write and about the world, lingering well past my self-assigned five-year sell-by date. I never made it to New York or Los Angeles, for the simple reason that I found way too many great stories to tell right here in Florida.

Thus, instead of the Great American Novel, I have produced reams and reams of nonfiction—articles and columns for the *Pensacola News Journal*, the *Sarasota Herald-Tribune*, and the *St. Petersburg Times*, now known as the *Tampa Bay Times;* stories for various magazines, including *Sarasota* and *Flamingo;* and freelance pieces for such online publications as *Crime Reads* and *Slate*. After my March 2020 layoff from the *Times*, I began writing weekly columns for an online news organization, the *Florida Phoenix*, and continued freelancing for *Politico*, the *Washington Post*, etc. Along the way I wrote five nonfiction books on such subjects as the destruction of wetlands, illicit orchids, and endangered panthers. One of them did make it onto the *New York Times* bestseller list—for a whole week!

This book, then, is a distillation of what I've been doing with the tools and techniques that Dean Hall (and, later, Dean Judy Means Wagnon, whom we students called "Judy Means Business") tried to teach me about the inverted pyramid lede and the "POW-aaahhh of the PRAY-uss."

Don't call this a "best-of" collection. It includes none of the stories that won national and state awards. Those ended up being turned into books of their own, so including them in a collection would be redundant.

Instead, what I've gathered here are some of my quirkier pieces: a deep dive into Florida's mermaid industry; a love story involving the most tattooed lady in the world; a wild ride with an audacious con man. There are some serious pieces, too, including a meditation on those Florida mug shots we often laugh about; an obituary for Florida's most famous manatee; and a profile of a fugitive whose second life was far more satisfying than his first. I wrote about Florida institutions, like Jack Rudloe and his Gulf Specimen lab, and Florida influencers you may never have heard of, like M. C. Davis and Donald J. Sobol. There are scientists tracking a fabled beast and a radio pundit who had to fake his death. There is also a lady who got arrested for shoplifting while dressed as a turkey.

My hope is that, taken together, these pieces paint a vivid picture of this amazing state we're in—my native state, my favorite state, the state that inspires me to write. A lot of people treat it like it's the Punch Line State, but I contend it's really the Most Interesting State. This is a place that's easy to caricature and disregard. But there's more going on here than is dreamt of by all your stereotypes, and if you're ever bored here, that's your own fault. Sometimes it's wild and dangerous, sometimes it's inspiring and gorgeous, and a lot of times it's all of those at once. To me, Florida is an evolutionary test—if you can survive this, if you can thrive here, then you *are* the fittest.

part 1

FLORIDA MEN AND FLORIDA WOMEN

WORKING FOR SCALE

Tampa Bay Times, July 1, 2018

Florida's best-known industries include citrus, seafood and selling tacky souvenirs to tourists. But there's one booming Florida industry that hardly ever gets a mention from the Chamber of Commerce folks.

Mermaids.

All over the state there are now scores of women—and a few men— who regularly pull on prosthetic tails and pretend to be those mythical creatures made popular by Hans Christian Andersen and Walt Disney. Some do it for fun, but quite a few are diving into it as a business, charging by the hour to appear at everything from birthday parties to political events.

"This mermaid industry has just skyrocketed. It's crazy," said Eric Ducharme, aka "the Mertailor," whose Crystal River–based business is making high-quality tails. "I don't know if it's a fad, or if it's here to stay."

To judge how crazy the mermaid business is right now, consider this: Ducharme, a Lecanto native, sells custom-designed tails for up to $5,000 each. He's working on 80 now, each one designed to match the customers' personal measurements.

"Half of those people who have purchased those tails are just hobbyists," he said. "It's a way for people to connect to a different world, but not in a weird type of sense."

But for the rest, it's a business and they're all trying to make a splash. Their swimming may look leisurely, but they hustle for high-profile gigs. For instance, when Tampa played host to the Republican National Convention in 2012, a party at the Florida Aquarium featured mermaids cavorting in the fish tanks.

To see where Florida's mermaid industry started, you have to visit Weeki Wachee Springs State Park. That's where Ducharme got his start, too, although he quit when he was a teenager, blaming what he called "mermaid politics" for ruining his dream job.

A former Navy frogman named Newton Perry created this Hernando County roadside attraction in 1947 by cleaning all the old refrigerators and other junk out of the spring and building an underwater theater full of hidden air hoses. Then he hired nubile women to perform a languid, aquatic ballet in the crystal-clear water, to the delight of the ticket-buying public.

In the 1950s, Weeki Wachee was one of the nation's most popular tourist stops, but it nearly went belly-up in the 2000s when the profits (ahem) tailed off. In 2008, the Florida Department of Environmental Protection bought it and turned it into a state park.

As a result, Florida is the only state where the list of government jobs includes "mermaid." Starting pay is $10 an hour.

When Weeki Wachee held auditions in January 2018 for six new mermaid positions, 60 people showed up, despite the cold. In maybe the most Florida thing ever, a manatee surfaced in the spring right in the middle of their swimming trials.

Stayce McConnell, 38, the lead mermaid at Weeki Wachee, grew up watching the mermaid shows and marveling at the way they glided through the water. Now, after 16 years on the staff, she oversees the training for the newbies. It combines earning scuba certification, learning first aid and underwater choreography, plus "all the tests you have to take to be a state employee," she said.

The ones selected trained hard for three months before ever swimming in their first show. Their graduation was marked by performing a routine they designed.

"Once you know how to be a mermaid, it's something that's a part of you," she said. "You don't do it for the money. You do it for the experience."

But other mermaids are definitely in it for the money. In St. Augustine, Trina Mason started out playing around with underwater photography, which led to her becoming a mermaid for hire who also breathes fire and occasionally juggles. She's been doing it for six years, most recently at Wolf's Museum of Mystery.

She had to figure out the business on her own. She once caught her own chin on fire. She spent $400 on her first tail, and it caused an uproar among the other mermaids because it was a copy of someone else's. Her second, an original by the Mertailor, cost $2,600. She now charges $300 an hour to swim around in that 60-pound silicone-and-neoprene special.

Meanwhile, down in Fort Lauderdale, Marina Anderson regularly pulls on her tail to do snap rolls as she swims past the portholes in the historic Wreck Bar. She became fascinated by the life aquatic as a girl in Puerto

Marina Anderson (*center*), who goes by the names "MeduSirena" and "Marina, the Fire Eating Mermaid," poses with some of the mermaids she leads in underwater performances for the patrons of the Wreck Bar in Fort Lauderdale. Photo courtesy of Marina Anderson.

Rico, watching Jacques Cousteau documentaries and Esther Williams movies. She started free diving before she was 10 and later studied marine biology.

Now she considers herself "a dance performer" who models her mermaid moves on sea lions. She supervises a squad of 15 mermaids who put on seven shows a week at the Wreck Bar. Sometimes they perform underwater burlesque in which the tails come off.

She's even done some fire-eating (not to be confused with fire-breathing), earning her the nickname of "Marina, the Fire Eating Mermaid." She also goes by "MeduSirena." She's 47, and jokes, "It's a good thing water lifts!"

She wants bar patrons watching her show to become immersed in the illusion that they're watching a real mermaid.

"If I chill right in front of one of the windows and they aren't thinking about the fact that I'm not breathing and my eyes are being assaulted by chemicals, but they're just appreciating the artistry of it, then my job is done," she said.

Serena Woody, 29, of Pensacola, started off making mermaid-themed art, then began dressing as a mermaid to sell it at art shows, and then wound up running a business called Mermaids of Nue Blue Hues.

She's part of a "pod" of 15 part-time mermaids who, she said, like to get together once or twice a month to "take a break from reality and be weird and swim around for an hour or two and then go have lunch."

Six of them work for her, rotating duties as they show up at birthday parties and other celebrations for pay. If the event is on dry land, that's $150 for two hours. If they have to swim around, then they charge $250 for two hours.

"The mermaid community is bigger than people realize," Woody said. "Maybe it's because we're kind of below the surface."

A FLORIDA LOVE STORY (WITH TATTOOS)

Tampa Bay Times, February 13, 2018

This is a Florida love story.

It involves tattoos, of course.

Tattoos, along with citrus and sunburns, are modern Florida's most popular products. Ink, you might say, is in our blood. That's because, with our constantly warm weather, we tend to expose a lot of our skin here, so lots of people like to augment their epidermis with art.

When Florida cops look for distinguishing characteristics among their suspects, they can often count on distinctive ink to help them find the perps. There was the suspect who got his head tattooed to look like Tom Brady's New England Patriots football helmet (and boy howdy is he probably disappointed with this month's Super Bowl loss to the Eagles). Then there was the guy whose tattoo transformed his face into something resembling The Joker. Incidentally, he listed his profession as "tattoo model." In 2012, St. Petersburg police were able to track down a bank robber because he had the words "MOST WANTED" tattooed on his arms.

Tats are so identified with Florida culture that when author Lynn Waddell put together a book called *Fringe Florida* all about the Sunshine State's nudist resorts, UFO fans and exotic wildlife breeders, the cover featured the title tattooed across a woman's back, along with a pair of pistols.

Is it any wonder that the National Tattoo Association holds its annual conventions in Orlando?

But now we've got some good news about a Florida woman and her tattoos. The Guinness Book of World Records recently named her the Most Tattooed Woman Alive (that last word is an important distinction).

No, her name is not "Lydia" (sorry, Groucho Marx fans). It's Charlotte Guttenberg. She's 69, a fifth-generation Floridian now living in Melbourne. According to Guinness, she's covered 98.75 percent of her figure with designs, leaving only her face and a part of her hands untouched by the needle.

Until she was 56, she didn't have a single tattoo. Her husband wouldn't allow it, she said. He had tattoos himself but didn't think they belonged on ladies.

A few years after he died, she finally got her first tattoo. She also saw a painting of someone with an entire body full of tattoos, and said, "That's what I want."

On her second visit, she got a detailed tattoo of a rose garden, four inches wide, that wrapped around her thigh. Creating it required her spending hours dealing with the pain. The tattooist asked a regular customer named Chuck Helmke to sit with her and help her get through it. He held her hand and talked to her for hours.

Afterward they talked and talked on the phone. Helmke's wife had died, so he was alone too. The next time he saw her, he took her in his arms and gave her a big, bend-over-backwards kiss.

"He's a pretty good kisser," Guttenberg said. "That sealed the deal."

The pair have been together for more than a decade. Helmke, 76, now holds a Guinness record as well, as the Most Tattooed Senior Citizen (Male). Last year they were declared the Most Tattooed Senior Citizen Couple, which I like to think of as the "Do Not Go Gentle Into That Good Night Award."

Incidentally, Ms. Guttenberg's LinkedIn account lists her occupation as "Writer; Lifestyle Coach; Weapons Trainer/Range Safety Officer at The American Police Academy, Hypnotist." She's penned a series of novels in which, she says, tattoos play a major role.

A UPI dispatch notes that the couple "also each hold an additional record as Guttenberg has the most feathers tattooed on the body with 216 and Helmke has the most skulls tattooed on the body at 376."

When I asked her what had kept them together, though, Guttenberg said, "Not tattoos! That's just a fraction of our lives. We're together because we love each other."

In case you're wondering, though, neither of them has a tattoo that matches one on the other's body. Each of them is unique.

OF NUDISTS AND THEIR PACKAGES

Tampa Bay Times, March 13, 2018

The other day some folks at a Florida nudist resort in Pasco County made headlines because, they said, their letter carrier refused to bring their mail inside the front gate. They blamed discrimination.

About 150 people live at the clothing-optional Eden RV Resort in Hudson, according to one of the owners, who said his name was Dan—just Dan. (Apparently Eden is also last-name-optional.)

Most mail for Eden residents goes to a row of boxes by the gate, Dan said. But if there's a package, then the letter carrier is supposed to schlep it inside the gate and deliver it to the recipient's door.

One letter carrier refused to deliver packages in Eden, apparently because she didn't like seeing the residents dressed like the original residents of Eden, Adam and Eve. The U.S. Postal Service's famous "neither rain, nor snow, nor sleet" credo doesn't cover "seeing things that would require pouring bleach into the carrier's eyeballs."

In a five-minute interview, Dan said four times that the resort itself has no problem with the postal service. Just a couple of residents had complaints, he said, but "they were legitimate."

The postal service better watch out. Florida's nudist resorts could be a politically powerful force if they wanted to be. According to the American Association for Nude Recreation, Florida has more nudist resorts than any other state—29 registered clubs, well ahead of second place California's 14.

We've got every kind of nudist resort you could ask for. We've got high-end, expensive ones—although how you can tell that they're expensive if nobody's wearing clothes, I do not know. We've also got, at the other end, a resort run by a group called "the Bare Buns Biker Club," which sounds like a really bad idea. The word "chafing" comes to mind.

They can be public-spirited folks, albeit ones in need of more sunscreen than the average Floridian. As Hurricane Irma bore down on us, one Florida nudist resort offered to take in evacuees. And none of them would have had to pack any clothes, either.

Florida has so many nudist resorts that the American Association of Nude Recreation is headquartered in Kissimmee. Also located in Kissimmee: the American Nudist Research Library, in case you want to go read about the history of nudism while you're naked. (Be sure you bring a towel so you don't stick to the chairs.)

The Florida nudist resort that's been around the longest is the Lake Como Family Nudist Resort, originally chartered in 1941 as the "Florida Athletic and Health Association." Among its amenities is a bar called "The Butt Hut" (I assume that means smoking is allowed). It's in Pasco County, which has its own claim to naked fame.

"Pasco County has several large communities . . . and is considered the 'nudist capital of the U.S.,'" said Mark Haskell Smith, the author of *Naked at Lunch: A Reluctant Nudist's Adventures in the Clothing-Optional World.*

Pasco has so many nudist resorts that a Realtor discovered she could specialize in selling to nudists and make big bucks. She even landed her own reality TV show, which deserved a special Emmy just for its artful editing.

Smith said he's never before heard of nudist resort residents complaining of discrimination because someone who's clothed didn't want to enter their gates.

"The complaints are usually the other way around," he said, citing as an example concerns about nudists showing up not at a resort but at a public beach.

I'm hopeful the Eden folks and the postal service can work this out. When you strip the situation down to its bare essentials, this whole brouhaha isn't such a serious disagreement after all. It's only skin deep.

―――――――――――――――――――――――――――――――――――

Note: In June 2020, I wrote a story for the Washington Post *about how Florida's nudist resorts were coping with coronavirus. One of the people I interviewed was Eric Schuttauf, who heads up the American Association for Nude Recreation, based in Kissimmee. He told me that thanks to everyone wearing masks, "We'll have tan lines, but in a different place."*

PANACEA AMID A PANDEMIC

The Florida Phoenix, May 21, 2020

Usually, when you see Jack Rudloe in the spring, he's surrounded by schoolchildren and sea life. Usually the parking lot of Gulf Specimen Marine Laboratory, the only tourist attraction in the coastal town of Panacea about 40 minutes south of Tallahassee, is packed with school buses and cars with out-of-state plates.

Usually, Gulf Specimen's founder wanders around with a broad smile, answering questions and offering encouragement as children stick their hands into touch tanks or try to pick up enormous horseshoe crabs.

But these days his parking lot is bereft of buses and no one's lined up at the touch tanks to see what a starfish feels like. Worse, the various science labs that for decades have paid him to catch electric rays and other sea creatures for study have cut their orders.

"We've been in continuous operation for 56 years—until the coronavirus," Rudloe, 77, told me last week.

Rudloe, who launched Gulf Specimen in 1963 with encouragement from marine biology fan John Steinbeck, has been struggling to keep the doors open with just 10 percent of its normal income. What's fueling its continued existence, he said, is "pure stubbornness."

Gulf Specimen is a throwback to the glory days of the Florida roadside attraction, when you could watch regular shootouts at Six Gun Territory, buy a gnarled wooden clock from the Cypress Knee Museum, or gasp in amazement as Ross Allen handled rattlesnakes at his Reptile Institute.

Most of them faded away in the '70s and '80s in the face of competition from corporate entertainment behemoths like Disney and Universal. Only a handful, like Gulf Specimen, still hang on.

Like Allen, Rudloe is a classic Florida character—knowledgeable, feisty, sometimes profane, often at odds with developers and politicians. He has as many stories to tell as there are fish in the Gulf of Mexico.

Jack Rudloe (*center*), leading schoolchildren on an excursion to study marine life. He launched Gulf Specimen in Panacea in 1963 with encouragement from marine biology fan John Steinbeck. Photo courtesy of Jack Rudloe.

Some of those stories can be found in his books, which have titles like *The Sea Brings Forth, The Wilderness Coast, Time of the Turtle, The Living Dock at Panacea,* and *The Erotic Ocean.* (My mom, an avid reader, shared some of his books with me when I was younger, but never mentioned that last one.) Other entertaining yarns he has spun landed him on *Today* and *Good Morning, America* or in the pages of *National Geographic.*

Consider the tale of how he met his wife, Anne.

In 1969 she was a graduate student at Florida State, the institution that had given the Brooklyn-born Rudloe the boot for bad grades before he finished his freshman year. She was diving in the gulf to collect marine life for her studies, and after one trip had stopped at a gas station in Panacea, still in her wet suit.

"I determined that was a female in that thing, and invited her up to my lab," Rudloe said. She was unimpressed with him until he picked up a bright red sea squirt she had caught and said, "Oh, great, a *Polyandrocarpa maxima!*"

Because he knew the scientific name, Rudloe said, "instead of my etchings, she came to see my specimens and we went from there."

They wed in 1971 and she earned her Ph.D. eight years later. Rudloe credits her with the idea of converting his marine supply business into a showplace that offered educational experiences for the public. She died of cancer in 2012, a hard blow that—like hurricanes and the 2010 BP oil spill—Gulf Specimen somehow survived.

Rudloe got his start working on shrimp boats, picking up from the more experienced hands where to look for odd and unusual creatures found beneath the surface. Then he'd collect those and sell them to places like Harvard and Yale. He still refers to himself, somewhat tongue-in-cheek, as a mere fishmonger.

He's picked up other names over the years. He has been characterized as both a "nut" (by a county commissioner) and a "Gulf Guardian" (by the EPA).

Once, while he was at the microphone in a public meeting objecting to a paper mill's plans for a pipeline to dump pollution into the gulf, he was hauled off by a sheriff's captain. There's a species of jellyfish named after him. He has joked that it's because they're both so prickly.

In a way he reminds me of Johnny Appleseed, but instead of trees he plants in young minds a fascination with marine biology. Take, for example, acclaimed Tarpon Springs mural artist Christopher Still, whose work often features detailed depictions of Florida sea life. He credits Rudloe for that.

"When I was 8 or 9, my father took me over to meet him," Still told me. "He started pulling stuff out of the touch tanks and showing it to me—sea hares and sea cucumbers. . . . That Jack took the time to sit there and pull stuff out and show those things to me, it meant a lot. People who are excited about what they do excite other people, and children are attuned to the genuineness of it."

With the usual crowds of field-tripping kids kept away by the pandemic, Rudloe has been trying to fill the gap with live Facebook videos showing off some of the wet wildlife he finds so fascinating. One about seahorses drew more than 600 viewers. But Facebook Live videos don't pay the bills.

So here's hoping "pure stubbornness" is enough to preserve the endangered species that is Gulf Specimen, the pride of Panacea—if not for Rudloe's sake, then for the sake of all the kids who haven't yet learned just how amazing it can be to see a horseshoe crab up close.

5

THE KETCHUP MURDER

St. Petersburg Times, November 2, 1992

Ben Henry Pooley just can't shut up.

In 10 minutes he will go on the air with the latest edition of "Ben Henry's News and Views," and the fans in Pace and Pea Ridge and Chumuckla will tune in to hear his outrageous comments. So Pooley sits in front of a microphone in the broadcast booth at WECM-AM, glancing over his notes, deciding which politician he will hammer like a luckless nail.

Meanwhile, the loudspeakers above Pooley's head are blaring a minister's sermonette that ranges from the Book of Ruth to the presidential race.

At the mention of politics, Pooley's head snaps up. The minister drones on, but Pooley starts talking to the other people in the booth about Ross Perot's charge that President Bush tried to smear him.

"He's a loose cannon!" Pooley bellows. "To accuse the president of something like that without one iota of evi . . ."

Just then Peggy Dorsey, who answers the station's telephone, sticks her head into the booth. "They can hear that on the air!" she hisses.

Pooley clams up. After a few minutes, though, he starts talking again. Again Mrs. Dorsey whispers, "They can hear you!"

Pooley simmers down, but not for long. Fortunately, the sermon ends, and it's time for his show to start. He can speak his mind at last.

The man has got to talk. If Pooley ever caught laryngitis it would be a fatal disease.

Actually, that might be the only thing that could do him in. Nothing else has.

Four times somebody has come after Pooley, trying to shut him up permanently, and four times he has survived—although the bomb that went off near his head 13 years ago did leave him deaf in one ear.

Pooley treats the murder attempts as lightly as if they were crank calls, joking that he has never had trouble getting insurance.

"I'm a good risk," he says. "You can't kill me!"

Then he turns serious. "I never knew that I rubbed on people that bad," he says.

But the fact is he did rub on people, people who disagreed with him over local politics.

In other parts of the country, local politics might be ho-hum. But in rural Santa Rosa County, it can be a matter of life and death. Nobody knows that better than Pooley.

Yet he, too, says he is puzzled about the motives of the man accused of trying to silence him: Clifford Wilson, a former county commissioner who 50 years ago played high school football with Pooley. They were more than just teammates then—they were best friends.

"It's hard to believe," Pooley said, "that anybody you grew up with would want to kill you."

☼

Pooley hails from a village called Bagdad, population 500, just outside the county seat of Milton. Bagdad was a lumber town, but Pooley's father worked for the Milton police force, a job Pooley said he got by knowing the chief.

Wilson was born in the piney woods miles from Milton, in a tiny settlement named Harold. His father dug up tree stumps and sold them to a plant that extracted their chemicals. It wasn't much of a living during the Depression, but the family never went hungry.

"The woods was full of 'possums," Wilson said. "We'd eat 'possum and sweet potatoes."

Life was hard and diversions were few. Campaign rallies drew people for miles around, and the candidates, Democrats all, would entertain the audience with stories and wisecracks.

Pooley displayed his talent for talk at Milton High as half of a two-man debate team that placed second statewide. He also played fullback for the football team. Blocking for him was Wilson.

The teammates became fast friends. When they joined the military after graduation, Airman Pooley corresponded with Seaman Wilson—a couple of country boys comparing notes.

After World War II, Wilson came home to Harold and started his own sawmill, a business he runs to this day. He is perpetually coated with sawdust, from his sweat-stained cap to his cracked work boots.

Pooley, however, went to the University of Florida on the GI Bill. Then he got a job with the county, inspecting dairies and cafes and installing septic tanks—and making contacts.

After six years, Pooley mounted his first campaign for public office, running for clerk of the court. He won that race but missed re-election by four votes. He never ran again, and even now fumes, "My election, it was stole."

But retired county property appraiser F. M. "Bubba" Fisher snorts at Pooley crying foul over an election. "Son," Fisher says, "he stole as many as was stole from him."

※

For all its entertainment value, politics in those days was a rougher sport than high school football.

Pints of whiskey would change hands before the polls opened—in a dry county, mind you. A winning candidate could pass out jobs and favors afterward.

Shrewd politicians calculated their support according to who was related to whom. "You could pretty well count on your family connections," recalled Wilson, who first won his seat on the county commission in 1956.

But a new era was about to dawn. Clayton Mapoles, owner of WEBY-AM, gave Pooley a radio show. Suddenly, in this society that placed so much emphasis on the gift of gab, one man could talk to every corner of the county.

"He had the megaphone all right," Fisher said.

Pooley made the most of it, employing his acid wit like an early Rush Limbaugh. He would talk about politicians by name, tagging them with labels like "the young gas-guzzling commissioner from Harold."

That, of course, was his old friend Wilson. Pooley implied that "Super Octane" Wilson gassed up his logging trucks from the county's fuel pumps, a bit of innuendo that infuriated Wilson. Mad as he and Pooley's other targets might have been, though, they listened every day to see what this wild man would say next.

"Thirty years ago, everybody who was anybody taped Ben Henry," Fisher said.

One morning deputies arrested Pooley because they found moonshine in his car. Pooley's police officer father saw his son dragged into the courthouse.

"If they'd got me upstairs they'd have really put a good whipping on me," Pooley said. "But Dad cocked his .38 and said, 'He's never been upstairs before and he's not going now.'"

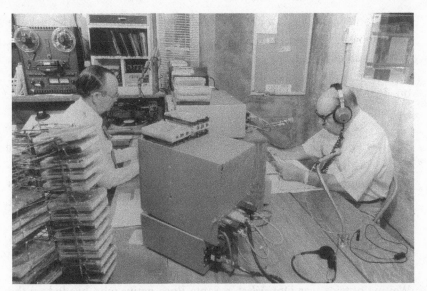

Radio show host Ben Henry Pooley (*right*, with WECM announcer Roy Dorsey) was the target of four assassination attempts. He joked that he had no trouble getting life insurance because "you can't kill me." Photo by Vicki Braun, used by permission of the *Tampa Bay Times*.

Set free, Pooley took to the airwaves to blast the people he said framed him. A grand jury refused to indict him.

His legal troubles weren't over. Wilson filed a $50,000 slander suit but lost. Then Wilson and several other politicians complained to the Federal Communications Commission. But the agency tossed out their complaints because Mapoles had offered everyone a chance to respond to Pooley—a ruling scholars cite as an important step in developing the Fairness Doctrine.

Fisher, who rarely sided with Pooley, figures the FCC made the right call.

"I'm not a fatalistic person by any stretch of the imagination, but some things have to be," he said. "Sometimes you need a Ben Henry Pooley. He keeps people honest."

Still, Santa Rosa split over the radio show. Fisher remembers going out to campaign and being asked where he stood on Pooley.

Finally, in 1968, the FCC yanked WEBY's license—not because of what Pooley said, but because Mapoles submitted false evidence defending himself against complaints about Pooley.

So Pooley found a new job, working for the county commissioners he had lambasted. He was hired as mosquito control director on a 3–2 vote. Wilson voted no.

Wilson and others repeatedly attempted to oust him, but Pooley hung on. Then somebody tried to do more than just fire him.

☼

The way Pooley describes what happened in 1979 is: "One morning about 2:30—BAM! The world exploded."

Eight sticks of dynamite, planted under his mobile home, blew his bathtub sky-high. The glass that held his dentures wound up on the roof of the trailer, with not a drop of water spilled.

Pooley walked away without a scratch, saved by a closet full of coats that muffled the blast. No one was ever charged with the bombing.

Then, one morning in 1984, Pooley heard a knock on his front door. Waiting outside was Don West, a Santa Rosa native who headed up the Florida Department of Law Enforcement's Pensacola office. He told Pooley someone had put out a contract on him.

What followed was an elaborate ruse designed to capture the man who had told an FDLE informant he would pay $10,000 to see Pooley's head blown off. The FDLE even set up a fake crime scene.

FDLE agents took Pooley out into the woods near his home, poured a bottle of ketchup on his head and snapped pictures of him lying on his back, looking dead. Then they spirited him off to a motel in Pensacola.

The deception worked too well. TV and radio reporters picked up rumors of Pooley's death and broadcast them as fact. Santa Rosans reeling from that shock then got another one: Pooley was alive, and the law had arrested Leroy Johnson, a former commissioner and father of state Rep. Bolley "Bo" Johnson.

Johnson swore he was innocent, even though he had stashed close to $10,000 in his car. He said it was for his re-election campaign.

Johnson never went to trial. Six days after his arrest, he died of a heart attack. Public sympathy turned against Pooley. Some people whispered that Johnson was framed.

What didn't come out at the time was that the FDLE suspected someone else of supplying the cash. Agents had trailed Johnson to Wilson's sawmill before they arrested him. Johnson didn't have the money before he went there, West said, but he did after he left. They had Johnson on tape saying his backer had told him, "I want the lights put out on that m——f——."

But they couldn't prove it was Wilson.

Three years passed. Suddenly, somebody was out to get Pooley again. This time the FDLE arrested William Chester Cole. An escaped felon named Curtis "Boo" Adams said Cole asked him to kill Pooley for a man named Wilson. In exchange, Adams said, he would get $7,000, and Cole would get enough lumber to finish his house.

A jury convicted Cole and sent him to prison for 35 years. But again the FDLE couldn't make a case against Wilson.

Finally, in 1988, the FDLE arrested Wilson. Agents said he had tried yet again to hire someone to kill his boyhood friend.

☼

Fisher never believed Wilson wanted Pooley dead—at least, not at the hands of a hit man.

"If he'd wanted to kill Ben Henry, he would've done it himself," Fisher said. "He's a gutty thing, a gritty old thing."

But taped conversations between Wilson and a Pace logger named Charles Faulk seemed to indicate otherwise—that not only was Wilson willing to pay Faulk $8,000 to kill Pooley, but that he was behind the previous murder attempts as well.

In person, though, Wilson denied everything and blamed his arrest on politics. "They all was in cahoots against me—the judge, the prosecutor, the whole bunch," he said.

He spent $60,000 to fight the charges. In the end, a jury agreed he was innocent.

"I can't understand how he walked," West said. "It was an overwhelming case. If it had been tried in any of the other 66 counties in Florida, the verdict would've been different."

But to Pooley it makes perfect sense. Faulk had a lengthy arrest record, so nobody believed him. Wilson was a respected businessman and former commissioner.

For his part, Wilson still denies he ever tried to kill Pooley.

"I never solicited nobody," he says. "They solicited me."

About a year ago, Wilson spotted Pooley in the parking lot at Hardee's and called him over.

"We agreed my problem wasn't with him and his problem wasn't with me," Wilson said. "We shook hands and buried the hatchet."

☼

Instead, Wilson said, his problem was with West, the now-retired FDLE agent. Both Wilson and West mounted campaigns for sheriff this fall and all Wilson's campaigning was aimed at defeating West. He warned voters they didn't want a sheriff who would deceive people about whether someone was dead. West lost and although Wilson didn't win, he was happy.

"I guess he satisfied that vengeance in his heart," West said.

Wilson is 67 now and Pooley 69. They won't ever be as close as they were in high school, but at least they're on speaking terms again.

"I think it's behind us," Pooley said.

Almost all the people Pooley battled long ago are dead or retired. But he's got a new crop of politicians to pick on, because last year he went back on the radio again for the first time in 25 years.

His drive to the station each day carries him past a graveyard, but he doesn't worry about winding up there. Shortly after he left the air in the '60s, Pooley was ordained as a Baptist minister, and he says he won't die until God is ready for him to stop preaching.

Although Pooley has popped up on national TV as recently as last week talking about his flamboyant career, he is no longer the celebrity he used to be in his hometown. Thousands of new people have moved into Santa Rosa in recent years, turning farm towns into suburban enclaves.

"If you were to walk into some of the more recently developed subdivisions in Pace and call the name of Ben Henry Pooley and Clifford Wilson, the common person wouldn't know who you were talking about," West said.

Still, as Pooley rambles through his 25-minute program, he fields several phone calls from admiring fans, old-timers like himself. At the close of the show he ends with his trademark slogan: "What you don't know *will* hurt you!"

Just then Mrs. Dorsey pokes her head through the door one last time. "A lady called and said to tell you she loves you," she says.

Ben Henry pushes back from the microphone and mutters, "I'm glad to hear *somebody* does."

Note: Ben Henry Pooley finally died for real in May 2003—at home, and not from dynamite or an assassin's bullet. All the newspaper obituaries mentioned "The Ketchup Murder." The makers of Heinz Tomato Ketchup did not send a wreath, though.

6

THE HOUSE OF TURTLES

Tampa Bay Times, October 22, 2017

OVIEDO—In a small town about 5 miles from the University of Central Florida, there stands a two-story yellow house built in the 1920s. A modest sign mounted on the wall next to the front door says, "Chelonian Research Institute."

Step inside that door and you'll find the largest private collection of turtle and tortoise specimens in the world—13,000 individual pieces from 100 different countries, hanging on every inch of the walls and lining every table and shelf. Live ones crawl slowly around enclosures or swim in ponds around back.

The institute and its vast array of shells, skulls, skeletons and live creatures are the life's work of Peter C. H. Pritchard, a lanky and erudite scientist who has been called "the Jane Goodall of turtles." One of his many adoring colleagues refers to him as "the Turtle God." *Time* magazine declared him "A Hero of the Planet," although one of his children asked his sometimes-distracted dad, "Which planet?" Disney-bound tourists stepping off a plane at the Orlando airport see a huge photo of him holding a turtle. Worldwide, four species of turtle are named for him.

But Pritchard, 74, now suffers from Alzheimer's disease. The robust and perpetually inquisitive explorer who once climbed mountains and snorkeled beneath the sea chasing specimens is now rail thin and frail. During a visit earlier this month, he was unable to speak and seemed hesitant to take a step without someone helping him.

His vivacious wife, Sibille, 72, says his days of lecturing students are over. His vintage Rolls-Royce—a prized possession because family lore says one of his ancestors introduced Mr. Rolls to Mr. Royce—hasn't been cranked in months.

He now sits in his home across the street from the institute and flips idly through his own books. He perks up a bit when his wife puts on a BBC documentary about the time in 1971 when he helped discover Lonesome George, the last remaining Pinta Island tortoise and an icon for Galapagos Islands conservation.

His deteriorating condition raises the question: What will become of his collection, assembled over five decades?

Will it remain in little Oviedo, a hidden gem displayed according to Pritchard's own idiosyncratic system? Or will it wind up being absorbed into a museum or university, perhaps one outside Florida? Mrs. Pritchard says the institute's board has talked with several institutions, but nothing's resolved.

"We've got to come to grips with how to preserve it," said one institute board member, Orlando environmental consultant Mike Dennis. "The general consensus of the board members is that it's extremely valuable, and we need to find a long-term home, and a method of curating it."

When Pritchard was 10 years old, his grandparents took him to the London Zoo. He saw, for the first time, a turtle. He was thunderstruck by the exotic creature.

"I didn't even know there were such things before," he explained years later, his British accent clipped but genial.

He began reading everything he could find about them. The more he learned, the better he liked them.

"Turtles are not trying to dominate Earth," Pritchard once said. "They're just trying to survive."

Soon he was raising some as pets. When he was at Oxford University studying chemistry, he kept a tank full in his dorm. He kept meat to feed them, and he turned up his heater to maintain the proper temperature. It did not make him popular.

"You could smell those things from 20 yards away," his brother, Michael, said. "But Peter always did his own thing. He was going to do what he was going to do, and the rest of the world would have to adjust."

Eventually, Pritchard decided that instead of chemistry, he should study turtles. He moved to Gainesville to learn all he could from legendary University of Florida sea turtle expert Archie Carr, for whom the Archie Carr National Wildlife Refuge in Brevard County was later named.

Pritchard earned a Ph.D. in zoology there in 1969, and went on to write more than a dozen books, including *The Encyclopedia of Turtles*, a standard reference among scientists, and even a children's book, *Cleopatra the Turtle Girl*. He also wrote *Saving What's Left*, a manual on conserving environmentally sensitive lands in Florida, and helped write the first recovery plan for the endangered Florida panther.

But his passion remained turtles. He traveled the globe chasing them, pursuing snake-necked turtles in New Guinea and pond turtles in Myanmar, traveling throughout Asia and Africa filming a documentary called The Turtle Planet.

"I never asked him if he'd been somewhere," said his current assistant, Zach Burke, an Oviedo native. "Instead I would ask him when he was there."

Pritchard was determined to collect only already dead turtles and tortoises, instead of killing the specimens the way some scientists did, Burke said. That led to some odd situations.

Once in India, he found some rare remains near the Taj Mahal and snuck it back into his ritzy hotel. He began scooping the mostly liquefied carcass into the toilet so he could keep the shell. Meanwhile, according to Allen and Anita Salzberg of the publication Herp Digest, six hotel staffers were banging on his door because of complaints about the odor.

He didn't care. He got his shell.

Pritchard met his wife, a journalist, at a party in Guyana, where he was researching turtles. She had no interest in his favorite subject, but she found him fascinating. After all, how many men keep turtles and crocodiles in a bathtub, or dodged death in a sinking boat in the Galapagos? They married and had three children.

Pritchard was something of a throwback to the Victorian model of scientist, said Florida gopher tortoise expert George Heinrich. These days the trend in science is toward specialization in one region or one species, but "Peter's interest and knowledge was global and encyclopedic."

In 1998, on 15 acres in Oviedo, he opened his institute, named for the scientific order that covers turtles, tortoises and terrapins. He filled it with his still-growing collection, as well as books and research papers and live creatures, and invited anyone who was interested to stop by and see it, free of charge. Lots of people did, including Girl Scout troops, government officials and celebrities.

"You never knew who was going to show up," recalled a former assistant, Tim Walsh, now assistant director of the Florida Turtle Conservation Trust. "I'd be packing up to leave for the day and he'd say, 'Oh, you should stick around. Miss America is stopping by.'"

Anyone who tours the institute is, in a way, seeing into Pritchard's mind and personality, explained Simona Ceriani, a marine turtle expert with the state's Fish and Wildlife Research Institute in St. Petersburg, who regards Pritchard and his wife as her surrogate parents.

"That place is really him," she said.

He organized the displays to highlight not just the specimens themselves but also artwork and native crafts that give them a cultural context. There are plenty of shells and skeletons—and even one taxidermied loggerhead—that can be touched rather than merely observed.

"When he set it up, he didn't want it to be like a museum," Burke said. "He wanted it to be like visiting a friend's house."

And he delighted in playing tour guide, giving as much time to answer questions for a curious 4-year-old as he would to a visiting scientist. At one point several years ago, while Ceriani was trying to work with him on a project, he leaped up to show visitors around so frequently that she finally blurted out, "How do you get anything done?"

But now all that is changing.

Alzheimer's had already begun taking its toll on Pritchard when he experienced a bad reaction to an antibiotic recently. It has, for now, robbed him of speech and the ability to walk unaided, his wife said.

"When he was well, he would come over here every day to work," she said while showing visitors around the institute. She is hopeful those days are not forever gone.

The loss of Pritchard playing tour guide and mentor has already changed the experience of visiting the institute. Moving the collection to a university or museum would alter it even further, Ceriani said.

Without him, "you lose that personal touch and that relationship," Ceriani said. Pick up any piece in the collection, she said, and "Peter would tell you the story of how he got that sample."

Dennis said the board has held two meetings to discuss what to do about the institute's future, so far without figuring out an answer.

"We don't know what's going to happen" said Mrs. Pritchard, who's also on the board. "We are trying to preserve it—and keep it in Florida."

Note: Pritchard died February 25, 2020. In February 2021, the family announced the collection will be moved to an institute in Ojai, California.

7

THE BALLAD OF ALLIGATOR RON

Tampa Bay Times, February 3, 2019

Florida has had some colorful public servants over the years: a governor who claimed the Pope had sent hit men to kill him; a congressman who took payoffs from a fake sheik and then claimed he was collecting evidence for his own investigation; and, more recently, a U.S. senator who flew on the space shuttle and also went python-hunting.

And then there is Ronald "Alligator Ron" Bergeron, a former state wildlife commissioner whom Gov. Ron DeSantis just appointed to the South Florida Water Management District governing board this past week.

Bergeron tops them all.

For a hint of why, call up his office in Fort Lauderdale. The hold music is country star Tanya Tucker wailing a song called "Alligator Man."

It's about Bergeron.

"Wrestling alligators is his fame . . . He's the leader of our clan," the song goes. "He's the Alligator Man."

"She's a personal friend," Bergeron explains.

☼

Alligator Man only hints at Bergeron's many qualifications to be the most Florida of all Florida officeholders.

He's a gator-wrestling, python-hunting, rodeo-winning, airboat-piloting son of the Everglades. He's usually seen wearing a 10-gallon hat and a Texas-sized belt buckle, driving a black Hummer with gold trim that he calls his "Cowboy Cadillac."

Ask him his age, and Bergeron will say, "I'm 75, but you don't want to rassle me, OK?"

Bergeron is a mass of contradictions: An avid hunter who as a state wildlife commissioner cast the lone no vote against holding the first bear hunt in 21 years. A rancher who professes a love for Florida panthers, even though they have eaten some of his calves. A developer who says his great passion is restoring the Everglades.

"His commitment to the protection and restoration of the Everglades is unmatched and I think he will be a tremendous leader for South Florida," DeSantis said in a statement announcing Bergeron's appointment. DeSantis had previously demanded every water board member resign for approving a lease favoring the sugar industry over Everglades restoration.

However, Bergeron may face a conflict of interest. According to his website, one of his companies, Bergeron Land Development, has a $79 million Everglades restoration contract with that same water agency to build stormwater treatment areas to clean up pollution in farm runoff.

Bergeron has come a long way from the boy who watched his parents build their first home using old freight boxes salvaged from the nearby port. That house flooded often, back before the Army Corps of Engineers rejiggered South Florida's plumbing with canals, pumps and levees. Back then everyone would just head for high ground until the flood receded, then clean up and start over, Bergeron said.

At 18, he left his home in Davie with just $235 in his pocket. He was a millionaire by age 25 but kept living in a trailer until he was 41 so he could invest his profits. Now he's the CEO of a group of companies with interests that range from highway construction to rock quarries to hurricane debris cleanup.

He's also a rodeo champion who shows off his roping skills every Wednesday night at the Davie rodeo arena that bears his name, the Bergeron Rodeo Grounds. When he was thinking of running for governor last year, he joked that if he won, "they're going to have to put a hitchin' post at the governor's mansion." (Ultimately he and life partner Ali Waldman, an attorney, decided he should not run, and so he backed DeSantis.)

The family member who influenced him the most was his grandfather, an Everglades game warden named Lonnie P. Harvey. When Bergeron was a small boy, his grandfather brought him out into the River of Grass and showed him its majesty in those pre-Corps days.

"I will never forget the beauty he showed me in the woods and the environment," he said.

☼

Whenever dignitaries from Washington want to view the Everglades, it's Bergeron who always plays tour guide, piloting his airboat around what's left of the world's most famous marsh. Party doesn't matter. He took both Bush and Obama Administration officials around in his boat. When

Rodeo champ and onetime state wildlife commissioner Ronald "Alligator Ron" Bergeron helps release a rehabilitated Florida panther. He got his nickname from wrestling a gator that tried to kill him. Photo by Tim Donovan, courtesy of the Florida Fish and Wildlife Conservation Commission.

then-U.S. Sen. Bill Nelson, a Democrat, went on a python hunt, Republican Bergeron was his machete-swinging partner. (The snakes somehow managed to elude them and their large press contingent.)

During his 10 years on the Florida Fish and Wildlife Conservation Commission, Bergeron helped cook up the state's python hunt, argued for maintaining current protections for the panther and led the fight to make sure there wasn't a second bear hunt.

He is the only wildlife commissioner ever appointed to the board after being investigated for molesting an alligator—the source of his nickname.

In 2006, Bergeron was giving visitors a tour of his 5,000-acre Hendry County ranch when he spotted an alligator sunning itself near a pond. Although the gator appeared to be 7 feet long, Bergeron "demonstrated what he called 'an old cracker tradition' to his guests" and "began to wrestle with the alligator," an investigator from the state wildlife commission later wrote.

The gator wrapped its tail around Bergeron's leg, rolled him into the water, bit his left hand, "and proceeded to take him to the bottom of the pond," the official investigative report says. "Bergeron stated he began to strike the alligator on the nose as he was taught as a boy, several times."

The gator let go. Bergeron swam to the surface and went to a nearby hospital, where his fingers needed stitches.

State law forbids attempting to take, pursue, molest or capture an alligator without a license, and Bergeron basically confessed to the wildlife investigator about jumping on the reptile.

But when the investigator met with prosecutors in La Belle, they declined to pursue the case because "there was not enough evidence . . . to prosecute the subject."

While his fingers were still bandaged, Bergeron attended an event at the White House and met then-President George W. Bush. Bergeron explains what happened next.

When the president asked what caused his injury, Bergeron told him, "I was rassling an alligator."

Bush leaned in close and said: "You're kidding, right?"

Note: A review by the state Ethics Commission cleared Bergeron of accusations of a conflict of interest.

8

OH, SNAPP!

St. Petersburg Times, March 30, 1992

Note: When I worked in the St. Petersburg Times*'s Palm Harbor bureau, every spring an editor in Clearwater named Roy LeBlanc picked one reporter to come up with feature stories about spring training baseball. For a month you'd get paid to go to spring training games—what a scam! The year it was my turn, this story was my favorite.*

CLEARWATER—Mark Eddinger was collecting autographs around Jack Russell Memorial Stadium last week when he saw a white-haired man in a Philadelphia Phillies jersey sitting on a bench behind home plate.

Eddinger, 24, knew this was one celebrity's autograph he just had to have.

"Would you sign my glove?" he asked, clearly in awe. "You're kind of a legend to me."

The man took Eddinger's mitt and looked for a spot that hadn't already been filled by such big-name players as Dale Murphy and Mookie Wilson. Finally he found a space and wrote, "Wilbur Snapp, Three Blind Mice organist."

"This happens about 10 times a day," said Snapp, a big-name player in a league all his own.

Snapp, who lives in St. Petersburg, has been the official ballpark organist for the Phillies in Clearwater for 10 years. At 72, Snapp still plays the organ for the major-league team during spring training and for the minor-leaguers through the summer. He's as much a part of the national pastime as peanuts and Cracker Jacks.

One minor-league game gave him his 15 minutes of fame. In 1985, a 22-year-old umpire made what Snapp thought was a bad call at the plate, a call that went against Snapp's Phillies. Snapp responded with a rendition of "Three Blind Mice."

Clearwater Phillies organist Wilbur Snapp made a musical comment about an umpire's call, and what happened next cemented his place in baseball history. Photo by Joan Kadel Fenton, used by permission of the *Tampa Bay Times*.

The ump pointed up at the organist, then made a heave-ho motion with his thumb. Translation: You're out of the game.

Snapp's ejection made him a folk hero. He fielded phone calls from around the country. Weatherman Willard Scott mentioned it on NBC's *Today* show, and Paul Harvey talked about it on his syndicated radio show.

Clearly, the organist had struck a chord.

Seven years later, people still ask for his autograph, or take his picture, or just shake his hand. And Snapp, ever gracious, always obliges them, even on days when he's not feeling much like a star.

On the day Eddinger got his autograph, Snapp was battling an ear infection, a cold and a fever. A stiff breeze blowing in from the outfield made the temperature seem lower than the official 68 degrees. Snapp's wife, Janice, wasn't sure he should be outdoors, much less at the stadium.

"I feel like less than 2 cents," Snapp acknowledged. Nevertheless, he showed up before 10 a.m., determined to be at his Kawai organ during the game that afternoon. "People expect to see me here," he explained.

Snapp used to own a music store in Ohio. He taught himself to play the organ when he was 35. He plays by ear because he can't read music. He counts that as an advantage. On a windy day like this one he wouldn't be able to hang onto sheet music, much less read it.

He boasts a 3,000-song repertoire, mostly pop tunes from the '30s, '40s and '50s. Atop the organ he keeps a small notebook filled with song titles to jog his memory.

Often he uses the music to comment on the action. When the manager yanks a pitcher, Snapp may play "There'll Be Some Changes Made." Once, when Detroit Tigers manager Sparky Anderson got into a heated argument with an umpire, Snapp played "I Love You Truly" and cracked them both up.

Snapp has so many fans that he made a tape of his music and sells it at the ballpark. "My husband keeps your tape in his Walkman," Jeanenne Radabaugh told him before the game.

Lenny Dykstra led off the Phillies' batting order by smacking a homer. As Dykstra rounded the bases, Snapp went wild with the organ's sound-effect buttons, making electronic wow-wow-wows over and over.

Later, though, when the Tigers scored several runs, Snapp didn't touch the keyboard. "Hey, where's the organ?" asked some Tigers fans.

"They don't pay my salary," Snapp said. He often closes up the organ and leaves the park while the visiting team is at bat.

When the Tigers came up in the top of the seventh, Snapp wandered down to the tables that he and his brother-in-law, Elmer Finley, had set up before the game. The tables were covered with bats, broken Louisville Sluggers that Snapp has turned into wall racks, desk caddies, toy cars, mallets, and tomahawks. He makes thousands of dollars selling his home-made souvenirs.

Working at the tables during the game was Floyd Cassaday, 70, who met Snapp five years ago.

"We had season tickets and sat right in back of his organ," Cassaday said.

The Cassadays live about 30 miles north of Philadelphia. They got to be such good friends with the Snapps that they visit every spring. The Snapps reciprocate during the summer so they can see a few regular-season Phillies games.

The top of the seventh ended abruptly when the Phillies turned a double play. As the Tigers took the field, 7,350 people stood up and looked around for the organist. He was supposed to play "Take Me Out to the Ballgame" so they could sing along.

But on this day they stretched in silence. Snapp was still down by the souvenir tables. By the time he realized what had happened and scrambled back up to his bench, the game had resumed.

"I don't think I ever missed a seventh-inning stretch until today," Snapp said, shaking his head. "But while I was goofing off I sold $40 worth of bats."

If Snapp ever disappeared for more than just an inning, Peggy Celler would miss him. For eight years, the Dunedin resident always has held a ticket for Section 19, Row 12, Seat 4, putting her next to Snapp's organ.

She has visited other ballparks where there was no organist, and the fans had to listen to canned music. That leaves her cold.

"I prefer this," she said. "It makes it feel like a real ball game. The other is too artificial."

A spirited Snapp treatment of "When the Saints Go Marching In" failed to revive the Phillies, and they fell to the Tigers 8–3. As the crowd streamed toward the exits, Snapp kept up a peppy medley of anthems— the "Battle Hymn of the Republic," "God Bless America." People stopped to put a dollar or two in the jar on his organ, or to pat Snapp on the back.

He wound up with "There's No Place Like Home." But just as he was about to close the lid, some fans asked him to pose for another picture, and a guy with a video camera asked him to play "Take Me Out to the Ballgame" one more time. Snapp, aching to get out of the wind, nevertheless did as they asked. Finally they all left.

Snapp's brother-in-law was helping him pull a tarp over the organ, to protect it until the next game, when a man wandered up and asked a question Snapp has heard a hundred times.

"Excuse me," the man said. "Are you the organist who got thrown out of the game?"

Note: When Snapp died in 2013, his obituary in the New York Times *ran under the headline: "Wilbur Snapp, 83, Organist Ejected by Ump."*

9

GAMBLING ON NATURE

Tampa Bay Times, September 6, 2015

M. C. Davis was a gambler, a hard-nosed businessman, a guy determined to get his way—and a man who swooned over Florida nature.

His savvy and money saved thousands of acres of forests and swamps across the South and preserved more than a few species. For the past two decades he did this without attracting attention, until this year, when he was written up in *Smithsonian* and profiled by National Public Radio.

Last week he was saluted by the state wildlife commission. He will be honored this month at a national conference where he will be awarded the National Private Lands Fish and Wildlife Stewardship Award.

But Davis won't be there.

The man who spent much of his life avoiding the limelight killed himself this summer as he battled inoperable cancer.

"He's probably one of the most influential people you never heard of," said Julie Hauserman, a former *Times* reporter who worked for him as an environmental consultant for seven years.

Marion Clifton Davis grew up in bucolic Santa Rosa County. "I'm a dirt-road Panhandle guy," he told *Smithsonian,* which described him with a string of adjectives that included "jovial," "rumpled" and "forceful."

Davis's father died when he was young. To support his mother and two half-sisters he began hustling pool, then graduated to backroom poker games. He put himself through college and law school with his winnings, said his son-in-law, Pat Chisholm.

He practiced law a bit, didn't like it, tried other things—trading in commodities like timber, and oil and gas rights, buying up run-down companies and turning them around.

But his life had a hole in it. He'd made millions and married his high school sweetheart, a proper Southern lady named Stella. They'd raised three daughters and sent them off into the world. Now what? What was the point?

Then one rainy evening about 20 years ago, he got stuck in a typical Tampa tie-up on Interstate 4. He figured he'd pull off the highway and let the traffic clear. He spotted a marquee at a high school that advertised a lecture on bears. So he went.

Inside, he later recalled, was "an old drunk, a politician . . . and a couple of Canadians looking for day-old doughnuts and coffee." Up on stage were two women, Laurie MacDonald and Christine Small of Defenders of Wildlife, talking earnestly about Florida's black bears—then on the state's imperiled species list—and what it would take to save them.

Davis was surprised to learn Florida had bears. He stayed for the whole talk. The next day he gave Defenders enough money to keep its bear campaign going for two years.

He'd found his calling.

He began meeting regularly with MacDonald, giving her fits, peppering her with questions, challenging her to prove she was right. His conversion from right-wing capitalist to a self-professed nature nut was not an easy one.

"He had the steepest learning curve I've ever seen," MacDonald, a St. Petersburg resident, recalled, laughing. "We would begin with little debates. They were a little testy but fascinating."

She gave him a reading list. He soaked up the writings of John Muir, Henry David Thoreau and E. O. Wilson. He also started quietly buying up environmentally sensitive land—a lot of it in Florida, but also in Louisiana, Mississippi, Tennessee, Alabama, Georgia and the Carolinas.

He bought bat caves in three states to save their inhabitants. He bought 2-mile-long strips of land on either side of a Florida highway and built an underground crossing for freshwater turtles so they could get from one lake to another safely. He added thousands of acres to national forests and wildlife refuges, said Manley Fuller of the Florida Wildlife Federation.

Environmental groups might trumpet their plans to preserve land, only to see the price get jacked up. Not Davis. He'd sidle up, apparently just another good ol' boy timber buyer, and maneuver the seller into giving him a good price, not revealing his intentions until the deal was done.

"He was very good at staying quiet," Chisholm said. "He was always telling us, 'Don't tip your hand.'"

He worked behind the scenes to stop Florida's pay-to-pave program that let developers write a check in exchange for sealing up gopher tortoises in their burrows. He was a major supporter of the Amendment 1 ballot initiative, which set aside state money for conservation, and a strong opponent of the wildlife commission's recent decision to allow a bear hunt for the first time in 21 years.

He would see a problem and then "throw more money at it than anybody else," recalled Vivienne Handy, another environmental consultant he befriended. "When he saw something that needed to happen, he went right out and made it happen."

His crowning achievement was the Nokuse Plantation, 53,000 acres of Panhandle peanut farms and pulpwood forests near Eglin Air Force Base that he bought and turned into a center for biological preservation. It's the largest block of privately owned conservation land east of the Mississippi.

He hired experts to begin bringing back the longleaf pine forests from pre–Civil War days, a key to making it an ideal bear habitat, while creating a haven for gopher tortoises pushed out of other areas.

At Nokuse (pronounced no-GOO-see) he opened the E. O. Wilson Biophilia Center, named after the Pulitzer-winning biologist and naturalist who grew up in Alabama. The center was designed to educate Florida schoolchildren about the natural world.

Wilson became a major supporter of his work, and a friend. The two were laying plans to take Davis's work global, linking parks and preserves together around the world, when the bad news arrived.

☼

Last fall Davis was diagnosed with stage four lung cancer. He tried chemotherapy and radiation to no avail. The cancer spread to his brain. He was fading fast. He didn't want to die in a hospital bed, Chisholm said.

On July 11, he slipped away from his family and made his way out to the Nokuse piney woods he loved so dearly. The man who always wanted to be in control had picked the place and the time of his death, and he carried out his plan, Chisholm said, declining to give further details.

Before he killed himself, Davis had set up a plan to keep Nokuse going. It will be run by a foundation, its board made up of his family.

If Davis were still around to hear all the accolades coming his way now, Handy said, "he would have pooh-poohed it all. He would say, 'Keep all this legacy crap—and leave my bears alone!'"

10

THANKFUL FOR THE TURKEY LADY

Tampa Bay Times, November 19, 2017

The other day, I had a lovely chat with a lady who was arrested on charges of shoplifting . . . while she was dressed as a turkey.

I guess you could say that she's been accused of doing the wrong kind of stuffing.

The lady's name is Irene and she lives in The Villages, the largest gated over-55 community in the world, a place where everyone rides around in golf carts, even people in turkey outfits.

More on her in a minute, after a word about that special day we will soon celebrate.

Thanksgiving always seems like the briefest of holidays, squeezed into a few hours between the sugar-fueled fantasies of Halloween, the frenzy of Black Friday and the feel-good pageantry of Christmas. It's there and it's gone, with nothing to mark its passage but a fridge full of leftovers and the occasional acrimonious glare from that uncle whose NFL team lost to yours.

Yet it's the holiday that depends the most on putting aside our differences and coming together as one, which is something we as a nation desperately need these days. Granted, the cause that unites us is stuffing our faces, but still, it's a start.

Everybody knows the story of the first Thanksgiving in 1621: The Pilgrims, saved from starvation by kindly Native Americans, invite them to a feast, yadda. The only problem is that it wasn't really the first Thanksgiving celebration held in the New World.

Nope, the first one was held here in Florida.

More than 50 years before the Pilgrims, some 800 Spanish settlers led by Pedro Menendez de Aviles landed at what became St. Augustine. As curious members of the native Timucuan tribe watched, the first Spaniard to wade ashore was a priest, Father Francisco Lopez, who carried a cross. When Menendez joined him on dry land, the conquistador knelt and kissed the cross.

They all gathered around a makeshift altar, where Lopez conducted a Mass to thank God for giving them safe passage across the Atlantic Ocean. Afterward, they feasted, and at Menendez's invitation, the Timucuans joined in.

"It was the first community act of religion and thanksgiving in the first permanent settlement in the land," University of Florida history professor Michael Gannon wrote in his book *The Cross in the Sand.*

Turkey was not on the menu. Instead the settlers dined on leftover garbanzo stew made with pork, garlic, saffron, cabbage and onion. The Timucuans may have brought alligator, bear, turkey, venison or even oysters, turtle, catfish or mullet.

So you could argue that Thanksgiving—the day that's supposed to make us count our blessings instead of our calories—is the most Florida of holidays, because we started it.

We have so much to be thankful for here: our postcard sunsets, our gorgeous beaches, our fast-flowing springs and deep forests. The end of November marks the end of hurricane season, so we've got to be thankful for that, especially this year. Plus, we're blessed to live in the Most Interesting State in the U.S., a place full of sinkholes and shark bites and machete-waving road ragers, where every day the news headlines make you say, "Wait, what?"

Which brings us back to Irene and her turkey outfit.

She's 67, a retired GM employee and faithful church member, she told me. She said she bought her costume from a catalog several years ago on a lark. Then she added several feather boas, so that now it's "really a striking outfit," she said.

"I would wear it to pass out candy to the children," she said. "I do it for my neighborhood. It's just something fun to do."

On Nov. 10, she put on her costume and rode over to Belk's "to pass out candy," she said. She wore the outfit "because it's Thanksgiving." She hadn't been invited by the store to do that, so I guess you could say she was winging it.

As for her arrest, she's a little vague, saying that "somehow things got a little bit confusing."

The Lady Lake Police Department arrest report says surveillance cameras caught her swiping purses, an electric snow globe, jewelry and a waffle maker. She said she plans to fight the charges.

"I was hoping to wear my costume to court, but now I don't think that's a good idea," she added. "I don't think that would impress the judge."

I am hoping she reconsiders that decision, because I'm pretty sure the judge would be very impressed by a defendant brave enough to dress as the bird Ben Franklin called "much more respectable" than the bald eagle.

And then everyone in Florida would have one more thing to be thankful for.

Now pass me some of that garbanzo stew.

11

ONE FOOT IN FRONT OF THE OTHER

Tampa Bay Times, June 11, 2017

Jim Kern has hiked trails all over the globe. He just got back from walking around Corsica. He's clambered across the mountains in Nepal and trekked through the jungles of Borneo. He's 83 and still pulling on his boots to wander the woods around his St. Augustine home whenever he can.

But the most important hike he ever made took place in 1966. He lived in Miami then, scraping by as a fledgling real estate broker. Kern had joined his family in North Carolina for a vacation and gone on a 40-mile hike on the Appalachian Trail. He returned home hankering to hike some more.

There was one very big problem: Florida didn't have any hiking trails of its own.

So he set out to make one.

"The idea," Kern says, "was to dramatize the need for a trail in Florida."

His wife dropped him off at a spot on the Tamiami Trail known as the 40-Mile Bend. This was in March, so the temperature was in the 50s. He carried equipment that now seems antique: a canvas-frame backpack, a sleeping bag, a little Campmor camp stove and an aluminum cup.

By the end of 12 days, Kern had hiked to Highlands Hammock State Park, near Sebring in Central Florida—a distance of 170 miles.

With that hike, Kern launched the Florida National Scenic Trail, which now stretches more than 1,000 miles from the Big Cypress National Preserve in swampy South Florida to the Gulf Islands National Seashore in the farthest northwestern reach of the Panhandle.

The Florida Trail is one of only 11 federally designated scenic hiking trails in the United States. It attracts 355,000 people every year, according to a University of Florida study. It is also the only warm-weather winter trail in the United States.

"It's kind of the hub of our entire hiking trail system" in Florida's three national forests, said U.S. Forest Service spokeswoman Denise Rains.

But the trail has gaps, about 2,800 of them, totaling 300 miles.

Right now, that is what's on Jim Kern's mind—closing the gaps in the trail he started so long ago. One last thing to do before he can't hike around anymore. And the Florida Legislature, he said, isn't helping.

☼

Kern wasn't alone in blazing his trail in 1966.

For the first leg, he took along a Miami-Dade Community College professor named McGregor Smith Jr. They started off hiking along the levees the Army Corps of Engineers had built to hold back the Everglades, stopping frequently to snap photos, whistle at birds and swat away mosquitoes.

One night as they camped, they were surrounded by owls Kern had summoned with a mating call.

Smith's feet soon sprouted blisters galore. Kern seemed unfazed. During one stop, Smith wrote, "while I plastered my feet with ointment, 'Leather-Foot Jim' kicked off his shoes, trotted down the oyster shell bank and dove into a murky looking canal."

"Boy, this is great," he shouted. "Yell if you see any gators."

Smith bailed soon afterward, but other companions took up Kern's cause. A troop of Boy Scout Explorers accompanied him for a weekend, and later he was joined by noted Florida reptile expert and showman Ross Allen.

Florida newspapers carried Smith's account of Kern's 1966 hike, which also mentioned that he had formed a group called the Florida Trail Association. Within six months, his group had attracted 70 dues-paying members. Now the membership numbers more than 4,000.

"He's a networker and quite tenacious, good qualities for soft-spoken environmental advocates to have," said Sandra Friend, an avid hiker who wrote *The Florida Trail Guide* in 2015 and *The Florida Trail: The Official Hiking Guide* in 2004. "But most importantly, he promoted a dream that caught fire with other people. He didn't have to carry the torch alone for very long."

Kern set up more hikes through North Florida, creating new legs for the trail he was proposing. He figured out his path so that it would go in stages through Ocala, Osceola and Apalachicola national forests, touching on state parks, as well.

At one point, he went to federal Forest Service officials to tell them what he had in mind.

Miami real estate salesman Jim Kern made a hike in 1966 that guaranteed others would follow in his footsteps, as he blazed the path of the Florida Trail. Photo by Bob Self, used by permission of the *Tampa Bay Times*.

"They smirked," Kern recalled. "They thought, 'Who's going to hike in Florida?'"

Hiking was for mountain terrain, not for Florida's flat and swampy landscape.

They didn't object—but they did tell Kern he was on his own.

But by then the word about Kern's project had reached an ex–Green Beret and onetime Eagle Scout from Tampa named Fred Mulholland, who decided to lend a hand.

Mulholland, a GTE project manager and a dedicated backpacker, had been building things with wood since he was 8. He organized a crew of volunteers that included family members and Boy Scouts.

Over a series of weekends, he led them in building an actual 26-mile footpath, complete with wooden bridges, along the route through Ocala National Forest that Kern had mapped out.

"Now we were up and running," Kern said. "After Fred finished, we publicized it, and people began to show up and ask, 'Where's the trail?'"

The Forest Service officials who had scoffed "had egg on their faces," Kern said, chuckling.

They also made him change the route.

"That was painful," Kern said. The whole thing had to be redone.

Today, although the federal Forest Service manages the trail, "there's a huge group of volunteers who do much of the maintenance—they do 99 percent of it," Rains said. "The Florida Trail is probably one of the biggest volunteer success stories in the state."

But Kern and his volunteers haven't been able to stitch the whole thing together.

Not yet.

☀

At 83, Kern isn't leaping into any gator-infested canals these days. He's had hip-replacement surgery and other medical issues. When he walks around through the woods near his home, he limps a bit.

He has a lot of accomplishments he can look back on with pride. He started the American Hiking Association and served as its first president. He started an organization to help inner-city kids visit the wilderness. He started *American Hiker* magazine and published a coffee table book with his nature photography.

But he's not spending his remaining years looking behind him. Instead, he's facing forward, putting one foot in front of the other, pushing to complete his first big project, the Florida Trail:

> We're coming to the government at a point where far more of the trail has been completed by volunteers than by anyone else, and we're saying, "If you want this trail to be around for posterity, you need to do something—now."

Buying the land that's needed won't be cheap. Kern estimates the price at $200 million, or "about the cost of two large interstate interchanges."

And he knows it's a bad time to be seeking federal funding, given the current White House drive to slash spending for all the environment-related agencies.

Florida is supposed to be able to help. The state had a politically popular land-buying program called Florida Forever that acquired millions of acres of environmentally sensitive land for its award-winning state parks and state forests.

But in recent years, legislators have repeatedly stripped money out of the program and spent it on other purposes. So environmental advocates came up with Amendment 1, a constitutional amendment requiring them to fund Florida Forever. The measure passed in 2014 with the support of 75 percent of the voters.

Yet legislators have yet to change their ways. In this year's budget, they put down zero for Florida Forever.

"If there was any money in Florida Forever, that would have helped," Kern said.

Legislative leaders, as they have done repeatedly in the past, promised to come up with money for the program next year.

Kern isn't sure how long the trail can wait, though. He doesn't know how long he can wait, either.

Ask if he expects to live long enough to see all 1,300 miles of trail connected, and Kern gave an answer that's the equivalent of a shrug: "I don't know. I would love to."

He paused, then added: "Of course, I can only state a preference."

12

ELVIS AND THE FLORIDA MAN

Tampa Bay Times, July 29, 2018

Tucked into a back corner of the sprawling campus of the Humane Society of Tampa Bay on Armenia Avenue is a scattered collection of stones and statues with an odd connection to Elvis Presley.

It's a pet cemetery. And it's about to get dug up.

What's the connection? The cemetery and the King were, in a way, both the creation of one man—a Florida man, of course.

While Elvis hailed from Mississippi and lived in Tennessee, his stardom owed a lot to Florida. According to author Bob Kealing's book *Elvis Ignited: The Rise of an Icon in Florida,* the Sunshine State helped launch his career.

His first song to hit No. 1, "Heartbreak Hotel," was written by a Jacksonville woman named Mae Axton. He filmed a movie in Central Florida called *Follow That Dream,* during which he met a young Tom Petty, inspiring the boy to become a rock star, too. And a photo of him performing one of several shows at a Tampa armory show became the iconic image on the cover of his debut album.

But this Tampa pet cemetery is the weirdest Florida connection of all.

It involves a man who was born in Holland under the name of Andreas Cornelis van Kuijk. In the 1920s he made a hasty departure from his homeland and found his way into the United States as an illegal immigrant.

He worked in sideshows and carnivals, learning the ins and outs of show business. Then he joined the U.S. Army under a phony name and soon earned a promotion to private. While stationed at a base in Pensacola, he went AWOL for five months. His punishment: solitary confinement for two months. It wasn't exactly "Jailhouse Rock."

When he was released, he seemed a mess—incoherent, full of rage, all shook up. Doctors who examined him threw up their hands. He was classified psychotic and released. It's not easy to get an honorable discharge after being convicted of desertion, but he pulled it off.

He found work at a carnival based in Tampa, showing horses, reading palms and putting on stunts like a phony marriage atop the Ferris wheel. He also sold "foot-long" hot dogs that weren't, hamburgers that were mostly filler and raffle tickets for a ham that always went home with him. He wed a Tampa woman, although as with many other things he did, there's some question about whether it was legal.

Between tours he found other ways to scrounge up a buck in Tampa. For instance, he buried a pony up to its knees in the dirt, put a curtain around it and charged people to see "The World's Smallest Horse."

He was a classic Florida hustler, and money was always on his mind. That background proved valuable when in 1940 he landed a new job as a "field agent"—i.e., dogcatcher—for Tampa's Humane Society.

The job not only brought him a steady paycheck, but also provided his family with a rent-free apartment above the Humane Society's shelter. His employer furnished him with a uniform and cap as he went on "ambulance runs" to check on reports of cats in trees and boys shooting at birds.

According to his biographer, he started telling people to call him "doctor." He invited local merchants to donate money for pet supplies—although that ended when they figured out he was instead buying food for his family.

He engineered stunts to get the Humane Society's name in the paper. He dressed up as Santa and gave away puppies to children. He dug a deep but narrow hole, put a dog in it, told reporters that the dog had fallen in and invited people to send in contributions so he could hire a circus midget to rescue it. The shelter was in bad financial shape when he started, and within a year he had it out of the red.

Then he started the pet cemetery, which, as Kealing puts it, "was totally a scam." The biographer called it "his most inspired and creative money-making scheme."

The "doctor" was aided by a gofer named Bevo Bevis. He bestowed on Bevis the title of "General Manager for Perpetual Care for Deceased Pets," then told him his first assignment was to clear weeds and debris from the site. Then, Kealing said, he had Bevis build small coffins from wood scraps.

To seal the deal, the dogcatcher fast-talked a monument maker into giving him a small tombstone for free, inscribed with "HERE LIES SPOT, A BELOVED AND FAITHFUL COMPANION." He had Bevis dig a hole, then refill it so the dirt made a mound, then stuck in the phony headstone.

The fake grave made for a dandy sales pitch for bereaved dog and cat owners. The "doctor" charged them up to $100 for each "Fido funeral,"

Kealing said. He used headstones that cost him only $15, and decorated each plot with daisies he had gotten as castoffs from a local florist.

How much of the profit went to the Humane Society? Nobody knows, but Kealing said, "My money is on (him) keeping a ridiculously high percentage for himself."

Soon, the dogcatcher found a new way to make money: organizing a fundraising concert for the Humane Society starring country music star Roy Acuff and comic Minnie Pearl. The concert at the Homer Hesterly Armory in Tampa, where Elvis would later get his picture taken, was a huge success.

Concert promotion proved to be where his true genius lay. He began promoting more shows, but not for charity. Soon he was neglecting his duties at the shelter because country music paid better. He trained himself to present more of a Southern-fried image, wearing string ties and drawling at all times, as he moved into managing big-name country stars.

Then, in 1955, he laid eyes on the hunka-hunka burning talent that was the young Elvis. Through some shrewd gamesmanship, the onetime dogcatcher maneuvered Elvis away from the people who had been overseeing his career up until then and took over his management. He shaped and guided the young singer's image, his career, his whole life, until the King died in 1977.

By the time he met Elvis, the former private had gotten a promotion. He was known as Col. Tom Parker, the rock 'n' roll Svengali who would grow fat by taking 50 percent of his client's profits.

The Humane Society of Tampa Bay, a far more respectable organization these days, maintains what's left of Col. Tom's pet cemetery. No new graves have been added since the 1980s because now people generally cremate their pets, said CEO Sherry Silk.

Some of the cemetery had to be moved or dismantled years ago when the society expanded a dog play area. Now, Silk said, because of a recently announced $11 million expansion, "we will have to relocate the headstones to another part of the property."

The society staff keeps on the office wall a big photo of Col. Tom Parker from his "doctor" days with one of his canine clients. His life is proof that any Florida man can be a success, even if, at heart, he ain't nothing but a hound dog.

part II

CRIME DOES NOT PAY (ENOUGH)

13

"THE PHONIEST SUMBITCH THAT WALKS"

St. Petersburg Times, March 7, 1994

ST. PETERSBURG—Joe Bujan spun the most amazing tales. He talked of wealth, his grand adventures, his powerful friends. And all the guys at Derby Lane believed him—all but an old oil field worker named Johnny Boyd.

One day at the track the conversation turned to how much money greyhounds earn. Bujan claimed one dog had won $3 million.

Impossible, Boyd said. No greyhound had ever won that much.

But even when Boyd showed his friends a book that proved Bujan wrong, the other guys refused to believe it. To them, good old Joe was a family man with eight children and a million-dollar house on Tampa Bay, a well-connected home builder, a smart bettor who often won big. He *must* be right.

"He had them so bumfuzzled they would believe anything he told them," Boyd said. "But I was always telling them, 'He's the phoniest sumbitch that walks!'"

Boyd was right, and not just about the dog.

Last week Bujan stood exposed in a Pinellas County courtroom as a man with an astounding talent for persuading naive friends to swallow a string of lies, a thief who has stolen hundreds of thousands of dollars armed only with his vivid imagination.

Although Bujan said he owned a house on the bay, he actually lived in a duplex in a scruffy part of St. Petersburg.

Although he said he had eight children, he really had six—two with his wife, Jean, and four with Ella Collins, the woman he married while still wed to Jean.

Bujan was not a builder. He wasn't even much of a gambler. A lot of the cash he flashed around came from another Derby Lane regular, George "Pop" Ashwell.

Everyone at Derby Lane thought Bujan was taking care of Ashwell, 75.

It was the other way around. Ashwell says he gave Bujan $130,000, most of his life's savings.

Ashwell thought he was lending money to Bujan's corporation. All he got in return was a business card for a non-existent company.

"I look at it now and say, 'Jiminy Cricket! Why did I believe him?'" Ashwell said.

His only consolation is that over the years Bujan's fantastic stories have fooled plenty of others.

Bujan once told a Tampa race-car driver he could swing a $30,000 sponsorship deal with Radio Shack if the driver gave him a $5,000 kickback. The driver had painted "Radio Shack" on his car before he learned Bujan was a fake and had no connection with the company.

Bujan persuaded several St. Petersburg bankers to give him $10,000 to finance a racing team he said he managed. He didn't repay the loan, but persuaded them to give him another $20,000 before they learned the truth.

He made a Thonotosassa businessman believe he held $90 million in bonds spirited out of Cuba when Castro took over, and needed help converting them to cash. The businessman gave him $20,000 and a new Mercedes-Benz before figuring out the story was fiction.

And when Bujan was arrested for swindling a Clearwater car dealer out of a brand-new Lincoln, he made bail, swiped the Lincoln from the dealer's lot and disappeared. Months later he was pulled over in Alabama doing 85 mph in the stolen car.

The police officer who stopped him nearly let him go. The fast-talking Bujan almost convinced him the whole thing was a silly mix-up.

"If you met him today he would tell you the most outrageous lie in the world, and he'd tell it to you so emphatic that you'd have to believe him," Boyd said. "Nobody could think up lies like these."

☼

Once when a scam landed him in court, Bujan sobbed, "I was just trying to make it . . . to be somebody."

But which "somebody" he is depends on whom he's talking to.

At various times he has called himself Jose Bujan, Jose Bulan, Jose Latti and Joe Bulah. He says he was born Nov. 29 in either 1942 or 1944. He sometimes claims to be from Spain, sometimes from Cuba.

He told the guys at Derby Lane he was a professional jai alai player whose career ended when an injury left him unable to raise his right arm. But his wife told a judge his arm has been like that since birth.

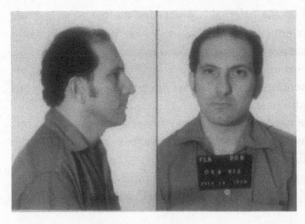

Con man Jose "Joe" Bujan, seen in this 1979 mugshot, stole thousands of dollars armed only with a vivid imagination. Photo courtesy of the Florida Department of Corrections.

When Bujan befriended Ashwell at Derby Lane, he spun a new identity, tailored to appeal to the older man.

A retired welder, Ashwell was the richest of the retirees who hung out together at the track, with a nice nest egg from selling some family property in Ohio. But Ashwell lived simply, and because his family was still up North, alone. He savored the camaraderie he found at the track.

Bujan presented himself to Ashwell as a family man with a problem. His three oldest sons ran his business, he said, but their bank account had been frozen by the savings-and-loan crisis. Bujan & Sons needed money to stay afloat. Could his buddy throw him a lifeline?

Ashwell gave him a few thousand, then a few more, then still more. Bujan promised to build him a home. Ashwell took him at his word.

Bujan began driving Ashwell around—to Lake Tarpon to see a house Bujan said he had been hired to build; to Interstate 75 in Tampa to look over property that Bujan said belonged to him; to Miami's Calder Racetrack to bet on horses Bujan said he owned. Ashwell didn't suspect he was lying.

Bujan also offered to introduce Ashwell to his friends—Tampa's top FBI agent, Calder Race Track's hottest jockey. Ashwell, a shy man, always said no, thanks. It didn't occur to him Bujan didn't know them.

Bujan made Ashwell feel like part of his family, even giving him pictures of his children—although Ashwell never met them.

"The more I dealt with him, the more I trusted him," Ashwell said. "He had me programmed."

Another retiree Bujan met at the track was Ernie Giannini. In their modest home Giannini and his wife, Marie, cared for their mothers, both suffering from Alzheimer's disease. Bujan told Giannini that he too was caring for ailing parents. Even their Alzheimer's symptoms were the same.

"He really played up the paternal instincts and all that American pie stuff," Giannini's daughter Pat said. "He must have been a really good judge of character to know just which buttons to push."

When the Gianninis decided to add a room to their house, Bujan offered to build it, presenting himself "as a very rich man who was doing us a big favor," Mrs. Giannini said.

But Bujan said he needed money to buy materials, so the Gianninis gave him $9,000. Days passed. No construction crews showed up. On the phone, Bujan was full of excuses.

"The last time he spoke to me, it sounded like he had a grin on his face," Mrs. Giannini said. "He said, 'Do you know what's going on?' And I said, 'I got a feeling, Joe.'"

✿

Crushed, Ernie Giannini complained to Gulfport police. They charged Bujan with grand theft.

But when the con man went to court in late 1992, "he walked in there just as cocky as if he owned the joint," Boyd said.

Bujan's attorney told the judge his client would like to plead no contest and be put on probation. But Circuit Judge Susan Schaeffer said no. Because of Bujan's past record, she said, he would go to prison.

The con man started crying.

Bujan pleaded innocent and arranged with Largo bail-bondsman Frank Kopczynski to get out of jail. As collateral, Bujan handed Kopczynski the title to a new car.

Then Bujan disappeared, and Kopczynski discovered that the car belonged to a rental agency.

Judge Schaeffer put out a warrant for Bujan. If caught, she said, he should be brought before no judge but her, and his $50,000 bond should not be reduced.

Kopczynski began hunting the fugitive, who was spending his way across the South. He ran up a $75,000 tab on stolen credit cards, then switched to a more creative financing method.

On a piece of paper, Bujan drew a picture of a check. Then he ran off hundreds of photocopies and used them to rent cars, buy groceries, even stay at fine hotels, the bail-bondsman said.

Although fleeing the law, Bujan and his girlfriend, Ella Collins, stopped off in Butts County, Ga., to see a judge.

The judge married them.

Jose Bujan knew Largo bail bondsman Frank Kopczynski was chasing him, but he told his girlfriend that his pursuer was a Mafia hit man. Photo courtesy of Frank Kopczynski.

But there were two problems. Although Jean Bujan was seeking a divorce in St. Petersburg, Bujan was still married to her.

And, according to Kopczynski, Bujan paid the judge with one of his homemade checks.

☼

Bujan knew Kopczynski was chasing him. He told Collins his pursuer was a Mafia hit man, Kopczynski said.

One night, while Collins was staying with relatives in Gadsden, Ala., a bomb exploded by the house, Kopczynski said.

Bujan was in Atlanta at the time and called Collins to blame the blast on the "hit man." But Collins hadn't told him about the bomb. The only way he could have known about it is if he had staged the explosion.

Realizing she had been duped, Collins told Kopczynski she would help nail Bujan. She told Bujan to meet her at an interstate rest stop near Pell City, Ala. When he pulled in, deputies grabbed him.

When Kopczynski went to fetch Bujan, Alabama authorities were glad to be rid of the con man. Complaining of chest pains, he had run up a big medical bill for the jail.

As they started back, Bujan wailed that without medication he would die. Kopczynski, a former hospital administrator, scanned the list of pills. They were all for high blood pressure.

"Blood pressure is a silent killer," Kopczynski told Bujan. "Shut the hell up."

☼

Kopczynski brought him back to the Pinellas County Jail in October, but Bujan didn't stay long.

Despite Schaeffer's order, Bujan's bond was reduced by another judge two weeks later, after prosecutors and defense lawyers agreed to it.

"I don't know where the state attorney's office was on this one," Kopczynski said. "This guy was a fugitive, for God's sake!"

Assistant State Attorney Evan Brodsky, who prosecuted Bujan, couldn't explain the mistake. With his bond lowered, Bujan arranged with another bondsman to get out of jail. As collateral Bujan gave him title to some land—land that turned out to belong to someone else.

Bujan disappeared again, and Schaeffer again put out a warrant for him and ordered that he be brought back only to her.

This time Bujan was not hard to find. After a month he was nabbed in Gadsden, buying a used car with a bad check.

Now sporting a beard, Bujan walked into Judge Schaeffer's court in December chewing his lip, looking worried. In addition to the grand-theft charge, he had been accused of swiping a rental car in St. Petersburg Beach, writing bad checks in Georgia and ducking a court hearing.

But his attorney sailed ahead with explaining why his bond should be lowered. Bujan didn't show up for court, he said, because the notices had been sent to the wrong address.

Kopczynski sat in the back row of the courtroom with Boyd, Ashwell and Pat Giannini, whose father had died while Bujan was on the lam. The bondsman glared at Bujan and muttered, "He's a lying sack of s—!"

Judge Schaeffer gazed down at Bujan. "I wonder what Mr. Bujan thought was going on down here in Pinellas County while he was up in Alabama," she said. "Did he think his charge was just going to go away?"

"I never have run from the law," Bujan said. "Nobody ever told me I was supposed to be here."

The judge, a gospel-singing former IRS agent, exploded.

"You conned your lawyer, you conned the bondsman and now you're trying to con me!" she snapped.

Bujan didn't make bail again. He pleaded guilty to all the charges Wednesday. Schaeffer sentenced him to 10 years in prison and ordered him to pay back what he stole from Ashwell and the Gianninis.

Before he left the courtroom, Bujan looked at the judge with a straight face and, sounding wounded, told her, "I think you have the wrong opinion of me."

Note: Bujan spent four years in prison. He was released in 1998 and died a year later, still a wanted man in at least two states. At least, that's what the records say. With this guy you could never be sure.

14

ENCYCLOPEDIA BROWN AND THE CASE OF THE MYSTERIOUS AUTHOR

Crime Reads, May 1, 2019

Let me tell you about the most popular mystery author you've probably never heard of.

He sold 50 million copies of his books worldwide. His work was translated into a dozen languages. The Mystery Writers of America gave him a special Edgar. The character he created became a cultural icon—spoofed by *The Onion,* the star of a short-lived television series, and the subject of a nasty lawsuit over the movie rights.

His name was Donald J. Sobol. He was a World War II veteran and New York City native who moved to Florida in 1961. Two years later he created his "Sherlock in sneakers," boy detective Leroy "Encyclopedia" Brown.

Smarter than the Hardy Boys and wittier than Nancy Drew, Encyclopedia Brown solved mysteries for nearly 50 years and never charged more than a quarter. Although "born" in 1963, young Brown remains forever 10.

His beat is an idealized Florida beach town named Idaville. It exists in the era before cellphones, video games, and Ariana Grande, when kids went fishing or rode bikes for fun. He runs his cut-rate detective agency out of his family's garage on Rover Avenue.

Sobol's sleuth has a keen eye and a prodigious memory for arcane facts—hence his nickname. (These days he'd have to be Wikipedia Brown, which just doesn't sound as authoritative.) He solves small mysteries for his friends and sometimes helps out on big cases that baffle his police chief dad, exposing robbers and con men by spotting the clue everyone else missed.

I loved the Encyclopedia Brown books as a kid, not just because I loved the idea that a kid could be smarter than the adults. I also loved it because of a clever gimmick that Sobol used.

Each book contained ten stories. In each story, someone would present

Encyclopedia with a puzzle. He would carefully examine the clues, listen to what the witnesses said, then compare that with his vast store of knowledge gleaned from reading as well as his own common sense. Then he would indicate he had the solution—but he wouldn't explain it, not right then.

Instead, the reader would have a chance to figure out what it was. If you couldn't—and usually I couldn't, but that didn't stop me from trying—then you could flip to the back of the book, where Sobol explained how his pint-size private eye had solved the puzzle.

But the real mystery wasn't inside the books. The real mystery was: Who's Donald J. Sobol?

☼

Most authors would love to be a big name—a Stephen King, a James Patterson, a John Grisham. People buy their books not for the title or cover image or first page, but because it's the new King, the new Patterson, the new Grisham.

Not Sobol. He preferred nobody know who produced all those books.

"What I really wanted, and couldn't achieve—it was just a pipe dream—was to remain anonymous," Sobol once told his college alumni magazine. "That never worked."

He came close, though. He never gave a single television interview. When he talked with newspaper and magazine reporters, he did so by telephone. That way they couldn't take his picture or even describe what he looked like. A photo of the author only appeared in one book, and he said that was by mistake.

"I am very content with staying in the background and letting the books do the talking," he told the *Oberlin Alumni Magazine* in 2011.

Most of his personal appearances were among people who couldn't care less about his name. They only cared about his character.

"He would go into the elementary schools and talk to the children," his daughter Diane told me. She tagged along once. "He presented a case and he let the elementary school children attempt to solve it. He loved working with and talking to children."

He was the most unlikely of authors, joking once that "I am totally unqualified to be a writer. My childhood was unimpoverished and joyful. Even worse, I loved and admired my parents."

Donald J. Sobol—the *J* was just that, no middle name, just an initial—was born and raised in New York City, where his father owned gas stations. As a child, he was more like Brown's frequent nemesis, inept gang leader Bugs Meany, than his hero, "but only in that I thought up devilish pranks. I never had the courage to act out on them."

He didn't read mystery stories. Instead, he was attracted to tales of adventure. As a kid he wanted to be a police officer, or a firefighter, or a shortstop for the Yankees. In high school he tried his hand at sculpting.

In World War II, he was part of a combat engineer battalion, then attended Oberlin College on the GI Bill. He took the college's only creative writing course, and was hooked. After the last class, he asked the professor if he could take an advanced writing course. The professor explained that there wasn't one. Sobol said later he just stared at the professor "like a dim-witted penguin watching water freeze."

Then the professor asked whether he'd seen action during the war. They talked about that a bit, and finally the professor agreed to teach an advanced writing course for just one student.

"Without his help, I probably never could have had a career as a freelance writer. I owe him so much," Sobol told the alumni magazine. Not only did the professor help him become a better writer "but he instilled faith in me, in myself. I will always be grateful."

Two of the stories Sobol wrote for his advanced class wound up selling to the pulps, and he was on his way. He became a copy boy for the *New York Sun* and worked his way up to becoming a reporter there and at the *Long Island Daily News*. He married Rose Tiplitz, who had earned degrees in math and physics at Brandeis University. She worked in computers at IBM in the 1950s.

Sobol's first foray into the dark genre started when he began writing a syndicated column called "Two-Minute Mysteries." Those flash fiction columns helped him hone his ability to sprinkle clues through a very short story.

Once they had three children, the Sobols decided to raise their kids someplace warmer than New York. They picked Miami, which then had a population of 291,688 (it's now 463,347). There they stayed, all through South Florida's evolution—first as a refuge for Cuban exiles, then as a shooting gallery for Cocaine Cowboys, then as a haven for South American strongmen and Russian gangsters. (It delights me to imagine 1980s Sobol perusing his morning *Miami Herald* and reading headlines like "Drug Dealers Masquerading as Cops Arrested by Cops Masquerading as Drug Dealers," then going off to write another story where his hero solves a bank robbery thanks to his knowledge of Civil War trivia.)

✵

Upon arriving in Florida, Sobol decided to devote himself full-time to writing. In addition to his "Two-Minute Mysteries" column, which ran for 10 years, he produced more than 60 books, including non-fiction books for kids on the American Revolution, the Wright Brothers and the Knights of the Round Table. He and his wife co-wrote a book for children explaining stocks and bonds, too.

None of them proved to be as popular as Encyclopedia Brown.

Sobol cranked out the first book in the series, *Encyclopedia Brown, Boy Detective,* in just two weeks. That first book contained all the elements that would show up in all the other books: the idyllic setting, the 25-cent fee, the roster of regular baddies like dimwitted Bugs Meany, leader of the Tigers gang.

In inventing his hero, Sobol started with Brown's nickname, then fleshed out the character from there. "I wanted a name that would appear on the cover and tell readers that this was a book about a smart youngster," he told an interviewer in 1984.

The author made it clear right from the start that Encyclopedia wasn't just smart but was socially adept, too.

"Old ladies who did crossword puzzles were always stopping him on the street to ask him questions," Sobol wrote. When one asks him to name a three-letter word for a Swiss river that begins with A, he pauses a moment and then says, "Aar."

"He always waited a moment," Sobol wrote. "He wanted to be helpful. But he was afraid that people might not like him if he answered their questions too quickly and sounded too smart."

Sobol wanted kids to identify with Encyclopedia, describing him as looking like any other fifth-grader. He also decided that his detective needed a flaw, so he made him brainy but not brave. He'd shy away from physical confrontations.

That meant he needed a tough sidekick, a Hawk to his Spenser. Sobol first tried including a big brother character, but that didn't feel right. Then he tried making his sidekick a reformed bully. That didn't work either. At last, inspiration struck in the form of a cat-suited Diana Rigg, playing TV secret agent Emma Peel.

"Along about that time," he told the *Denver Business Journal,* "there was a TV program out of England called 'The Avengers' in which the heroine did all the judo work. I said, 'Well it works for TV, it ought to work for Encyclopedia Brown.' So I brought in a young lady named Sally Kimball, a neighbor, and she was his junior partner."

Sobol's daughter Diane said her father also drew on personal experience in creating Sally. When he was young, she said, "his big sister really looked out for him . . . He did tell me that when he was growing up, his sister really stood up to some bullies on his behalf. His mother was a very strong woman, too. If you look at his whole body of work, you'll see he included a lot of strong women."

Sally was "the prettiest girl in the fifth grade and the best athlete," Sobol wrote. She had also punched out Bugs Meany, who wasn't eager for a re-match. Encyclopedia regarded her as more than just muscle. She was his best friend.

As for his back-of-the-book solutions gimmick, Sobol got the idea for that from a library mix-up. While doing research, he asked a librarian to bring him four books. Three of the ones she brought were ones he'd re-quested, but not the fourth. That one was a puzzle book. In glancing at it, Sobol realized it had the solution for each puzzle in the back. It dawned on him that he could use the same idea in writing mystery stories.

Once Sobol was done with that first Encyclopedia Brown story col-lection, he was sure he had a winner. Yet the manuscript was rejected by more than two dozen publishers. Once it finally found a home, though, it took off with young readers. The Encyclopedia Brown mysteries have never been out of print.

They have been around long enough that their original audience has passed them along to their own children and grandchildren. When my kids were old enough, I started reading them the Encyclopedia Brown stories at bedtime. They ate them up just like I had when I was their age.

Some of his fans have gone on to write their own mysteries. For in-stance, Laura Lippman (*The Lady in the Lake*) told *Topic* magazine re-cently: "What I really liked (as a child) were the Encyclopedia Brown sto-ries, where the reader was asked to solve the mystery. I really loved the fact that Encyclopedia was the brain and his friend Sally was the muscle—she was the one who had to beat people up when they were threatening Ency-clopedia Brown."

☼

Sobol wrote every day, taking about six months to produce each of the En-cyclopedia Brown books. The title always included the detective's name: *Encyclopedia Brown Solves Them All*, *Encyclopedia Brown Sets the Pace*, *Encyclopedia Brown and the Case of the Mysterious Hand Prints*.

He'd start writing each morning before his kids woke up and still be tap-tap-tapping away when they went to bed. The one time of day they saw him was at dinner, when he would entertain his family with all sorts of tales.

"He usually had a funny story to tell," Diane told me. "We used to love to listen to him tell stories. He always knew just where to pause."

He frequently tested out mystery ideas on his children. "We would talk about it sitting around dinner," his son John said. "My mom also helped inject humor into the stories."

And there were so many stories. By the time he died in 2012, he had written 29 books, each one with 10 stories. That's 290 mysteries over 49 years—an astonishing output, especially when you recall he wrote other books too.

Although the puzzles Sobol concocted were always eminently fair, the clever writing is what kept his readers coming back.

"Sobol turns out to be a deft storyteller," Kevin Burton Smith wrote in a profile on his "Thrilling Detective" website. "Each story is a little gem, rich in atmosphere, with plots that are often quite inventive, full of jokes and metaphors."

What helped keep the books popular is that they showed how kids could be smarter and more observant than adults. Sobol himself learned that lesson anew in 1990 when second-graders in Philadelphia found an error in one of his stories and wrote to him to point it out. He had to change the story.

But here's the question I put to his daughter: In those pre-Internet days, when you couldn't just google any arcane fact, how did he manage to fill his main character's brain with all that important trivia? Was he the real Encyclopedia?

"He had a lot of reference books," she explained. With his background in reporting, he knew how to track down the facts he needed. Meanwhile the non-fiction books he wrote often supplied him with fodder for his clever detective to use in foiling a criminal, she said.

"That was his gift," she said. "He knew how to put that together in a way that was unique to him."

She said there had been talk about someone else in the family taking over the series after he died, but so far nothing has come of that. Unless and until that happens, Donald J. Sobol will remain the sole proprietor behind the Encyclopedia Brown Detective Agency.

"Readers constantly ask me if Encyclopedia is a real boy," Sobol said once. "He is, perhaps, the boy I wanted to be—doing the things I wanted to read about but could not find in any book when I was 10."

15

MUG SHOTS

Tampa Bay Times, March 31, 2016

Since 1949, Florida prisoners have been stamping the words "Sunshine State" on our license plates, despite most of our cities getting more annual rainfall than famously gloomy Seattle.

These days, though, the Legislature should change our nickname to "The Punch Line State." We're constantly producing stories about kooky crooks, crooked politicians and other wackiness that get circulated worldwide.

Friends of mine know how much I relish these tales, so they tag me on Facebook when they see one.

One afternoon my buddy Bill in Miami tagged me so I'd see a story from South Florida about a guy caught prowling a strange neighborhood armed with brass knuckles and a knife.

What made this funny was his mug shot. He had smeared dark grease all over his face and looked kind of dopey. I laughed about it, so I tweeted his picture and called it our Florida Mug Shot Du Jour. It was retweeted by other folks who found it amusing, and that was the end of it—or so I thought.

The next day I got an urgent call from Bill.

"Take it down," he said.

"Do what?" I asked.

"That guy's mug shot. Take it down," he said.

Bill explained that since tagging me, he had learned that the guy was a military veteran who had served three tours of duty in Afghanistan. Friends said he had post-traumatic stress disorder. He was on 100 percent disability and having trouble adjusting to civilian life.

Knowing all that made his photo not quite as funny anymore.

I deleted the tweet, but I couldn't delete the implications inside my head.

As a lifelong Floridian, I know that in this state, tragedy often wears the mask of comedy. A man wins a Deerfield Beach pet store's cockroach-eating contest, then keels over, and the medical examiner says he choked to death on insect parts. Someone attending Zombicon in Fort Myers is shot and paramedics can't find the victim because everyone's made up to look like the walking dead. A burglary suspect hiding from the cops is attacked and eaten by an alligator.

I laughed about each of those stories and never gave much thought to the families of the victims and how they felt. But with so many strange things happening here every day, chances are good that eventually one of those "Only in Florida!" stories may involve you or someone you love.

In the Miami suburb of Kendall, two men got into an argument over dog poop, and one shot the other dead. The man who died was the uncle of someone I knew, a very sweet woman who was devastated by what happened. Just as with the grease-smeared veteran, once you saw the pain behind the dog-poop shooting, it didn't seem amusing anymore.

It's human nature to gawk and giggle at absurdities, then pass the wildest ones along to a friend or co-worker. But sometimes when we do that, we forget that real humans are involved who are dealing with serious problems, and that hee-hawing about their misfortune makes it worse.

Case in point: In 2013 my colleague John Pendygraft wrote a brilliant story about a Brandon couple. They'd been hog hunting together, and the man accidentally shot his girlfriend in the leg. She barely survived and a year later still walked with a limp.

Headlines about the shooting were ideal fodder for all the aggregation websites and late-night comics: "Florida Man Mistakes Girlfriend for a Hog, Shoots Her." The stories were generally illustrated with a picture of a hog, not a human.

Dealing with strangers' cruelty about the shooting became part of the couple's ordeal. Bubba the Love Sponge sent his radio listeners to the victim's Facebook page to see if she really looked like a hog. Vicious comments piled up on the page until family members took it down. When the page disappeared, though, some of her friends feared she had died.

The derisive laughter didn't let up for weeks. "They really wouldn't leave it alone until that guy ate a man's face in Miami. Then it just disappeared," the man told Pendygraft.

Listen, I'm not saying we shouldn't laugh at the crazy stories that happen in Florida. Some of them really are funny, like the one about the Marion County burglars who mistook urns of human and animal ashes for drugs and snorted them.

I'm just saying that from now on, when I look at the mug shots of people involved in weird Florida crimes, I'm going to make myself repeat an old phrase we seldom hear anymore: "There but for the grace of God go I."

"AN ALIAS NAME"

St. Petersburg Times, November 24, 1996

They say it's impossible to keep a secret in a small town. Everybody knows you, knows your family, knows your business.

In the towns south and east of Raleigh, N.C., little towns like Faison and Warsaw and Wilson and Roseboro, everybody knew Curtis Jackson.

They knew he was a steady, well-liked employee of the Cates Pickle plant in Faison, a friendly guy who played on the company basketball team. They knew he was an ordained elder in his church, preaching the Gospel to everyone he met. They knew he had married a woman who worked at the Wilson Police Department, and that the couple had separated.

But they did not know everything.

One day in late September, Detective Sgt. Tim Jones of the Duplin County Sheriff's Office showed up at the pickle plant with a warrant.

Turned out, Curtis Jackson of Warsaw was actually Calvin Jackson, a fugitive wanted for murder. Witnesses said he shot a man in the back in Pinellas Park, Florida, after he was taunted with racial slurs. Detectives had been hunting him for 10 years.

Caught at last, Jackson did not resist. Just the opposite.

"He took a deep breath and he let it out," Jones said. "It was like he'd had a ton of cinder blocks lifted off his shoulders."

Because the pickle plant is Faison's biggest employer, plenty of people saw Jackson led away in handcuffs. The word spread quickly in breathless phone calls, barber-chair chatter, beauty-shop whispers. To say everyone was surprised would be an understatement.

"It's kind of tore a lot of people up," said the Rev. Dennis Culbreath, pastor of the First Baptist Church of Roseboro.

But nobody was as shocked as Jackson's estranged wife, Van, a police records technician.

That her husband was a liar did not surprise her. Despite his sterling reputation she had long ago figured out he was hiding something. She just never imagined it was anything as big as possibly killing a man.

"He fooled me worse than he fooled everybody," she said bitterly.

☼

To be known by his real name, to be called Calvin once again, has taken a little getting used to, Jackson said last week. But he likes it. He declined to discuss the shooting on the advice of his attorney, but he said that, although now that he's locked in the Pinellas County Jail, he feels freer than he has in years.

"As a fugitive, your heart is never settled," he said. "You can never have peace."

At 33, Jackson is a slender man with a quick smile and the unhurried manner of someone at ease with himself—even dressed in the blue uniform of a prisoner.

Jackson has spent time behind bars before, but only as a minister, visiting inmates to tell them about Jesus. Except for the murder charge his record is clean, said Sgt. Mike Darroch, chief of detectives for the Pinellas Park Police Department.

That is one reason he was so hard to find, Darroch said. Most fugitives break the law again and get caught. By staying clean, Jackson stayed hidden.

He was smart to stick to small towns where people are more likely to take you at face value than to check a resume or a computer record, Darroch said. He was smart not to share his secret, instead wearing his false face 24 hours a day. Jackson said he did not want to drag anyone else into his pain.

"I could never bring myself to tell anyone," Jackson said. It was "part of my burden of my heart."

As a minister, he was supposed to speak out against injustice. But he feared attracting attention so he kept silent, and that hurt, he said. He wanted to speak out for truth, even though he was living a lie.

"An alias name does not take the truth from a man's heart," he said.

☼

Ten years ago, Jackson hardly seemed a candidate for divinity school. He drank. He used cocaine. He went to strip joints.

Recently discharged from the Air Force, the 23-year-old Jackson was living in a Texas mobile home park with a buddy named Philip "Joe"

Totora, 23. They hooked up with Michael Dulus, 26, and decided to pull up stakes, live off the land, work only when they had to and sleep in a van. When they got to Florida they needed money, so they signed on with a Pinellas Park company that provided day labor.

On July 23, 1986, Jackson worked with a man known variously as Toby Brown, John Brown, Howard Brown and Donald Rice. Brown, 31, of St. Petersburg had served time for cocaine possession.

After work, Jackson met his friends at a tavern to cash their checks, and Brown dropped in. As they drank and played pool, Brown promised to take them "to a place where we could take our own beer and watch girl dancers," Totora later said.

They spent four hours at a club, ogling women and drinking steadily. One woman later told police that Brown, who was White, kept taunting Jackson, who is Black, with a racial epithet.

Police said Jackson told her that if Brown "didn't get off his back and stop calling him a n——, he was going to go get his gun out of his truck and kill him."

But when they left the club about 11 p.m., Brown kept needling Jackson, calling him "a dumb n——," Dulus and Totora said.

Jackson's friends, both White, told Brown to cut it out. Finally, Dulus stopped the van in a parking lot on 66th Street and ordered Brown to get out. He refused, even when Totora pointed a rifle at him.

Totora and Brown struggled until Brown smashed Totora in the face with a full beer can, leaving him stunned and bloody. Jackson quickly loaded the rifle and aimed it at Brown, who by then was walking away, Dulus said.

"Joe (Totora) looks up, sees Calvin pointing the gun and says, 'Shoot him! Shoot him!'" Dulus testified. "Calvin shot him."

As the three friends fled in their van, Dulus said he told Jackson, "I can't believe you did that."

"He looked at me and smiled," Dulus recalled.

Panicked, they left Pinellas County as fast as possible. They stopped in Apopka to pawn the gun for gas money, then drove to the Atlantic Ocean.

Totora had a friend in New Smyrna Beach, and they holed up with him until Totora got a call from his mother. A detective was looking for him, she said. Something about a murder.

Totora decided to surrender, but Dulus and Jackson headed north. Totora told police that Dulus and Jackson wanted to turn themselves in too but "they are very scared."

They stayed for a while with Jackson's brother Robert, just outside Daw-

Calvin Jackson fled a murder warrant in Florida and built a better life under a new name. He was ordained a church elder and married a police employee. Photo by Kathleen Cabble, used by permission of the *Tampa Bay Times*.

son, Ga. Then Dulus hit the road again for Alabama. That's where police nabbed him. He had painted the van, but kept the same license plate.

Totora and Dulus were charged with first-degree murder. Totora eventually pleaded guilty to manslaughter and was sentenced to 2 years in prison and 13 years' probation. In 1994, a judge granted a request to end his probation early.

Dulus pleaded guilty to being an accessory. He was sentenced to nine months in jail and 5 years' probation and completed his sentence in 1992.

After Dulus's arrest, detectives asked him where to find Jackson. He said Jackson had told him he was going to take a bus to Detroit. Dulus said he asked Jackson how long he planned to keep running.

"Until I get caught," was the reply.

For years the search for Jackson was assigned to a series of detectives, but the trail just grew colder. At one point police even tried to persuade *America's Most Wanted* to broadcast his picture.

Twice, police thought they had caught Jackson only to learn they had the wrong man. Instead it was "some idiot" who got drunk and claimed to be Jackson, Darroch said. The second time Darroch confronted the impostor, the frustrated detective blurted out, "Not you again!"

☼

Actually, Jackson had not traveled far. Instead of Detroit, he bummed around Atlanta for two years, then went to North Carolina as a migrant farm worker. He liked what he found there.

"It was quiet," he said. "People treated me real nice. I didn't know anybody, but they began to reach out to me. The love they showed me made me stay."

The Rev. Carl Faison found him hunkered down in an abandoned house. He gave Jackson food and persuaded him to go to church. There the sinner on the run found a new destination: heaven.

"He fell on the altar and he was crying," Faison said. "Ever since then, his life has been different."

The people he met through church helped him get his job, found him a new home, invited him to preach once he announced he had been called to the ministry. He even found his wife at church.

Looking back, she now sees that something was not right. When she asked to meet his family, he told her that "when he left Georgia, he had no intention of going back," Van Jackson said.

When his relatives missed their wedding in 1992, she said he told her they had had to go to a reunion. She said all questions about his background met with the same answer: "My past is something I am not going to discuss with you."

Then she got pregnant. At six weeks, complications led to a doctor's recommendation that they abort the pregnancy to save her life, she said. Jackson rejected the diagnosis, she said, and when she went through with it he told her: "I won't live in the same house with a murderer."

They reconciled, but eventually her long-suppressed doubts bubbled to the surface.

"Who are you?" she demanded

"You know who I am," he told her.

Two weeks later he moved out, she said. Now she wonders if his entire life in North Carolina was not a cruel fiction, including his devotion to the church.

"He used the church as a front," she contended. "He knew someday he'd be caught. . . . If he was so deep in his religion, why didn't he turn himself in?"

☺

In the end, it took the FBI to nail Jackson. Although spokesmen for the agency would not give specifics, they said agents uncovered information that he was in Faison and passed it along to local authorities.

In eight weeks at the jail, Jackson said he has saved six souls. He said he conducts prayer meetings in his cell, counseling the troubled, showing them verses in his well-marked Bible.

Like many inmates, when he goes to court he carries an envelope of legal papers. But on his envelope he has written some of his favorite verses. It is easy to see why some of the verses might have special meaning. One from Colossians says: "For ye are dead, and your life is hid with Christ in God."

His supporters in North Carolina write him frequently. Laura Morrisey mailed defense attorney John Trevena a list of 38 character witnesses.

"I don't know Calvin," she said, "but I know Curtis."

He may need every witness: Prosecutors could seek the death penalty.

Still, Jackson said he has hope. When he bows his head in his cell, he said, "I'm praying for my freedom. I'm trusting God that I'm going home. It may look bad right now, but I'm going home."

———

Note: In 1997, a circuit judge sentenced Curtis Jackson to 14 years in prison, which was more than the three-year term requested by his defense attorney but less than the 17 or more years requested by prosecutors. More than a dozen people traveled down from North Carolina to serve as character witnesses for the man they didn't really know. He was released in 2005—and moved back to Wilson, N.C.

17

THE BARD OF BOCA RATON

Crime Reads, April 9, 2020

> Now they were in Florida postcardland, surf and sunny sky, lush
> tropical greenery. Stick took it all in, watched it get better and
> better. . . . worlds away from a bleached house in Norman on an
> oil lease, or a flat on the west side of Detroit.
>
> —*Stick,* 1983

When he died, the papers called him "The Dickens of Detroit." Dutch
always hated that nickname. "What if I came from Buffalo?" he'd ask his
researcher, Gregg Sutter. "Would I be the Bard of Buffalo?"

So no, he wasn't Dickens. He wasn't the Bard either. He was just Dutch,
a guy who started off writing Westerns and then moved into crime stories
and hit the bigtime and got his picture on the cover of *Newsweek* and sold
a lot of his stories to Hollywood.

Some of his crime books were set in and around his hometown of Detroit, but a lot of them weren't. They were set in Florida, a place Dutch
knew quite well. He had absorbed the humid atmosphere and sketchy
cons firsthand. As a result, he created some of his most iconic characters
in books that were set in, or started off in, Florida including U.S. Marshal
Raylan Givens, the main character in the acclaimed TV show *Justified.*

So while the late, great Elmore "Dutch" Leonard would decline the
nickname of "the Dickens of Detroit," maybe he'd be okay with another
title: "Part-Time Florida Man."

"It was his Florida books, you could say, where he really made his
bones," Sutter told me.

☼

"It doesn't bother you," Nolen Tyler said, "you call this place the Coconut Palms, there isn't a single palm tree out there?"

"The high rise on the south side of us, nine stories, is called the Nautilus," Moran said, "but I don't think it's a submarine. The one on the other side, it's ten stories, is the Aurora. Tell me if you think it looks like a radiant glow in the upper atmosphere. That'll be thirty dollars."

—*Cat Chaser*, 1982

Start with his mom's motel.

Elmore John Leonard Jr. had been visiting Florida on vacation starting way back in the '50s. That was even before he began spinning Western yarns such as *The Bounty Hunters, Valdez Is Coming, Hombre* and *3:10 to Yuma*.

His dad, Elmore Sr., made a living scouting car dealership location for General Motors. That's how Elmore Jr. was born in New Orleans but grew up in Detroit. New Orleans was the hometown of his mother, Flora. She apparently was no fan of the Detroit weather, longing for a return to a warmer climate.

In 1969, her son bought her a four-unit motel in Pompano Beach, about 30 miles north of Miami. She lived in one unit and rented out the rest. Now Leonard had an even more compelling reason to visit Florida. A version of that motel later showed up in one of his earliest Florida stories, *Cat Chaser*.

"He thought that was funny, that she had this mom and pop place dwarfed on either side by behemoths. That was typical of him—he liked the little guy up against the system," said Les Standiford, a friend of Leonard's who founded the Florida International University Creative Writing Program.

The year he bought the motel was the same year he realized the market for Westerns was drying up. He shifted gears and penned his first crime novel, *The Big Bounce*. It and his next three novels were gritty Detroit stories with titles like *Unknown Man 89* and *City Primeval*.

But all that changed in 1980 with the publication of *Gold Coast*, his first novel set in Florida. *Gold Coast* features an attractive Mob widow hampered by her husband's punitive will that forbids her to so much as date another man or she'll lose her millions. She meets a onetime bank robber turned dolphin trainer who might have a plan to help her—or at least help himself. It became the first in a string of wild and woolly Leonard tales to be set in South Florida.

Leonard later explained that his visits to see his mom showed him Florida's potential as a crime novel setting.

"Visiting her, I found Miami a great locale," Leonard told *Rolling Stone.* "The high crime rate, the contrast in people—rich retirees, Cubans, boatlifters—all kinds of good things are going on there for me."

"I think the idea of the Florida landscape got his juices flowing," Sutter told me. "It's the land of psychics and strippers."

According to one of his friends, his move was born of desperation.

"Elmore showed up here in 1977 . . . with a colossal case of writer's block," Bill Marshall, a Coral Gables private investigator, told the *South Florida Sun-Sentinel* in 1985. "His recovery—no, his renaissance—came together in Florida because he was desperate for fresh ideas. I showed him around town, and he couldn't believe what he was seeing."

Florida, as it turned out, was a perfect example of a sunny place for shady people, occupied by both the obscenely wealthy and the desperately poor. Leonard opens his 1981 novel *Split Images* with a rich psychopath in Palm Beach shooting a Haitian immigrant dead—then hiring the cop who does a lackadaisical job of investigating the crime to help him pull off another, bigger murder.

"I didn't start paying attention to the contrast between the beauty on the surface and the corruption underneath till I started hanging out with Bill Marshall again," Leonard told the *Sun-Sentinel.* "In Miami Beach, you've got retired car dealers, dressed in bright yellow shirts and paisley pants, walking down the street—and right next to them are guys who just got out of a Cuban prison, *pachucos* with tattoos on their hands for killing people. I thought, what could happen in a tense setting like that? What characters would emerge?"

As it turned out, some pretty funny ones.

"He really grooved on all the quirky characters that are gravitationally attracted to Florida," said Neely Tucker, a friend of Leonard's who had been a reporter for both the *Miami Herald* and the *Detroit News.* "I don't think Dutch became fully Dutch until he put that Florida touch in there."

✳

What he saw from the window was timeless, a Florida post
card. The strip of park across the street. The palm trees in place,
the sea grape. The low wall you could sit on made of coral rock
and gray cement. And the beach. What a beach. A desert full of

people resting, it was so wide. People out there with blankets and umbrellas. People in the green part of the ocean, before it turned deep blue. People so small they could be from any time. Turn the view around. Sit on the coral wall and look this way at the hotels on Ocean Drive and see back into the thirties.

—*La Brava*, 1982

Leonard began writing about South Florida at just the right moment, just as it was changing from a seedy retirement mecca to a neon-spangled criminal haven. The Art Deco hotels of Miami's South Beach, once a magnet for elderly Jews from New York and New Jersey, soon got a fresh coat of paint and a new demographic thanks to the arrival of the Cocaine Cowboys of the '80s.

When Bill Marshall and Dutch Leonard were classmates at the University of Detroit in the 1950s, they visited Florida on break. Back then Miami was full of "gambling, girls and gangsters," Marshall said. "So he comes back in '77, and it's all Cubans and Cocaine Cowboys. He was disappointed. But then he says, quietly, 'Maybe we ought to get into the drug thing.'"

In *La Brava*, the novel that brought him his only Edgar Award for best novel from the Mystery Writers of America, that changing South Beach landscape and the flow of Florida history dating back to the 1930s give the story a potent context. The characters include a Cuban killer and sometime stripper who arrived during the Mariel boatlift, an elderly gallery owner who remembers the 1935 Labor Day hurricane, and a sneaky redneck security guard who had been involved in a major drug bust.

"Remember the town in North Florida that was in the news, where everybody's in the dope business and they built a new Baptist church from the profits?" Leonard told the *Sun-Sentinel*. "I had my White, hillbilly hustler . . . come from there."

If the idea of drug smugglers building a church seems absurd—well, welcome to Florida.

"You can hardly come to Florida and not be overwhelmed by the absurdity of it," Standiford said.

Leonard's Florida novels opened the door for more people to focus on the state's bizarre people and crimes. The first *Miami Vice* episode premiered in 1984, four years after *Gold Coast*. Charles Willeford's *Miami Blues* published in 1984 too. Carl Hiaasen's first wacky Florida crime novel, *Tourist Season*, came out in 1986.

☼

Sunday morning, Ordell took Louis to watch the white power demonstration in downtown Palm Beach. . . . Man, all the photographers, TV cameras. This shit is big news, has everybody over here to see it. Otherwise Sunday, what you'd have mostly are rich ladies come out with their little doggies to make wee-wee. I mean the doggies, not the ladies.

—*Rum Punch*, 1992

The thing is, the craziest stuff in Leonard's Florida books? It was all true.

"I'm reading these (Leonard books) and I think he's followed some of my worst clients home from their bail hearings, listening to their stories," a Fort Lauderdale defense attorney told the *Sun-Sentinel*. "The accuracy of the lifestyles is uncanny."

Leonard was meticulous about the details of life in Florida, said Oline Cogdill, a Raven-winning mystery reviewer for the *Sun-Sentinel*.

"When he used the South Florida area, he was very specific about the location," she told me. "You felt you were there. So the references were authentic. These include, among others, Southern and Okeechobee boulevards, the downtown courthouse complex . . . the Glades Correctional Institution, the Sheriff's Office and The Gardens mall. He didn't just drop these in but made you feel as if you were really there. Every time I go by the Palm Beach courthouse, I think of that scene in *Rum Punch* in which there is a White power demonstration in downtown Palm Beach."

That weird Nazi rally in the middle of rich Palm Beach actually happened, Sutter told me. He had been cultivating some sketchy Florida sources for Leonard and one of them paid off.

"Guy calls me up: 'Tomorrow there's going to be a Nazi-Klan rally in Palm Beach,'" Sutter said. "I grab my mini-camera and go down. Eighteen Nazi bikers and Klan guys and 200 cops getting OT. I brought it to him like a cat bringing a dead rat to his master. 'Oh Elmore's going to go for this.'"

Leonard dispatched Sutter all over Florida to bring him back information on Weeki Wachee's professional mermaids (four of whom were named "Kim"), the soothsayers of Cassadaga (known as the "Psychic Capital of the World") and the hippie-like Rainbow Family camping in the Ocala National Forest. All of it became grist for his Florida fiction.

Leonard once explained that his books start with him thinking about a particular character—for instance, Karen Sisco of *Out of Sight*: "I think of characters who will carry a story. The plot comes out of the characters, their attitudes. How they talk describes who they are. . . . In 1995 my researcher, Gregg Sutter, handed me a photo of a deputy U.S. marshal standing in front of the Miami federal courthouse, a pump-action shotgun held upright against her hip. 'She's a book,' I said to Gregg."

Leonard bought a condo in North Palm Beach where he spent part of the year writing and playing tennis and taking long walks. Meanwhile he collected fans and friends who could provide him with true Florida stories. One was a Florida Department of Law Enforcement special agent named James O. Born. Born served on the violent crimes task force that rounded up the escapees from the Everglades prison break that inspired the opening scene of *Out of Sight*. Later, Leonard encouraged Born to write his own Florida-based crime novels, starting with *Walking Money*.

Another was a Palm Beach County judge named Marvin Mounts, who would send Leonard full transcripts of hearings and trials where funny things happened, Sutter said.

Mounts helped with the creation of one of Leonard's wilder characters, a horny Palm Beach judge who's nicknamed "Maximum Bob" because of his tendency toward throwing the book at defendants. Maximum Bob wasn't based on the mild-mannered Mounts. Instead he was a gender-swapped version of a real Florida judge, Ellen "Maximum" Morphonios, who kept a toy electric chair in her chambers along with Toto, her diaper-wearing pet chimp. In her autobiography, the former model wrote of her extremely active love life: "I'm not going to lie about it: During (two) marriages I had a lot of boyfriends on the side. They were interesting guys."

She wasn't the only real Florida character to show up in a Leonard novel. Chili Palmer, the Miami loan shark who's the main character in *Get Shorty*, was based on Chili Palmer, a Miami private eye who had been a loan shark in the '70s. Leonard very politely asked the real Chili if he could borrow the name for the fictional character, figuring it was better than anything he could think up.

And then there are the Crowes—a whole flock of them.

※

Dale Crowe, Junior, told Kathy Baker, his probation officer, he didn't see where he had done anything wrong. He had gone to the go-go bar to meet a buddy of his, had one beer, that's all, while he was waiting, minding his own business, and this go-go whore came up to his table and started giving him a private dance he never asked for. . . . Dale was from a family of offenders, in and out of the system.

—*Maximum Bob*, 1991

When he wrote a book, Leonard would sometimes slip in references to people and places in prior novels, creating a sort of Extended Dutch Leonard Universe. He used the Leucadendron Country Club—where the members include both a wealthy drug dealer and a deposed South American secret policeman—in both *Stick* and *Cat Chaser*. Karen Sisco's private eye dad, Marshall, pops up not only in *Out of Sight* but also in *Cat Chaser*. Ray Nicolette, an Alcohol, Tobacco and Firearms agent who's dating Karen Sisco at the start of *Out of Sight*, first appeared in *Rum Punch*, which became the movie *Jackie Brown* (and, thanks to cooperation between directors Steven Soderbergh and Quentin Tarantino, was played by Michael Keaton in the movie version of both books).

But Leonard's main signal that his Florida books all take place in the same timeline is his inclusion of a family known as the Crowes. Once you start looking for them, you'll see a whole murder of Crowes.

The first, found in *Gold Coast*, was Roland Crowe, a backwoods thug in $350 cowboy boots and a cream-colored Coup de Ville. Roland's brother Elvin, described as "this big guy from the swamp in a cowboy hat," and his screw-up nephew, Dale Jr., appear in *Maximum Bob*. The judge, in sentencing Dale Jr., mentions sentencing his father too, "I've had Dale Crowe Senior before this court on several occasions in the past. Either caught poaching alligators or apprehended with quantities of marijuana in his boat, coming off the lake."

Another member of the Crowe clan, a killer-for-hire and sometime fishing guide named Earl, is a character in *Pronto* (1993) Leonard's first novel about Raylan Givens. Dale Jr. gets a probation violation curtain call in the second Givens novel, *Riding the Rap* (1995). A Crowe relative named Dewey later pops up in the Raylan-centered TV show *Justified*. Meanwhile, in Leonard's Spanish-American War novel *Cuba Libre*, the hero confronts a Florida-born bodyguard named Novis Crowe who's apparently the patriarch of the family.

Leonard regarded the Crowes as "swamp creatures," Sutter said, but let's call them by the name they would have today: Florida Men. They're felonious and full of themselves, constantly getting drunk and into trouble, never quite as clever as they think they are.

Take Elvin, for instance. In *Maximum Bob,* Elvin Crowe is ticked off that the judge sentenced him to serious prison time for a murder in which Elvin shot a stranger instead of the man he was aiming to kill. He contends that his lack of intent to kill the man he actually killed is an extenuating circumstance. Elvin explains to his probation officer how he wound up shooting the wrong man, then says he told her that story because "I want you to see I'm not some ordinary two-bit fuckup you got on your list." The implication being Elvin is more of an extraordinary one.

So when you read news headlines about a Florida man trying to get an alligator drunk, or fixing cars with Play-Doh, or running over himself during a road rage incident, just remember that that meme got its start in literature thanks to Dutch Leonard from Michigan, a part-time Florida man himself.

Leonard had no master plan for weaving in the Crowes, Ray Nicolette and the rest of his Florida reference points, Sutter told me.

"Elmore didn't plan," Sutter said. "He wrote and used what came into his head." Of course, the funniest stuff in his head always came from Florida. After all, Sutter told me, "It's kind of hard to avoid the freak show. It's just in the air down there."

> Chili didn't say anything, giving it some more thought. Fuckin endings, man, they weren't as easy as they looked.

—*Get Shorty,* 1990

18

UNINTELLIGIBLE AT ANY SPEED

Sarasota, August 27, 2017

The Federal Bureau of Investigation has been the focus of a lot of headlines lately. Between the president firing the director and the ongoing investigation of potential Russian interference in the 2016 election, the FBI is all over the front page.

Here's hoping this current controversy has a more satisfying conclusion than one that happened 50 years ago and involved a Sarasota connection.

The year was 1964. The upheavals characteristic of the '60s—assassinations, protest marches, the loosening of sexual mores—were just getting started. One Sarasota educator was sure he knew who was to blame.

A band called The Kingsmen.

The Kingsmen were one of several raucous rock bands that formed in the Pacific Northwest in the early '60s. The best known was Paul Revere and His Raiders. They all played songs that tended to be fast and loud and party-oriented. It wasn't unusual for several bands to record the same song.

Thus, in 1961, a Seattle band called Rockin' Robin Roberts and the Wailers cut a speeded-up version of a rhythm and blues tune called "Louie, Louie," and then in 1963, The Kingsmen and Paul Revere and His Raiders both cut singles of the same number. The original version of "Louie, Louie," was written and performed by Richard Berry, who also recorded the original version of "Money (That's What I Want)," later covered by the Beatles. In Berry's version, "Louie, Louie" was a Caribbean-flavored tune about a homesick sailor pining for his girlfriend.

But when The Kingsmen got hold of it, it became something *duh-duh-duh, duh-duh, duh-duh-duh* different. Or so the rumor went.

"Back in 1963, everybody who knew anything about rock 'n' roll knew that the Kingsmen's 'Louie Louie' concealed dirty words that could be unveiled only by playing the 45 rpm single at 33-⅓," rock critic Dave Marsh later wrote in his book about the song. "This preposterous fable bore no scrutiny even at the time, but kids used to pretend it did, in order to panic parents, teachers and other authority figures. . . . So 'Louie Louie' leaped up the chart on the basis of a myth about its lyrics so contagious that it swept cross country quicker than bad weather."

Somebody somewhere along the line jotted down the "dirty" lyrics. The homesick sailor now sang about having sex with his girlfriend. Instead of "Louie, Louie, me gotta go," it was "Louie, Louie, grab her way down low." Everything went downhill from there—the f-word showed up, among other things.

The lascivious "Louie, Louie" lyric sheets were soon being passed around, hand to hand, in the nation's schools—and one landed in the hands of a particularly touchy Sarasota educator.

Everything we know about him is contained in an FBI file that the agency has posted online. The file contains his letter of complaint and all the subsequent reports from FBI agents.

The educator had a teenage daughter. She bought the record and brought it home. Soon after, her agitated parent typed out an angry epistle to U.S. Attorney General Robert Kennedy dated Jan. 30, 1964—two weeks before the long-haired Beatles debuted on *The Ed Sullivan Show*.

"Dear Mr. Kennedy," the educator wrote. "Who do you turn to when your teen age daughter buys and brings home pornographic or obscene materials?"

The governor of Indiana had banned the song from Hoosier radio stations, noted the letter-writer, so he "proceeded to try to decipher the jumble of words." However, he declared in his letter, "The lyrics are so filthy I cannot enclose them in this letter."

He wrote that he wanted everyone involved prosecuted for distributing obscenity to impressionable children.

"We all know there is obscene materials available for those who seek it, but when they start sneaking in this material in the guise of the latest teenage rock & roll hit record, these morons have gone too far," the educator wrote. "This land of ours is headed for an extreme state of moral degradation what with this record, the biggest hit movies and the sex and violence exploited on T.V. How can we stamp out this menace???"

The biggest hit movie that week, by the way, was Disney's animated *The Sword in the Stone*, and the top TV show was *The Beverly Hillbillies*.

Nevertheless, the Justice Department took his complaint seriously. Thus the FBI launched an official investigation into "Louie, Louie." They wanted to see if it violated the laws against ITOM—"Interstate Transportation of Obscene Materials."

The first step: Send an agent from the Tampa FBI office to interview the person who complained.

The agent reported to FBI Director J. Edgar Hoover that the complainant worked at Sarasota High School and that "Louie, Louie" is "very popular with high school students, and he has been furnished lyrics for the song that are very dirty." Just listening to the record, the man said, "the words are hard to recognize," but by referring the dirty lyrics "it sounds like the lyrics are identical with the enclosed obscene lyrics."

The agent included the lyric sheet with his report to the director.

Yes, a Florida-based FBI agent sent dirty lyrics to J. Edgar—in a special envelope marked "Obscene."

Hoover soon dispatched agents to question the Kingsmen, Richard Berry, Paul Revere and the Raiders and record company executives. FBI laboratory technicians played the song at every conceivable setting. They—and the Federal Communications Commission, which joined the case—spent 31 months pursuing the "Louie, Louie" rumor and ultimately concluded the song was unintelligible at any speed.

At this point, Marsh wrote, the song "passed into legend, becoming the greatest example of rock's function as a secret language for its audience."

The one person the feds did not interview was the guy who sang the song. His name was Jack Ely, and he had left the Kingsmen to join the Army before their record became a hit.

Had they questioned Ely, they would have learned that on the day the band recorded "Louie, Louie," the microphone he sang into was hanging from the ceiling much higher than it should have been. Ely had to stand on tiptoe and tilt his head back, an awkward position for singing. He had strained his voice during a performance the night before. And during the recording, to get more of a "live" sound, his band mates stood around him in a circle, playing their instruments just as loudly as possible. Hence his half-shouted, half-gargled performance.

"Was there anything dirty in it?" an interviewer asked Ely in 2012.

"Not a thing," Ely replied.

The FBI files do not record whether anyone ever informed the outraged Sarasota educator of the inconclusive conclusion of the investigation, so we don't know his reaction. Sadly, his identity remains lost to history. The FBI redacted his name from its files, and the members of the Sarasota High Class of '64 whom I have interviewed said they could not say for sure whom it might have been. One remembered that the Kingsmen drew a good-sized crowd when they played at Sarasota's National Guard Armory—no complaints or protests.

One Class of '64 grad was historian Jeff LaHurd. He recalled "Louie, Louie" being a popular song but, like his classmates, he can't remember any teachers who seemed upset about it. As for the song, he laughed and said, "That song is probably one of the *minor* reasons the country has gone down the tubes!"

19

MISSION OF A LIFETIME

St. Petersburg Times, August 22, 1995

Susan Morrison has two nightmares.

One haunts her as she sleeps. She is somehow present at her father's murder. She hears him trying to call for help. But because he is a deaf-mute, all that comes from his mouth is an inarticulate cry of anguish.

In her other nightmare, the two men who killed her father are released from prison. That one haunts her waking hours, driving a crusade that has outlasted her marriage, her pursuit of a college degree, her dreams of a new career.

Lester Morrison was killed 21 years ago. For the past decade, his only child has attended every parole hearing for the two men convicted of murdering him.

"I will fight forever to keep them in prison," Susan Morrison said. "I'll go to my grave doing this."

Year after year she has made the trip to Tallahassee to speak for the man who could not call for help, to make sure his killers serve every day of their life sentences.

The records of the trial were long ago put on microfilm and filed away. The judge who imposed the sentence has retired. The lead prosecutor is dead. Morrison is the one constant. She will not go away.

No one keeps a record of attendance at parole board meetings. But Dix Darnell, the board official who works with victims like Morrison, says nobody else even comes close to her persistence.

It is hardly an enviable achievement.

"She's probably going to have to keep doing this for as long as she lives," said Wendy Nelson, a friend of Morrison's, whose daughter was murdered in 1980. "That's a horrible sentence she's been given. You can't let your grief have any closure with that going on. It's a wound inflicted 21 years ago that the system doesn't allow to heal."

Each time Morrison attends a parole board hearing, she relives her father's death. It leaves her so emotionally drained that for several days after, she lies on her couch, like a zombie.

Now she is girding herself for another trip to the state capital. The state Department of Corrections has recommended Gov. Lawton Chiles and the Cabinet commute the sentence of one of her father's murderers. The hearing is Aug. 28.

Sometimes people tell her she should give up the battle and get on with her life. Her reply is simple: "I tell them that's not possible."

☼

By April 3, 1974, Lester Morrison was 62. He had worked as a caretaker at Sylvan Abbey cemetery near Safety Harbor for about 15 years.

When the cemetery employees gathered for lunch in a warehouse full of tombstones, he would scribble notes or make signs that would crack the others up. Quick with a joke, he was even quicker to lend money to a friend. He often carried a lot of cash for emergencies, knowing that money could talk when he could not.

Arthur Copeland had worked at the cemetery for six months. He knew Morrison, even liked him—but he liked his co-worker's money more. Copeland, 29, had served prison time for forging checks but was released early.

Alfred Rosher, 22, also was out on early release. His crime: robbery. The pair met behind bars, and were close friends by the time they lay in wait together, before dawn, among the graves. A .22-caliber rifle in hand, they were waiting for Lester Morrison.

He arrived about 5 a.m., carrying apples. He never heard the shots. One bullet hit him in the arm, the other in the back. He dropped the apples and ran, dodging between the gravestones.

A woman who lived nearby later reported she heard something like a scream, shrill and perhaps not even human—the sound Morrison hears in her dreams.

Copeland boasted to his sister he had gunned down his co-worker. But after Copeland's brother-in-law turned him in, Copeland blamed his friend Rosher.

At the trial, Copeland testified that Rosher shot the deaf man, and they followed the trail of blood to where he fell. With a 2-by-4 they turned his body over. Then they rifled his pockets. They split about $85.

☼

Susan Morrison of Palm Harbor shows some of the files she has used at parole hearings in Tallahassee for the two men who killed her father four decades before. She made it her mission to keep them behind bars. Photo by V. Jane Windsor, used by permission of the *Tampa Bay Times*.

From her yellow house on a quiet street in Palm Harbor, Morrison plots her latest campaign—collecting petitions, asking friends and relatives to write letters.

She seems fully in charge, like a general marshaling the troops. But that appearance is misleading, according to therapist Lu Redmond, who runs the Crime Survivors Center in Clearwater and has written a book called *Surviving: When Someone You Love Is Murdered*. She says the murder of a family member brings much more than grief.

"It's a loss of control," said Redmond, who has worked with Morrison. "We believe we should be safe and sound and life should be fair, but murder shows that it's not."

It shows that our lives can be stolen at any moment by anyone too selfish or crazy to care about the continued existence of anyone else. Even now, 21 years later, Morrison's life is not her own. She is a prisoner as surely as are Rosher and Copeland.

"You realize your life revolves around a date and a time and a place that you didn't choose," Redmond said. "It continually puts control of your life in someone else's hands."

In 1974, a judge sentenced Rosher and Copeland to life in prison plus 50 years for second-degree murder. But in the language peculiar to the justice system, life did not mean life. It meant they would be eligible for parole by 1986.

Morrison found out by accident that Rosher and Copeland were about to be released. State officials sent her mother a letter in 1985, asking if the family wanted the killers to pay restitution when they were let out. Her mother was too fragile to fight, so Morrison stepped in.

Although untrained in dealing with the parole system, Morrison quickly learned how to get the board's attention. She called the newspaper and rounded up 700 signatures on petitions.

She was joined at that first hearing by top prosecutor Bernie McCabe, who has attended every subsequent hearing, plus a sheriff's representative.

It worked. It has worked ever since. And according to David Mack, that's an injustice.

☼

Mack represents Rosher. By all rights, he says, Rosher should have been freed years ago: "The system has been very unfair to Alfred Rosher."

In 21 years Copeland, now 50, has been written up 13 times for breaking prison rules. He recently wrote to the *Times* to say, "I feel that I have did enough time." But the parole board says he has to stay in prison until at least 2011.

Rosher is another story. Now 43, he has been written up just once in two decades. At Dade Correctional Institution, where he has been serving his time, the staff repeatedly has recommended him for release. He has the promise of a job on the outside.

"He's a lot older today, he's done a lot to improve himself as a human being and he has abided by all the rules," said Mack, a paralegal. The parole board has turned loose other murderers with records far worse than Rosher's, Mack said.

Morrison's continued focus on the crime itself instead of Rosher's progress in prison makes the case more emotional and political than it should be, he said. If it weren't for her, "he would be home."

Parole commissioners suspended Rosher's 1986 release date and have never set a new one. He keeps getting the same letter saying the board believes he needs "continued observation and treatment."

"They've been observing him for 20 years!" Mack said. "It's extremely frustrating."

Gene Strickland of the parole board said the commission's intent is clear: "They don't want to see him out. The commission believes he would still be a threat if released."

☼

For a time Morrison pursued a career as a professional victim's advocate, helping victims and their families deal with the court system.

She took college courses toward that end, but dropped it before she earned her degree. She says that bearing her own burden took so much energy that she couldn't bear anyone else's.

She divorced. The strain of her continuing crusade is not to blame, she said, "but it didn't make it any easier to deal with."

She's had plenty of run-ins with bosses who told her she couldn't have time off work to go to Tallahassee. She would go anyway. Now she sells insurance, a job with a flexible schedule.

She is living a race. If she outlives Rosher and Copeland, she thinks she can make sure they never leave prison. But she is older than both of them, and her life may run out before theirs does.

Should that happen, someone is waiting to take her place.

Her 27-year-old son, Kenneth Christian, has never attended a parole commission hearing. But he knows the drill and stands ready to go to Tallahassee to represent the grandfather he barely remembers.

"When the day comes," he said, "I wouldn't hesitate."

~~~~~~

Note: Copeland died in 2019, still behind bars. As of May 2021, Rosher remained in prison.

20

DOUBLE TROUBLE

St. Petersburg Times, February 22, 1997

Eight years ago, Ronald Davis stood before a judge who read off a long list of charges against him. Davis was astonished. He knew he had not committed those crimes.

Suddenly he realized what was happening.

"I have a twin brother," he told the judge.

"The whole courtroom just busted with laughter," Davis recalled last week. "Nobody believed me."

But it was true. Ever since they emerged from the womb eight minutes apart, Ronald and Rodney Davis have been mistaken for each other. They have the same eyes, same ears, same nose, same mouth. Similar burly build. Similar names.

Everyone gets them confused—including police and corrections officers, lawyers, court clerks and judges.

Anyone who calls up Rodney's files from Pinellas County's criminal court records will see Ronald's name listed as an alias. Anyone who asks for Ronald's mug shot from jail records gets a picture of Rodney.

"It's just a complete nightmare," one frustrated prosecutor said recently.

The American criminal justice system is based on the notion of individual responsibility: You do the crime, you do the time. But how can the courts determine whom to punish when the innocent and the guilty look alike?

So, after that disastrous court hearing, Ronald spent seventeen days in the Pinellas County Jail. His public defender said he should persuade Rodney to turn himself in. That would clear up the confusion, and he would be a free man again.

Instead Ronald bided his time until the mess sorted itself out and he was released. He refused to put his own brother behind bars, even to save himself.

"I'm just always going to feel like I got to protect him," said Ronald, 33, a restaurant manager. "I love him."

※

The Bible reports that the first twins, Jacob and Esau, struggled with each other even before they were born. Later Jacob donned goat skins and pretended to be the hairy Esau so their blind father would give him the blessing Esau should have received.

Nowadays the switched-identity trick has become a standard plot in soap operas: Evil twin appears in town, stirs up trouble, then leaves the good twin to suffer the consequences.

The myth that there is always a good twin and a bad twin has become fixed in the popular imagination, according to Patricia Malmstrom, director of Twin Services, a California-based resource center.

"We get calls to our help line from parents of newborns who say, 'I already know which twin is the good one,'" she said.

Sometimes, tragically, the labels stuck on by parents become the child's destiny, said Malmstrom, herself the mother of 23-year-old twins.

Actually, she said, twins will try out a variety of roles, experimenting with good-and-bad, follower-leader and bully-victim as they test the strengths and limits of their complex bond.

As with most twins, the relationship between Ronald and Rodney Davis is far more complicated than any soap opera plot.

When the Davis brothers were growing up, Rodney was considered the good twin—walking away from fights, dodging trouble—while Ronald was the bad one, always getting into mischief.

"I ain't never claimed to be no angel," Ronald said with a smile. He explained that the way to tell them apart is their scars. Rodney has just one, over his eye. "I have scars everywhere but my face," Ronald said.

Even before they began collecting scars, their mother, Margaret Denise Davis, could always tell them apart. "Mother's intuition," is Ronald's only explanation.

She died of a heart attack when the twins were 8, and all seven of her children left Atlanta and moved in with their grandmother in St. Petersburg.

Their grandmother, Mabel Davis, knew which twin was which, too. She even gave them different nicknames: Rodney was "Big Job," Ronald was "Little Bit." Rodney always was a little larger, Ronald explained, "and he would protect me."

Despite that closeness, Ronald and Rodney would constantly battle.

"We used to fight growing up, over everything: toys, clothes, money," Ronald said. "But it was a love kind of fighting."

They hated wearing matching outfits, so much so they would tear the clothes off each other. Yet adults kept trying to dress them alike until they were 13—fairly late in the development of twins' identity, according to Malmstrom.

Still, looking and dressing alike had its advantages at school, at least for the bad twin.

"I would be picking on people, and we'd get to the principal's office, and the person I was picking on couldn't identify which one of us did it," Ronald said.

The solution: Ship them off to different middle schools. Rodney went to Bay Point, Ronald to Madeira Beach. Ronald still feels responsible for the forced separation.

As they grew older the twins grew apart, particularly after Rodney discovered a taste for cocaine at age 22. "Once he started doing the crazy stuff," Ronald said, "I'd hardly ever see him."

Although they lived in the same city, Ronald said, there were times when he felt as if he didn't have a twin. The only reminder would come when a stranger would talk to him as if they were acquainted.

But the paths of Little Bit and Big Job crossed again in the court system.

✸

In Denmark, the government has registered every pair of twins born since 1870. In a study published in 1987, Danish scientists compared the list of male twins with national criminal records.

They found that when a male identical twin committed a crime, his twin was five times likelier than the average Danish man to commit a crime as well. When a fraternal twin committed a crime, his twin was three times likelier than other Danish men to break the law.

Does that mean a child's genes determine whether he will someday turn to crime? Or does it mean a similar upbringing produces children with a similar inclination to break the law? So far no study has answered that question.

Although the Davis twins both wound up with records, Rodney's crimes tended to be those of a man with little control over his desire for drugs, while Ronald's tended to be those of a man with little control over his temper.

In fact, it was after a 1989 bar fight that Ronald landed in jail facing Rodney's drug charges. And in a letter Rodney sent to Circuit Judge Nelly

Khouzam this month, he recalled being arrested on a drug charge and then being held responsible for his brother's record of violence.

"I was told they would get it right at the jail, but they did not," Rodney wrote. "So you see judge they thought that it was only one of us instead of two."

Rodney contended the confusion was not the fault of either twin. But Ronald says his brother sometimes pretended to be Ronald when arrested and also fudged his birthday and place of birth. Then Rodney would call and apologize for causing him trouble.

"It's created complete confusion," said Assistant State Attorney Nick Mooney.

Sorting out which case belonged to which twin required pulling every set of fingerprints the jail had ever taken of the pair and comparing them to the ones taken by the bailiffs in court, Mooney said.

Then, said Assistant Public Defender Bruce Johnson, "there were a long series of hearings on which were Mr. Rodney Davis's charges and which were his brother's."

Even now, Mooney said, "there are a whole bunch of charges out there that, frankly, we're not sure which brother is responsible for."

But while Rodney was sinking deeper into trouble, their grandmother was urging Ronald to change his ways for the sake of his children.

"Stop letting Rodney get you in the mess," she told him. And the sheepish Ronald had to tell her, "It's not all Rodney."

✿

By all accounts Ronald has heeded his grandmother and mended his ways. He has a steady job and a stable home. Probation officials praise his turnaround. His boss has promoted him.

His twin is another story. Last March 26, Rodney pleaded guilty to sale and possession of cocaine, and Circuit Judge Brandt Downey sentenced him to four years in prison as a habitual offender.

A teary-eyed Rodney begged the judge for a furlough. His girlfriend had had a baby and put the child up for adoption. Rodney said he and his family were trying to get custody, but to do that he needed to be free a little longer.

Downey granted a rare concession to a prison-bound defendant. He told Rodney to come back on April 15 to begin his sentence.

Rodney didn't get the child. And he didn't show up on April 15.

For nearly nine months Rodney remained on the run. Meanwhile the police kept stopping Ronald, thinking he was the fugitive. Each time he was able to establish his identity before they hauled him off to jail.

Finally, last month, the real Rodney was arrested. He told Judge Khouzam he didn't turn himself in because Ronald needed him.

Ronald had suffered a stress attack and was hospitalized. So Rodney stepped in to take care of his brother's children.

But even after Ronald came home, Rodney put off going to prison. He said he got hooked on crack again.

Khouzam asked for his Social Security number. Rodney gave a number different from the one in his records. The judge suggested fingerprinting him to be sure he wasn't Ronald. Mooney said that was not necessary.

Once again Rodney begged for mercy. But for failing to appear in court, Khouzam added five years to his four-year sentence.

While Rodney was waiting to be sent to prison, Ronald visited him in jail. What Ronald saw on the other side of the glass partition was unsettling.

"It was," he said, "kind of like looking in a mirror."

21

"THE MORNING FROM HELL"

St. Petersburg Times, February 25, 1996

*Note: One morning while on the criminal court beat, I showed up in misde-
meanor court to watch a specific case and became so fascinated by the crowd
around me that I stayed for the entire morning docket, taking careful notes
about everything I saw. The result was this slice-of-life story. Meanwhile, the
hearing on the case I was interested in wound up being postponed and later
the charges were dropped—no story.*

LARGO—They line up single file to pass through the metal detector,
stacking their keys, coins and cigarette lighters in white plastic trays, send-
ing their purses through the X-ray machine.

Past the snack bar and the restrooms, they round the corner and walk
down the hall to the last courtroom on the right, its blue walls bathed in
sterile fluorescence.

Once inside its tight confines they fill every seat on the six short rows
of hard oak benches, then spill out the door and jam the tiny vestibule. At
8:35 a.m. Pinellas County Judge Stephen Rushing, his gray beard contrast-
ing with his black robe, sweeps in and settles himself on the bench up
front.

Out in the hall a lighted sign clicks on. It says: "Court in Session."

It could add: "Look Out."

What follows is what one attorney calls "the morning from hell," a
frantic antemeridian of pathos, anger, confusion, numbing routine and
twisted comedy.

Rushing says that's a fairly typical mix for a Tuesday.

No one in the crowd is a mere spectator. They are all defendants or
victims, summoned to appear in Courtroom E of Pinellas County's misdemeanor courts complex on this particular morning for pretrial hearings
on 69 cases.

When court convenes, the people in the vestibule fold their arms, lean on the wall, stare at the gray carpet and strain to hear what's going on through the propped-open doors. A bleary-eyed man with a ponytail puts his motorcycle helmet on the floor and sits on it.

Most are dressed in jeans and sneakers, looking like a crowd of shoppers at the mall. But one petite 28-year-old St. Petersburg woman, wearing a diamond stud in her nose and an amazingly long set of fingernails, has squeezed into a white satin dress with more ruffles than a wedding gown. When her case is called, she stands up and tells the judge she had "an 8:30 appointment," as if he were a doctor and could write a prescription to cure her of her charges.

Across 49th Street, in circuit court, the cases involve brutal crimes such as rape and murder. A felony conviction can send someone to state prison for years, sometimes for life. A few even go to death row. Most defendants have been through the court system before, and rare is the case where no attorney speaks for the accused.

But in county court the crimes are more mundane. The docket for this day lists animal cruelty, shoplifting, trespassing—charges that, at most, could result in a year in the county jail. It's not uncommon for defendants to show up alone, determined to speak for themselves as best they can.

"It's kind of like People's Court," Rushing says afterward. "We get a lot of people who have never been in court before. Some of them were just in the wrong place at the wrong time."

Rushing calls himself a "local yokel," a St. Petersburg High School graduate who worked as a public defender and a prosecutor before being elected to the bench seven years ago. A county judgeship is usually a guarantee of obscurity, but Rushing's hobby has gained him some small renown. He draws cartoons, published in various periodicals under the title "Legal Insanity."

When judges face a courtroom full of victims and defendants, Rushing says, "Every decision we make hurts somebody." Drawing cartoons about the silly side of the law helps him maintain a sense of balance.

So far two books of Rushing's cartoons have been published. In the foreword to the second, Rushing quotes an old saw that says a judge needs only three attributes: "gray hair to look distinguished, thick glasses to look learned and inflamed hemorrhoids to appear concerned."

☼

Printed at the top of this morning's 24-page docket is a polite fiction. It says Rushing will deal with all 69 cases in just one hour. He will actually take more than four times that, yet will not spend more than a few minutes on each case.

In normal conversation Rushing, despite his name, weighs his words carefully before he speaks. But to get through his morning docket he sometimes talks so fast that whole sentences come out in a single whoosh: "Raiseyourrighthand. Doyoupromisetotellthetruth . . ."

At any time Rushing's division carries a load of more than 1,000 cases. With more coming in all the time, he has to dispose of 300 a month just to stay even. Under such pressure to push cases along, Rushing employs every tool at his disposal to keep the system from bogging down.

"The bottom line is to get it done," he says. "It's not an art."

This morning a 22-year-old Palm Harbor woman is ready to plead no contest to a charge of criminal mischief for running a key down the side of a man's car. But she says the victim has told her boyfriend he wants $350 to fix the damage, not the $800 that the state says she should pay.

Rushing turns to Assistant State Attorney Maria Woodruff, whose billowing blond curls have drawn expressions of admiration from several women in the gallery. Like Rushing, Woodruff, 32, is a St. Petersburg native. She has been a prosecutor for almost a year, all of it in misdemeanor court. Although another prosecutor sits at the prosecution table this morning, he is still in training. Woodruff handles each of the cases that come up.

Woodruff tells the judge she has tried contacting the victim to ask if he would accept $350 but he has not returned her calls. Rushing reaches for a phone sitting near him on the bench and asks Woodruff, "What's his number?"

The judge dials and leaves a message for the victim: "Hi, this is Judge Stephen Rushing . . ." Then he turns to the defendant and tells her, "You have a seat for a minute and we'll see if he gets back with us."

Rushing moves on to other cases. After five minutes his judicial assistant, Sherrie Morton, bustles into court and hands him a note. The victim just called the judge's office to say $350 was fine with him.

The Palm Harbor woman pleads no contest and agrees to pay the $350. Rushing has disposed of one more case.

In another case, a Clearwater resident stands before the judge facing a charge of soliciting a prostitute—actually, an undercover officer whom he offered $5 for sex.

This would be an easy case for Rushing to deal with, except the man is from Mexico and speaks little English. Calling for an official translator would take time. So when another man stands up in the back of the courtroom and offers to translate, the judge agrees—even though the impromptu interpreter is a defendant in another case.

Rushing swears in both men, then runs through the standard questions as his interpreter, a 35-year-old St. Petersburg grocery store employee, puts them into Spanish. The Spanish-speaking defendant enters a plea of guilty—"*petition de culpable.*" The judge puts him on probation for six months and orders him to stay away from the spot where he was arrested.

To repay his translator for his public-spirited aid to the legal system, Rushing calls his case next. The charge is domestic battery. The victim is the interpreter's girlfriend of 11 years, who is 2 inches taller and 90 pounds heavier than the 5-foot-7, 160-pound defendant. She tells the judge that, despite what the police report says, her boyfriend did not hit her. He only grabbed her sleeve.

The interpreter pleads no contest and Rushing gives him six months' probation, fines him $100 and orders him to attend a 12-week course to learn how to control his anger.

Later, the interpreter says justice was served in the solicitation case, but not his own. The counseling is excellent but expensive, he says. He thinks the judge should have dismissed the charge.

"I think the judge should've said, 'Do you two love each other?'" he says. He and his girlfriend have physically attacked each other in the past, he says. "But we're still together. We still love each other."

☼

More than a dozen of this morning's cases involve domestic battery, in every permutation: White couples, Black couples, Hispanic couples, Asian couples, gay couples.

The variety of domestic battery cases can be startling, Rushing later says.

"I had one where the spouse had hit him with a frozen raccoon," he recalls. "Evidently they had one in the freezer."

Today's cases are more sad than comic. In one from Largo, the defendant and victim are women. Though one had attacked the other, they are still a couple. The defendant pleads no contest, then begins to cry. The victim comforts her, holding her close and stroking her hair.

Some of the victims sit in the jury box, staying as far away as possible from the defendants. Some, like the interpreter's girlfriend, choose to sit in the gallery next to the person charged with beating them.

About half the domestic battery cases Rushing hears involve a victim who stands up to proclaim he or she is not really a victim and does not want the state to pursue the charges.

One woman tells the judge she lied to the police about being beaten up just to get her man in trouble. She sticks to this story even after Rushing warns her she might be charged with filing a false report.

In each case with a balky victim, Woodruff tells the judge the state is prepared to go to trial anyway. Rushing suggests that the defendant could plead no contest, admitting that the state could prove its case but not that he or she is guilty. In exchange, he will fine them $150, tell them not to have any "illegal contact" with the victim and order them to get counseling.

Most, like the interpreter, take the deal.

In one battery case the defendant is a woman from Seminole, the victim her husband. The man says he definitely wants the mother of his three children prosecuted. She insists she is innocent. Each has sought a court order barring the other from further domestic violence.

Rushing sets a trial date and the woman leaves. The husband sticks around the courtroom for another 30 minutes to make sure he doesn't bump into her in the parking lot.

Two weeks later, she files for divorce.

☼

Although Rushing's docket is arranged with the defendants in alphabetical order, he doesn't call cases A to Z. Instead, he starts with the people who have hired attorneys. That way, those defendants are not paying their lawyers to stand around.

After them will come the cases handled by the public defenders, then the people who came to court with no lawyer at all. Rushing hopes the people called last can watch the professionals and learn enough to represent themselves when their turn comes.

As the private attorneys run through their cases—one or two per lawyer—a pair of public defenders is already lining up their considerably longer list of clients. Each keeps tabs on 170 cases at any one time, a sometimes crushing load.

"The word I would use is hectic," says the veteran of the pair, Robin Kester. "From the minute you hit that door and you're in court, you're running. It's organized chaos."

Kester is a pale and intense woman with short, dark hair who gives her age as "no longer thirtysomething." She has worked for the Pinellas-Pasco public defender's office for nine years, but only transferred down from New Port Richey a few months before. Kester has been paired up with Sean Scott, a tall, slender man with expressive eyes who, at age 30, has been a public defender for just six months. In the virtually all-White Pinellas court system, Scott is one of the few African-American lawyers.

Scott stands toward the back of the courtroom softly calling out names. When a defendant answers, he takes the person to one of two tiny rooms that flank the courtroom's vestibule. There he and Kester sit down to talk to their clients, often for the first time, going over the case and explaining what may happen in court.

"The client may want to go to trial or he may want to negotiate," Kester explains.

Four or five names get no response, and the corners of Scott's mouth droop with disappointment. He knows the judge will put out a warrant for the no-shows, and they could face additional charges.

Meanwhile, Kester, battling a flare-up of persistent bronchitis, is running clients through the interview rooms as rapidly as possible. At one point, a man Kester is counseling decides he does not like what he's hearing. His voice grows louder, then louder still. Suddenly the man is shouting loudly enough to be heard in the courtroom, distracting the judge.

Bailiff Cassandra Breech, whose regal bearing and piercing stare are more intimidating than the cloth badge embroidered on her black uniform jacket, strides back to warn the shouter to keep his voice down. Like magic, quiet prevails.

Later, Kester says diplomatically that the man "was having a problem grasping his options. He became a bit vocal—not upset, just excited. We eventually worked it out."

But the frantic pace of preparation takes its toll. By 10:30 a.m., the last of the private attorneys has departed, briefcase in hand. It's time for Kester and Scott to take their turn. When Kester walks into court, Rushing greets her by noting, "It's been kind of a busy morning."

"It's been the morning from hell," Kester croaks grimly, "and I put that on the record."

☼

Several of Kester's clients are people caught driving under the influence. One is a 36-year-old St. Petersburg man arrested after a police officer spotted him weaving along Fourth Street N.

On the sidewalk.

On a moped.

This is the man's fourth DUI, though apparently his first involving something other than an automobile. Speaking in an eastern European accent, he pleads no contest. The judge puts him on a year's probation and revokes his driver's license for 10 years—the stiffest penalty Rushing will impose all day.

By now the crowd that once jammed the courtroom has thinned to the point where everyone remaining can sit in the gallery. That includes the bleary-eyed man with the motorcycle helmet and another man who keeps muttering that the court system is out to drain his pocket of money.

Meanwhile a big, burly man with shaggy blond hair gets up, sits down, changes places, goes out and comes back in. He keeps hitching up his jeans, which almost immediately slide back down.

This is Kester's shouter, a 35-year-old roofer from St. Petersburg. When his case is called, he decides he doesn't need her services. He will speak for himself. Tucking his T-shirt into his jeans, he steps forward and tells his story to the judge.

Three months ago, he got in a fight with his brother and hit him over the head with a 13-inch portable TV. Police charged him with aggravated battery, a felony. But after he spent 27 days in jail, the state attorney's office dropped the charge.

However, because police had found "a couple of joints on me," he says, he was charged with possession of marijuana, a misdemeanor. He launches into a complicated legal argument about probable cause for the search, but that's not what the judge wants to hear.

Then the roofer mentions that his son's mother just died. He would like to move back to Ohio with the boy, he says, if he can resolve this misdemeanor charge without paying a fine he can ill afford. Rushing suggests giving him credit for the time he served in jail. Does that suit the defendant?

"Let's go, babe!" the roofer says enthusiastically. He pleads no contest, they take care of the paperwork and he asks if he needs to see any other officials. Rushing says no, he's free to leave now.

"Okay, I'll see you, bro!" the man sings out as he bolts from the courtroom, hitching up his pants.

"Now there's a happy camper," Rushing quips. Although Rushing does not draw cartoons in court, he says later, this case tempted him.

☼

It is well past noon, and the sound of rumbling stomachs has grown louder in the gallery. But Rushing is not done. By now he has finished the cases with Kester and Scott and moved on to the people with no attorneys.

That includes the man with the motorcycle helmet, who has brought a sheaf of photos to defend himself against a charge of animal cruelty.

It is true, he says, that around midnight on Aug. 27 he shot a cat to death with a .45-caliber pistol. But the shooting was justifiable, he tells the judge.

"We're like a mile or so outside the rabies quarantine zone," says the man, 33. "I'm a nurse. I don't go around randomly terrorizing animals."

He shows the judge a photo of himself with one of his own cats. "It's not like I hate cats," he says.

He explains to the judge that the pistol is protection for his home and family. On the night in question, he says, he heard his dogs barking outside his daughter's window, ran out with the gun in hand and encountered the cat "being really weird," biting its own legs and falling down.

"The cat acted aggressively," he says. "It would not retreat. It acted strangely toward me so I shot him."

Rushing asks Woodruff if she has anything to say on behalf of the prosecution.

"It does appear that he shot the cat six times," she says quietly.

The defendant replies that he kept pulling the trigger because of "my military training."

Clearly copying what he has heard other defendants before him say, the man tells the judge he will plead no contest if he can avoid paying a big fine. Before replying, Rushing delivers a short speech.

"I live in a rural area, in Seminole," Rushing says. "I have a cat. I am one of the founders and a director of Save the Florida Panther, which, of course, is a cat."

The judge offers to assess him $100 in court costs and put him on probation for three months, and he can keep his gun. The man agrees. Before turning him loose, Rushing warns him: "If you do this kind of thing again, you better be sure it is a rabid animal."

After a few more cases, Rushing is done for the morning. It is now 1:10 p.m. Outside Courtroom E, the "Court in Session" light clicks off as Rushing dashes out. He's headed for what he calls "the health food store around the corner," namely Checkers.

He has to hurry.

His afternoon docket starts in 20 minutes.

22

BRADYS ON A TRAIN

Slate, February 6, 2018

"Here's the story of a lovely lady . . ."

If you've heard the theme song, you know the premise—or you think you do. A lovely lady with three very lovely girls meets and marries a man named Brady who had three boys of his own. That's the way they became the blandly blended suburban family in the tic-tac-toe square at the end of the opening credits. They had a genial housekeeper named Alice whose face filled the center square, though she didn't rate a mention in the song.

Every day after school I'd step off the school bus and let myself into our empty house. I'd smear peanut butter on some crackers and glance at the conspiracy-filled stories in the afternoon paper—Watergate, the Mafia working with the CIA against Castro, new evidence about who shot JFK.

Mom's rule was clear: No TV until my homework was all done. Of course, I broke that rule every day. The TV's blare filled up that quiet house, making me feel less alone. I'd race through my assignments during the commercials. One of the shows I often watched, broadcast in syndication, was the blandest sitcom ever conceived, *The Brady Bunch.* I came to know that earworm theme song by heart.

But after a while a question occurred to me: How did Mike and Carol hook up?

The show conveniently skips over that question. You never learn what happened to Mike's first wife or Carol's first husband. The kids never mention their original mother or father. The kids' grandparents never visit after the wedding. Only once, in the series' pilot, did anyone display a photo of one of the missing parents.

Clearly, something had happened to these two families that was so traumatic no one dared to bring it up. But what? Nuclear meltdown? Alien abduction? Evil clown attack?

One day, while watching another channel's afternoon movie—the Alfred Hitchcock classic *Strangers on a Train*—suddenly I saw, with a startling clarity, the answer to my mystery: Mike murdered Carol's husband and Carol killed Mike's wife. It was a crisscross killing.

No one would suspect a thing. Each lover would have an alibi for their spouse's death. Then, when the heat died down, they could marry and move in together.

That's really the way they became the Brady Bunch.

How did they do it? I had my suspicions: As an architect, Mike knew how to weaken a balcony railing or sabotage a staircase, making Carol's husband's death look like an accident. How did Carol off Mike's wife? A phony mugging outside Sam's meat market, perhaps. Given Carol's size, maybe she got an assist from Alice. That woman knew how to handle a knife.

You might ask, "Why not just divorce their spouses?" But these were the dark ages of the 1970s. Divorce still carried a stigma. It would have ruined Mike professionally. That minx Carol wouldn't have been welcomed by the PTA crowd. Another motive for murder occurred to me: How do you support six kids, two adults, and a housekeeper on one salary? You collect the insurance on two dead spouses, that's how.

Knowing what I now knew, I spotted things I hadn't noticed before. Mike was clearly a man desperate to hide a secret, one that apparently curled his hair. Carol displayed a nervousness that lent a certain hesitation to her manner. Because of my secret knowledge, the show took on an edge it hadn't had before. The once-tame laugh lines now carried a darker tone, even in the silliest dialogue about Davy Jones and Marcia's nose.

In those pre-internet days, I had no outlet on which to announce my theories. If I told my parents, they'd say I was watching too much TV. My pals at school would look at me as if I had grown a third arm. So I brooded on it, alone, as the show became a pop culture phenomenon, the subject of several revivals, even two feature films. By then, I had moved on—or thought I had.

Whenever I heard that song, it would all come flooding back. It happened again the other day. This time, I checked Google. A year before she died, Florence Henderson, who played Carol, was asked in an interview what happened to that lovely lady's first spouse.

"I killed my husband," she said. "I was the original Black Widow."

The interviewer thought she was joking. I knew better. I'd known all along. It had been much more than a hunch.

Note: I made a joke about this on Twitter, and an editor at Slate *replied by saying if I wrote that as a story, he would pay me to publish it. So I did.*

23

KILLING TIME ON DEATH ROW

St. Petersburg Times, July 6, 1996

RAIFORD—At 5 a.m. the lights go on, and Amos Lee King Jr. starts another day in limbo.

He does some yoga, followed by breathing exercises. Then he reaches for something to read—law books, health guides, the occasional history.

He might set up his chessboard and replay games by masters like Gary Kasparov, who outmaneuvered a computer. He might tune in PBS on his 10-inch black-and-white TV. He might roll a cigarette or debate religion with a neighbor.

At 11 p.m., the lights go out and King thinks: "This is the end of another miserable day."

This is how he has spent the past 19 years: locked in a cell on Florida's death row for the murder of 68-year-old Natalie Brady of Tarpon Springs.

When he was 22, King had a sort of fame. Participants say his was the first murder trial in Florida to allow cameras in court. Now most people have forgotten him. His girlfriend married someone else. His family hasn't been in touch in years.

At 41, King holds a different distinction. He has lived on death row longer than anyone else from Pinellas County.

When the U.S. Supreme Court reinstated the death penalty on July 2, 1976, everyone expected a flood of executions. Instead it's been more like a trickle. Of the 700 people Florida has sent to death row, only 36 have been executed.

On its 20th anniversary, this is the reality of the death penalty: Many are sentenced to die, but few walk that last mile. Some see their convictions overturned or their sentences reduced. Most, like King, wait for an executioner who may never arrive.

The waiting becomes the sentence.

People talk about capital punishment as if everyone sent to death row will die someday from a whiff of gas, a jolt of electricity, a shot of some lethal drug. But for most convicts there is nothing but a slow drip of indistinguishable days.

"It's not really what's intended," said Richard Dieter of the Death Penalty Information Center. "Somehow you get this other sentence of slow torture. . . . It's a strange system."

That the system works the way it does angers people like schoolteacher Donna Lee Demuth, who was on the jury that convicted King.

"There is no reason for him to still be alive," she said.

For the handful of convicts executed nationally, the time between sentencing and death has averaged eight years. But experts say no more than one in 10 death row inmates will be executed, and there is no way to tell who will die and who will hang on.

King is one of 360 men and six women awaiting execution in Florida. Ten have been waiting longer than King. The dean is Gary Alvord, who escaped from a Michigan mental hospital and killed three women in Tampa. He has been living on death row since 1974.

Many death cases end without a trip to the chair. Of the 700 Florida convicts sent to death row, 289 had their convictions overturned, 18 had their sentences commuted and 18 died. At least five committed suicide.

Dozens have followed King to death row from Pinellas. Only one has been executed: Raymond Clark, 1990. State Attorney Bernie McCabe prosecuted Clark in 1977. Ask him why Clark is dead and King is not and he will reply: "Boy! I don't have any idea."

"The system doesn't want to kill very many people, but it doesn't really care who it kills," said Hugo Bedau, editor of *The Death Penalty in America*.

A leading proponent of the death penalty, Fordham University professor Ernest van den Haag, compares the system to a lottery: "Chances are you won't get it, but there is the possibility."

How has King survived? Simple, says University of Florida professor Michael Radelet, who has done extensive research on capital punishment.

"Amos King is lucky," he said. "I saw Amos 10 years ago and I thought he was dead and buried."

☼

King doesn't feel lucky. His home at Union Correctional Institution is 6 feet by 9 feet. With no air-conditioning, he swelters in the summer. His only window, 10 feet away behind two sets of bars, looks out on what King calls "an extension of the dreariness inside."

The only work assigned to death row inmates is cleaning their cells. They "attend" church by watching services on closed-circuit TV—the only cable programing available.

They eat in their cells. A typical day might bring grits and eggs for breakfast, liver and sweet tea for lunch, noodles in gravy with a slice of cake for dinner.

Every other day they get to shower. Twice a week they spend two hours in the exercise yard. Otherwise, they are confined to their cells.

All the killers can do is kill time.

"Time is going to bring you to the end," King said, "but you're just consuming time."

King spends much of his time plotting his appeals, planning his moves like Kasparov battling the machine. So far the match is a draw.

☼

Some people might look at King and say: Like father, like son.

Amos King Sr. had a good job laying cable. But he and his wife Alberta drank heavily, fought often and beat their nine children.

"There was no real thought of cultivation," King said. "There was a lot of violence."

The violence reached its climax Dec. 4, 1971. During a drunken argument, Amos King Sr. shot his wife dead. He was charged with murder but pleaded guilty to manslaughter and got five years' probation. He met a violent end himself, stabbed to death in 1985. The woman who killed him also got probation.

King followed his parents into alcoholism and worse.

"At 15," he said, "I started with heroin."

By the time his father killed his mother, King was already a petty criminal. He believes her death hastened him down the road to death row—a dusty road that passed between the Tarpon Springs Correctional Institution and Natalie Brady's house.

☼

Everyone called her "Tillie." A widow, she lived in a one-story house at the end of Brady Road. She loved to play bingo, to hold her grandchildren, to knit sweaters for her family.

Then, over the protests of Tarpon Springs residents, the state opened a prison so close that she could see the inmates play baseball in the exercise yard. She told her family she was afraid.

"We tried to get her to move but she wouldn't," her stepson, Jay Brady, recalled. "She said there were too many memories there."

King was serving time in Tarpon for a parole violation. He had a work-release job washing dishes at a Clearwater restaurant, Nellie Kelly's. When his shift ended he was bused back to prison.

On St. Patrick's Day 1977, Nellie Kelly's had a big celebration. King may have consumed some alcohol. He may have abused some other substance.

"I had a feeling when I signed him in that he was on something," recalled James "Dan" McDonough, the only corrections officer working that night.

Later McDonough discovered King's bed empty. As he searched the grounds he could see a fiery glow in the distance. Then he spotted King. He says now that he noticed blood on King's white pants.

Armed with only a flashlight, McDonough herded King inside. Suddenly, McDonough said, King pulled a knife and attacked him. They fought for 40 minutes. McDonough was stabbed 24 times.

"I can remember the first few knife thrusts really hurt," McDonough recalled. "After a while, though, it felt like hypodermic pricks, because shock had set in."

The other inmates just watched, McDonough said, until one "grabbed his arm and said, 'King, don't kill him—they'll fry your ass!' He shook him off, but it gave me the opportunity to punch King."

King fled. McDonough clung to life.

"I could just not lie down and die," he said.

King won't discuss what happened except to say, "It was nothing but a scuffle. It wasn't like I was attacking him like some fiend."

McDonough radioed for help. Tarpon Springs police dispatched an officer, who noticed Mrs. Brady's house was on fire. The firefighters he called discovered her lying in the back doorway, dead.

She had been raped, choked and stabbed.

Eventually King surrendered. Now he wishes he had kept running.

He was indicted for first-degree murder. Just as the inmate had warned him, prosecutors wanted to send him to the electric chair.

☼

Prosecutors Paul Meissner and Doug Prior say there was little debate about whether they should seek the death penalty. As Meissner put it: "It was a no-brainer."

But they didn't know how to do a death case. Florida had not executed anyone in 13 years.

Capital punishment has been a part of the American justice system since colonial times. Some 20,000 people have been executed, not all for murder. Florida electrocuted 41 men for rape, 39 of them Black.

But by the '60s, the number of executions nationwide dropped below 50 a year. People began complaining about how long it took to execute a condemned prisoner—up to three years in some cases.

The main reason for the delay was the NAACP Legal Defense Fund, which attacked the death penalty in rape cases because virtually all those executed were Black men accused of raping White women. No one was executed for raping a Black woman.

The NAACP's arguments led to a nationwide moratorium on executions, and in 1972 the U.S. Supreme Court struck down all capital punishment laws as too arbitrary. Many of those laws, including Florida's, had allowed juries to recommend death or life in prison, but gave them no standards for making that choice.

Thirty-five states passed new laws. Florida was the first. Its law gave juries in murder cases a list of factors to be weighed for and against death, so ideally only the worst offenders would be executed.

Judges began handing out death sentences again, and lawyers appealed them. In 1976 the U.S. Supreme Court announced it would consider five cases, one from Florida: Charles Proffitt, who had killed a Tampa wrestling coach named Joel Medgebow.

The court upheld the laws like Florida's, saying they would ensure the death penalty would be applied fairly. (Proffitt, it turns out, won't pay that penalty. Because he stabbed Medgebow just once, an appeals court decided he deserved life, not death.)

A year passed in Pinellas with no murder trials. Then along came King. Prior said King's attorneys "came to us and said, 'Hey, can we plead this guy to life?' And I said, 'Hell no!'"

☼

Over the years King's attorneys—he is on his ninth—have tried various strategies for appealing his case, spinning stories like Scheherazade.

They said jurors should have heard that he was drunk the night of the murder, or that he suffered brain damage as a child. King dismisses those strategies with a wave of his hand.

"I don't want an intoxication defense or an I-fell-on-my-head-as-a-baby defense," King said. "My defense is simple: I didn't do the crime."

But appeals courts rarely deal with the question of guilt. They consider only whether the defendant got a fair trial and deserves execution.

Representing King at his trial were a pair of public defenders, Tom Cole and Anthony Rondolino. Neither had ever tried a death case. Rondolino helped with jury selection while Cole ran the show.

Until 11 days before the start of King's trial, Cole was consumed by another high-profile case involving a beauty queen stabbed with a fondue fork. His colleagues later testified he was so wrapped up in that case he failed to do essential work on King's case.

The state's case was circumstantial. Prior said this was the state's theory: King broke into Mrs. Brady's house to rob or rape her. He was probably surprised to find her still awake, darning socks. He didn't plan on killing her. Panicked, King torched the house to cover the murder and ran back to prison to give himself an alibi.

A knife set in Mrs. Brady's house was missing a paring knife. Detectives searching the woods near the prison found a paring knife they believed King used to stab McDonough. King contends it was planted.

The young medical examiner, Dr. Joan Wood, said Mrs. Brady could have been stabbed with the knife. Wood also found semen in Mrs. Brady's vagina that came from the same blood type as King's.

The trial began July 5, 1977, four months after Mrs. Brady's death, with Circuit Judge John S. Andrews reluctantly allowing cameras in. Though the lawyers and judge were nervous about the effect the cameras would have, Prior remembers they started King's trial a half-day early to beat another trial to be televised that day in Dade County.

Among those chosen for the jury was Demuth, a young mother of four whose father had been a police officer in Chicago.

"I was just a sheltered housewife," she recalled. "I had never dealt with anyone like King."

Mrs. Brady's relatives and friends filled the gallery. After Dr. Wood's testimony, Andrews said, they were "standing there just staring at Amos. . . . I told the bailiff to get him out of there quick."

King's jurors were shocked too. "He was like a mad, wild dog who killed this woman," Demuth said. "During the trial he didn't seem to react. He didn't seem to care."

King says he figured he didn't stand a chance "with an all-White jury being told by racist prosecutors repeatedly that here we have a Black person who killed a White and to do their duty."

The jurors took 3½ hours to find him guilty. Some returned to court wearing sunglasses. King and Rondolino say that showed the impact of the cameras. But Demuth said the glasses were to hide their eyes, puffy from crying.

Next came the key part of the trial under the new law. The state listed reasons for recommending death: the heinous nature of the murder, the escape, the rape and arson.

Then the defense presented reasons for mercy. Cole didn't mention King's drug abuse or his mother's death. His only witness was a minister who said King was a good person.

"No one was there to speak a good word for him but this preacher who didn't seem to know him," Demuth said.

The jury recommended death 12–0. Demuth remembers "coming out of it thinking, not that we had done something good but that I had done my job."

Andrews immediately sentenced King to die.

☼

Like all death sentences, King's was automatically appealed to the Florida Supreme Court. The court took three years to uphold it.

Every appeals court has taken years to make a decision on King's case. Radelet, the University of Florida researcher, blames the sheer number of death cases requiring careful review. He once asked Florida Supreme Court justices how much time they spend on death appeals compared to other types of cases. Death cases ate up 30 to 40 percent of their time.

If the death penalty were reserved for killers like Gainesville serial killer Danny Rolling, he said, appeals would take less time and executions would be more frequent.

Twice the state has come close to killing King. In 1981 then-Gov. Bob Graham signed a warrant for his execution and another one for Alvin Ford, who killed a police officer in Fort Lauderdale.

Both men were moved to the state's special death watch cells, where convicts spend their final hours. As they wait, they are measured for their burial suit.

"Death watch is so emotionally draining that those who survive it usually spend the better part of the following two days sleeping," King said.

Ford couldn't take the pressure. "He began to hear things," King said. "He'd say, 'You hear that?'"

Appeals courts stayed both executions, but Ford was never the same. When Graham signed another warrant for Ford, the U.S. Supreme Court said the state couldn't kill someone too crazy to appreciate his punishment. He died in 1991, still awaiting execution.

Gov. Bob Martinez signed King's second death warrant in 1988. He came within a week of execution.

"In the last week an officer sits in front of your cell and watches everything you do," King said. "He watches you eat, brush your teeth, everything. They don't want you cheating the state."

　　※

So far King has cheated death, although he has won only one round in his appeals: In 1984 a federal court found that King's lawyer—Cole, by then dead in a car crash—did such a poor job that King deserved a new sentencing hearing.

King's victory was short-lived. A new jury again voted 12–0 for execution. Circuit Judge Philip Federico sent him back to death row.

Preparing for the hearing, Dr. Wood pulled out the autopsy photos and noticed for the first time a bite mark on Mrs. Brady's jaw. Wood told both sides, but there was no way to measure the mark and compare it to dental records, so no one mentioned it in court.

King's latest appeal has been stalled in Tampa federal court since 1992. His new volunteer attorney, a New York insurance lawyer, had never handled a death case, so he needed time to catch up.

Then the court found King's appeal raised an issue similar to one pending in a higher court. Until it's decided, King's case is frozen in place, and so is he.

So much time has passed that the crime scene is now an auto salvage yard. Both judges who sentenced King to die have retired.

So has the man King stabbed. McDonough says he's on the list to witness King's execution, if there ever is one. At 62 he is in the same position he was in 19 years ago, clinging to life to see justice done.

"The will to live is strong to see him executed," he said.

Only one person is happy that King has lived so long on death row: the victim's stepson, Jay Brady.

"He's suffering more in prison than if he'd been executed," Brady said. "If they had strapped him into the chair and popped the juice to him, his suffering would be over in a minute or two. But he's had 19 years to suffer."

　　※

Time passes on death row, and leaves its mark.

"The death row population I would say is getting older now," King said. "We got a lot of guys in wheelchairs now."

King suffers from arthritis. In the exercise yard he gets in some calisthenics, maybe a short run. Most of the other men on his cellblock go out at the same time. Two or three refuse to leave their cells.

"They fall into a state of hopelessness," King said. "You can see them. They're like walking dead. I've had that sense. . . . You kind of like feel yourself being sucked in, like you're in a hole."

Not long ago someone in King's cellblock distributed 50 quizzes on geography with questions about places the convicts probably will never see. They competed against each other as if there were some prize at stake.

"The one who exemplifies considerable knowledge gets to feel superior for a spell," King said, comparing the quiz to an anchor, something to keep their minds from drifting back to thoughts of death.

When the lights go out at night, King finds sleep elusive. When his eyes do close, and he drifts away from hard reality, unconsciousness brings little relief.

"From time to time I have dreams of being executed," he said. "Whether you want to think about it or not, your dreams make you face up to it."

Then it's 5 a.m. again, and the lights go on. Time for another day on death row, a day like the day before. Does he sometimes wish it was over, one way or the other?

"Every day," he said.

Note: Amos Lee King Jr. was executed by lethal injection on February 27, 2003, more than a quarter of a century after he was sentenced to die. His last words: "I want the governor and the family to know that I'm an innocent man and the government had evidence to that effect." Gary Alvord, the longest serving death row inmate in the nation, died in prison of natural causes on May 21, 2013.

24

A FLASH OF GREEN

Crime Reads, April 3, 2019

Last fall, as part of the annual Bouchercon celebration of mysteries and their authors, one panel was devoted to discussing a writer who's been dead for three decades and a character who last appeared in a book when Reagan was in the White House. One of the panelists, Ace Atkins (*The Sinners*) showed up in a T-shirt that proclaimed: "BASTARD CHILD OF TRAVIS MCGEE." Immediately the other panelists clamored for identical shirts. I was one of them.

Now, let me tell you about Travis McGee.

I come from a family of mystery fans. My grandfather was hooked on Perry Mason, both the TV show and the Erle Stanley Gardner novels. My mother couldn't get enough of Agatha Christie. Growing up, I jumped from Encyclopedia Brown to Sherlock Holmes to Sam Spade.

One day when I was 14, my chain-smoking great-aunt took a drag on her unfiltered Camel and drawled, "I think you're ready for Travis McGee."

She handed me a well-thumbed paperback called *The Deep Blue Good-by,* first published in 1964. On its cover was a very shapely woman, topless, but seen from the back. I was a teenage boy, so I gulped and said, "Yes, ma'am, I believe you're right!"

She gave me three books about McGee, a Fort Lauderdale boat bum/salvage consultant who was catnip to women and a magnet for trouble. That was my introduction to McGee's creator, the prolific John D. MacDonald, who wrote 500 short stories and 78 books, 21 of them about McGee, his "knight in tarnished armor."

I soon learned there was a lot more to *The Deep Blue Good-by* and its colorfully titled sequels (*Nightmare in Pink, The Quick Red Fox,* etc.) than the lurid covers. Unlike the other mysteries I'd read, many of these books were set in Florida, my native state and MacDonald's adopted home. It had never occurred to me that a place that seemed so sunny could be so full of shady characters.

In the McGee series—which concluded with *The Lonely Silver Rain* in 1985—and many of his other novels, MacDonald wrote about Florida's beauty, the appeal of nature and the risks of ruining it. He had an MBA from Harvard and had worked for an investment house and an insurance company, so he knew how business worked, how conscienceless and corrupt it could be, how it could turn a gorgeous public resource like a bay into a lifeless ruin for private profit. He had also been a lieutenant colonel in the Army, so he knew about large bureaucracies and how they can grind an individual down.

The more I read, the more fascinated I became. MacDonald's books weren't just straight-ahead puzzle mysteries like my grandfather's Perry Mason books. This author digressed. He quipped. He had a lot to say about a lot of things—particularly about the greed and carelessness driving the bad decisions being made about my state. What he had to say was a revelation to teenage me. I'd spent lots of time hunting and fishing with my dad, as well as camping and canoeing with my Boy Scout troop. Until I read MacDonald, I didn't realize that the places I'd enjoyed visiting might someday be turned into cul-de-sacs and convenience stores, or that such changes might not be for the best.

My experience with MacDonald's writing is shared by a lot of my fellow Floridians.

"I read all JDM's books in my early 20s," non-fiction author Cynthia Barnett (*Rain: A Natural and Cultural History*) told me. "My father and grandfather had both read them all and it was a point of inter-generational connection for us. We didn't agree on many things, but Travis McGee and Florida and rapscallions, we could agree upon."

McGee's ruminations on the asphalting of Florida are a big reason why MacDonald's books still have a life beyond the time when he wrote them.

"His ability to so perfectly capture the shared Florida experience of watching your favorite stretch of wild Florida turn to shopping malls and condos, and indeed the outrage, is what makes him so appealing across generations," Barnett said.

MacDonald knew this subject firsthand. The Pennsylvania native moved his family from Mexico to the sleepy beach town of Clearwater, Florida, in 1949. Two years later they settled in the more upscale Sarasota, a town full of circus performers and eccentric writers and artists. Mac-Donald was drawn there by the "softness of the air, the blue of the water, the dip and cry of the water birds, the broad beaches."

MacDonald lived there until his death in 1986. His house sat on an island called Siesta Key, on a point of land with full water views to the north

John D. MacDonald, who lived in Sarasota, became an early environmental activist and often slipped messages about saving Florida into his crime thrillers, especially the ones about Travis McGee. Photo courtesy of Sarasota County Historical Resources.

and south, a place frequented by dolphins and manatees. In between putting in eight-hour days writing in a room over the garage, MacDonald enjoyed boating and fishing. He loved watching what he called "the armada of pelicans" wheeling above the waves. In a panther paw print, he saw evidence that wilderness had not yet been wiped out.

MacDonald became so enamored of his gorgeous surroundings that he became an early and extremely vocal environmental activist, battling dredge-and-fill projects that would harm his beloved Sarasota Bay and later taking on other issues, such as saving the Everglades and stopping the construction of the world's largest airport in what's now Florida's Big Cypress Preserve. Well before the first Earth Day in 1970 made the environment a fashionable cause, MacDonald was bombarding the local paper with letters to the editor and columns, and organizing his neighbors to oppose the forces of what he viewed as greed and stupidity.

"Having made the state his home, MacDonald sensed personal loss when . . . business and government leaders impaired the quality of life,"

Pulitzer-winner Jack E. Davis (*The Gulf*) noted in a scholarly piece on his activism. By 1979, MacDonald was grumbling that the air that once smelled of sweet orange blossoms now was so full of foul emissions it had begun "smelling like a robot's armpit."

MacDonald smuggled some of his environmental arguments into his thriller plots starting with snide comments about dredge-and-fill development in 1953's *Dead Low Tide*. His non-McGee novel *A Flash of Green*, featuring a crooked county commissioner pushing a ruinous dredge-and-fill project, has been hailed as America's first ecological novel. It was published in 1962, the same year as Rachel Carson's nonfiction blockbuster *Silent Spring*. MacDonald, who based its plot on a real Sarasota dredge-and-fill plan that he had unsuccessfully opposed, dedicated it to everyone who was "opposed to the uglification of America."

Modern-day Florida crime writer Tim Dorsey (*No Sunscreen for the Dead*) calls him "Florida's Nostradamus. He was writing about protecting our environment long before we knew it was an issue."

Sometimes life imitated his art. In *A Flash of Green*, MacDonald created a citizen's group called Save Our Bay, colloquially called the S.O.B.'s. About a decade later, when yet another corporation tried to get permits to dredge and fill part of his bay, the organization that rose up to oppose it (successfully, this time) called itself by that very same name.

In 2016, the Sarasota County library system held a series of events to salute MacDonald's 100th birthday, culminating in the unveiling of a plaque in his honor. Each event, especially the last one, was very well-attended, according to librarian Ellen India, who organized them. Meanwhile, the *Sarasota Herald-Tribune* published a series of columns from such writers as Stephen King and John Jakes about the influence he had on their life and writing.

MacDonald's grandson, Andrew, said he still fields plenty of queries from readers about his famous ancestor, a sign of how much people still value commentary from so far back.

"I think he remains relevant for people today because he was so far ahead on his side commentary, particularly around politics and the environment," the younger MacDonald told me. "Maybe there is some reassurance for the reader when we see this mess has been brewing a long time and someone else saw it coming—we were warned."

MacDonald's far-sighted concern for the environment marks him as more than just a sharp writer and storyteller, Atkins said.

"He always took on social ills," Atkins said. "He wrote about the environment, corruption and morality. His characters contemplate man's place in the world and how dirty little secrets can have a resounding effect on the present. The stories have classic themes. . . . Travis McGee lived at the tipping point of Florida, seeing so much of it disappear and warning us of the future."

(And yes, Ace gave us all T-shirts. In different colors, just like the Mc-Gee titles.)

25

FIFTY-FIVE SECONDS

St. Petersburg Times, October 19, 1997

Note: This story reconstructs the events of a 1996 police shooting by a White officer named James Knight of a Black teenager named TyRon Lewis, a shooting that led to riots in St. Petersburg. After a grand jury inquiry cleared the officer of wrongdoing, a source of mine tipped me off that there were some serious discrepancies. Our police reporter at the time, the late Tim Roche, and I went over all the witness statements, the autopsy report, the photos of the crime scene and the police reenactment of the shooting. We repeatedly listened to the tape of the police radio traffic, and then reinterviewed many witnesses—most importantly, the medical examiner. We fired the same type of gun that Officer Knight used and even tracked down the car involved and sat where Lewis had sat, and where he died. That's how we noticed the key detail about the mirror.

The 1980 Pontiac LeMans was nearly as old as the scrawny teen reaching for the keys. Rust bubbled on its hood. Its "Fremont gold" finish had faded to brown. Someone had knocked the mirror off its driver's door.

But 18-year-old TyRon Lewis—ex–Boy Scout, patient fisherman, petty criminal—wanted it. And he had something in his hand that would make it his.

About 8 p.m. on Oct. 10, 1996, a motel maid drove the two-door sedan to an intersection not far from downtown. The LeMans had been her late mother's, but it meant less to her now than the craving that rippled through her body.

The maid was White, Lewis Black. Crack bridged the racial divide. She wanted what he had because it offered the illusion of escape. He wanted what she had for the same reason.

"We didn't have no other way around," said Eugene Young, Lewis's friend since childhood.

They dropped the maid off at a bar. Lewis boasted he bought her car for 10 rocks of crack. A day later the maid told a police officer her car was missing, but he wrote she didn't want to prosecute the "unknown b/m" she gave it to.

Three people saw the car and called police. One said the driver was wanted. But police did not even enter it in the national crime computer as stolen.

Although without a license, Lewis drove the Pontiac to Childs Park to visit family; to Coquina Key to fish; to Treasure Island to ask a girlfriend to plait his hair; to an auto parts store, where he put in too much oil, which made the engine smoke.

On Oct. 24, he drove it to another intersection not far from downtown. In a confrontation that lasted just 55 seconds, he died in the driver's seat, shot twice in the arm and once in the heart by a White police officer.

It was 55 seconds that made an "unknown b/m" national news and led to two nights of civil unrest that forever changed the city. A grand jury concluded the officer was justified in killing Lewis, but the officer's superiors found he had broken department rules.

Even now, a year later, key questions about those 55 seconds remain unanswered. Despite what the grand jury concluded, Lewis probably wasn't even looking at the officer when the first two shots were fired.

☼

Lewis spent his last night in a ramshackle house in Childs Park with a willowy girl he had been dating for six months. When she left for high school he was still asleep, waking sometime before 3 p.m.

He should have been behind bars. Three different judges had ordered him arrested, partly because he missed court hearings while serving a year in a last-chance juvenile facility in the hills north of Ocala.

Two months before, he had run from a pair of officers. Caught and charged with loitering, he gave a fake name. By the time fingerprints revealed the ruse he had been released. In his mugshot his eyes had the look of someone who was lost and didn't care.

"The Ron I knew was a child of the streets," said his uncle, James "Randy" Lewis. "I called him the Wanderer. . . . There were no future goals for Ron, other than to live on the street."

He always ran from problems. By 11 he had run away so much he was put in foster care. A family offered to adopt him. But his single mother refused to give him up, so the would-be parents told state authorities to come get him.

Juvenile counselors tried to make Lewis something other than a delinquent. They even put him in a Boy Scout troop. In custody he was a good student, a leader. But at home he returned to the only life he knew, dealing drugs, taking after his absent father and two half-brothers. One of them also taught him to fish, a pastime he loved so much he once stole a pole.

On Oct. 20 Lewis visited his grandmother, a hardworking domestic servant. His uncle, a county employee, urged him to take care of his warrants.

"I'm going to do it," he promised before driving off in the LeMans.

☼

On Oct. 24 Lewis put on denim shorts that hung below the top of his striped boxers. He wore black and white sneakers and no shirt. In his right pocket was an old Superglue tube containing six rocks of crack.

He smoked some crack, but its effects soon dissipated. Later he smoked marijuana, a habit since age 10. He was still under its influence, slowing his reactions and distorting his perception of speed and distance, about 5:25 p.m. when Young says they got in the car to go buy hot crabs.

Between them was a black boom box. Lewis switched it on. As they rode past the bars and Baptist churches of 18th Avenue S, it played a plaintive R. Kelly song of lost love and regret: "I can't sleep babe, I can't think babe, I can't live babe . . ."

☼

About the time Lewis was waking up, Officer James Knight was slipping behind the wheel of a police cruiser. A short White man with a wispy mustache, he applied to join the force about the time Lewis racked up his first arrest nine years before.

In the passenger seat was Officer Sandra Minor. Both wore green shirts and shorts, but the similarities ended there.

Although Minor had seniority, her bosses had labeled her in job reviews as a follower. Knight's supervisors praised his ability "to be at the right place at the right time."

Minor, then 35, was the daughter of a Pinellas Park tile setter. Knight, then 34, came from Colorado. Before Minor became an officer she worked for a veterinarian, while Knight had been a military policeman in the U.S. Army. The gung ho Knight volunteered for the SWAT team, while Minor was one of the city's first community policing officers.

About 5:35 p.m., they saw a man drop a beer bottle near 18th Avenue S and 21st Street S. While they checked on that, the Pontiac zoomed past on 18th headed east in the left lane.

The Pontiac zipped by a Toyota driven by Willie Graham. One passenger, cousin Eddie Graham, saw the police car and the two Black teens in the LeMans.

"Damn," he said, "they're gonna get stopped."

The officers had no radar, but as Knight pulled out to tail the LeMans he guessed it was doing 70 mph, enough to charge the driver with recklessness.

The LeMans stopped behind another car at a red light at 16th Street S, where men sat on a wall by a deli drinking beer as dozens of cars rolled by. Knight stopped about 4 feet behind the LeMans. Willie Graham stopped in the curb lane, next to the LeMans.

Minor called in the tag. Knight was already walking to the LeMans. Minor opened her door to join him.

The 55 seconds had begun.

☼

"There go the police," Lewis said. Surrender did not appeal to him, but for once he could not run away. He locked his door and told Young to do the same.

Knight tapped on the driver's window and asked him to roll it down. Lewis did not respond. Knight told him to turn off the car and get out. Lewis pushed "pause" on the boom box. Minor tried the same routine on the passenger side, with the same result.

The officers tried to open the locked doors, then Minor radioed for backup. Both said later they had trouble seeing through the tinted windows, and Knight said he believed he was in "a danger zone."

A number of witnesses later testified that they could see in just fine. But the grand jury that investigated the shooting accepted the officers' story.

What Knight did next later got him in trouble with his department: He stepped in front of the car and drew his gun.

Although he now faced the setting sun, Knight wrote, "I could get a better vantage of the inside of the vehicle. . . . I could see what I believed was the silhouette of 2 b/m's."

Knight said he stood in front of the car and pulled his gun as "an intimidation" to the driver. He insisted he was following training, but training officials said no course condoned what he did.

He had faced down cars before. "Everybody usually stops," he said.

So many officers had gotten into similar confrontations that the department produced a video warning them not to stand in front of a suspect's car. Knight saw the video a month before the shooting, but said he did not remember any such command.

Knight said he could think of no other way to see into the LeMans. But Minor did.

The light turned green. The car ahead of the Pontiac drove away. Minor tried to use the cruiser to block the Pontiac but abandoned the idea and ran to the driver's side of the Pontiac. She peered around the window post and looked through the windshield.

She saw more than silhouettes. She saw Lewis with his hands on the steering wheel, shaking his head. She could even see his gold teeth.

According to Young, Lewis was shaking his head at Knight and yelling, "Please don't shoot, please don't shoot, I ain't even got nothing!"

Then, 23 seconds after her first radio transmission Minor shouted: "He's trying to run over Knight, try to get over here!"

☼

Lewis let the car roll at a speed one witness compared to a baby's crawl. With automatic transmission, he could have simply taken his foot off the brake.

Young told Lewis to stop, but his panicked friend said, "F— that s—, man, f— that s—!"

Knight said the LeMans was "jumping forward," pushing him back. He held the gun in his right hand and put his left on the hood. He said Lewis might have been "just playing, you know, trying to intimidate me: 'Hey, maybe if I just bump him, he'll move.'"

Minutes after the shooting, Knight told a sergeant the car hit his legs "several times." Later he told homicide detectives it hit him a total of nine times. He told Det. Lisa McKinney from Internal Affairs seven times. He told prosecutors seven or eight times.

What Knight told grand jurors is secret, but they concluded the car hit him four times. State Attorney Bernie McCabe would not say how they reached a conclusion at odds with Knight's other statements.

There is some question whether Knight was bumped at all. Neither Minor nor Young saw any bumping. Most witnesses saw no contact, and some say the car only rolled forward. Among those who say the car touched Knight are people who saw things that did not occur, such as Minor shooting Lewis.

Pictures of Knight's legs taken three hours after the shooting show no marks. When McKinney asked Knight where the car hit him, he said, "I don't know." He said he had "no visible injury."

When he complained his right knee bothered him, a doctor at Edward White Hospital prescribed an over-the-counter cream. A photo taken a day later shows two faint red marks on the knee.

If Lewis struck Knight he committed battery on a law enforcement officer, a felony. So was Knight bumped or not?

"It's hard to say," Det. McKinney said. She said she was glad the grand jury had to answer that question, not she.

☼

Knight said the car bumped him harder so he yelled, "Stop or I'll f—ing shoot!"

Because of the car's oily engine smoke, Knight still could not see clearly. He could tell the passenger had both hands up and the driver's left hand was raised. But he could not see the driver's right hand.

Because the Pontiac rolled forward, Minor was now even with the car's left rear window. Because the Pontiac had no driver's side mirror, where Minor now stood was, for Lewis, a blind spot. He could not see her unless he turned around. She produced a metal rod and flicked her wrist. Sounding like a shotgun being racked, the rod popped open into a baton.

At Knight's urging Minor used it to break a window, which he called "an attention-getter." She smashed a 6-inch hole in the window behind Lewis.

Investigators now speculate the shattering glass so startled Lewis it set off the final chain of events. "Did he think it was a gunshot?" McKinney wondered.

As it shattered, Minor said, the car veered left and "he just started to floor it," so she jumped back.

"After she breaks the window," Knight said, "that is when the car drives into me and knocks me off balance and up onto the hood. And that's when I fired." He said he feared for his life.

An officer may shoot a fleeing felon who poses a threat of serious physical harm to the officer or others, said University of Florida law professor Fletcher Baldwin, an expert on police use of force cases. It is not legal to shoot a suspect who has not committed a felony, is not fleeing or poses no threat.

McCabe said the standard is whether the officer reasonably believed he was in danger, a highly subjective test that makes prosecution extremely difficult.

The grand jury found that when Knight was thrown onto the hood he "was in reasonable fear of imminent death or great bodily harm. . . ."

But the first time Knight told his story he did not mention being on the hood. Minor did not see him on the hood. Young, who is uncertain about other events, is sure he was not on the hood. No one in Graham's car saw him on the hood or saw the Pontiac lunge forward.

Of 28 other witnesses questioned by police, only two reported seeing Knight on the hood. One said Knight was on the hood with his feet on the ground as the Pontiac rolled, stopped and rolled again. The other said Knight climbed onto the hood on his knees and shot Lewis in the head, pausing between shots to warn someone to stay back.

How could the grand jury go against so many witnesses? McCabe said jurors judged who they found credible. He would not give his own opinion except that he is "comfortable" with their report.

To determine Knight's position, crime scene technicians could have tested the Pontiac's windshield for gunshot residue. If he fired as he lay on the hood, his shots would leave more residue than if he were standing back from the windshield. No test was done before the car was moved.

Technicians did dust the Pontiac's hood for fingerprints. During a re-enactment of the shooting Knight showed he had been thrown so far onto the hood his feet dangled in the air and he put his left hand near the back of the hood. But on the Pontiac, his only handprint was close to the front of the hood.

McCabe would not comment on Knight's credibility. Knight and Minor declined to talk to reporters about the shooting.

※

With each pull of the trigger, flame blossomed from the muzzle. Knight said he did not aim: "It was just point and shoot."

The three shots sounded like a series of pops, so close together Knight could not tell how many times he fired—or that he had just lit the fuse on the city.

The first two bullets burst through the windshield through nearly the same hole, blowing tiny bits of glass into the car. The bullets drilled into the side of Lewis's right arm an inch apart, while the glass stippled the skin on his arm, torso and back of the shoulder.

As the third bullet punched through the windshield, the glass stripped off its metal jacket. Both pieces caught Lewis in the chest, making two wounds, one superficial, one lethal.

"Dog, I'm shot!" Lewis cried twice.

The location of the first two wounds and the stippling indicate that when Knight opened fire, Lewis was probably not facing him, said Dr. Joan Wood, Pinellas-Pasco's chief medical examiner. Instead Lewis had to be turned fairly far sideways in his seat, with his right arm across his body about chest high.

He probably was looking back at the breaking window, she said.

"I don't know what sound that would make but it might make a pretty big pop," Wood said. "He could've been looking behind him to see what it was."

A second possibility, Wood said, was that Lewis was at last reaching to unlock his door.

Wood told Internal Affairs investigators Lewis was not steering the car with his right hand when he was shot. Because Knight said Lewis had his left hand up, that would mean he had neither hand on the wheel.

Yet the grand jurors said Wood told them that when Knight fired, Lewis had to be turning the wheel with his right hand. Because he was steering straight at Knight, they said, Knight "reasonably believed that he was in danger of being run over by the Pontiac or thrust into oncoming traffic at the time he fired his weapon" and therefore Lewis's shooting was justified.

Wood says the grand jury report of her testimony is wrong. She said she did not recall the panel even asking her if Lewis was steering.

Told of Wood's statement, an astonished McCabe said, "Wha-a-a-?" He insisted the grand jury report was accurate.

If Lewis was not steering the car at Knight, he posed no threat.

"What the person was doing with the wheel at the time would be the issue," said Baldwin, the law professor. But McCabe contended that no matter what Lewis was doing, what counts is whether Knight believed he was in danger.

After Lewis's arm was broken it fell limp, Wood said. Once the third bullet found his heart, "he's got seconds to unconsciousness."

Fifty-five seconds after Minor had reported the traffic stop, she said in an agonized voice: "Shots fired. . . . Shots fired, get me rescue!"

☼

Knight said he stopped shooting because "the threat was gone. The vehicle stopped." He scrambled over to handcuff the frightened Young, who had thrown himself from the car.

Knight glanced in at Lewis, then walked away. Backup officers came roaring up. Knight put Young in a cruiser and sat on the ground, looking dazed.

Minor leaned through the open passenger door to shut off the engine and unlock the other door. Then she went to check on the still unidentified driver.

She found him "gasping for air," she said. "I pretty well knew that he probably was going to die right there. There was really nothing I could do."

The boom box had fallen off the seat and was blaring: "I can't live, babe . . ." Officer Karen Demick switched it off and stood by Minor, already the target of angry bystanders. Then, Demick wrote, Minor "stated to me that she no longer felt a pulse and again asked about the whereabouts of rescue."

Paramedics arrived and immediately pronounced Lewis dead at 5:45 p.m. Demick suggested they put him on a stretcher. She draped a blanket over him but did not cover his face to avoid inflaming the crowd.

The paramedics drove the body to Bayfront Medical Center, where crime scene technician Roy Kirby took pictures of it. Police policy says documenting a shooting victim's condition is of paramount importance. As a result Kirby didn't get to the scene of the shooting for an hour, and was soon forced to retreat by flying rocks and bottles.

But before Kirby's arrival an officer altered the crime scene. Someone—investigators never established who—moved Knight's cruiser to block traffic.

Although the grand jury cleared Knight, the department suspended him for 60 days without pay. A disturbance ensued among those upset with the grand jury, an outburst McCabe termed "inevitable." Meanwhile people outraged by Knight's suspension donated enough money to replace his lost pay.

Police returned the Pontiac to the motel maid's father. The city paid him for the damage the officers had done to the glass.

Six months after the shooting, the only markers on Lewis's grave were some faded silk flowers and a rusted lapel button that showed a dove split between black and white, with the slogan: "St. Petersburg—Together."

Now even that is gone.

26

THE WONDERFUL WORLD OF WILLEFORD

Crime Reads, October 18, 2019

Orphan, hobo, painter, poet, boxer, book critic, decorated tank commander, actor, truck driver, teacher, author and inveterate prankster—Charles Willeford led a life that could provide him with a zillion stories, each one touched with his distinctive view of the world. He spent three decades cranking out pulp fiction classics like *Pick-Up* and *Cockfighter* that earned him very little money and hardly any notice from the critics.

Then, in 1984, he wrote a poker-faced comic thriller called *Miami Blues* that suddenly made him a hot commodity. He followed it up with three more off-kilter books about his unlikely hero, the leisure-suit-wearing Sergeant Hoke Moseley of the Miami Police. On the strength of those four books, the *Atlantic* magazine dubbed him "the unlikely father of Miami crime fiction."

One of the Hoke Moseley sequels was called *Sideswipe.* His widow Betsy says that not long after that book came out, Willeford got a package in the mail. When he opened it, he found a hardbound copy of *Sideswipe* that someone had shot. Accompanying the book was a note, written in all-caps, saying "It's a crime to charge $15.95 for shit like this." It was signed, "A Dissatisfied Customer."

When Willeford mentioned this to some friends they became concerned for his safety. One asked, "Have you alerted the FBI?" He replied, "No, it's always good to get feedback."

There are plethora of Willeford anecdotes, but I think that one might be my favorite. (Incidentally, Mrs. Willeford recalled that the book had been shot once, but a 1988 news story said five times. Fortunately the Broward County Public Library has Willeford's papers, so I checked with them. Librarian Erin Purdy sent me photos showing that that copy of *Sideswipe* had SIX bullet holes.)

These days few readers care quite so passionately about Willeford's writing. He is a cult figure to some, and otherwise just occasionally mentioned among the roll call of hard-boiled writers. But Willeford's work is due for a revival now that his 1971 novel *The Burnt Orange Heresy* has been made into a film starring Donald Sutherland, Elizabeth Debicki, Claes Bang and, in a small but crucial role, Sir Mick Jagger. The film had its world premiere in September at the 76th Venice International Film Festival. A *Variety* review calls it "a marble-cool art-fraud thriller."

"Cool" is not an adjective often associated with Willeford, born 100 years ago this year. "Quirky" is the one that Lawrence Block used. A couple more might be "droll" or "tongue in cheek." James Crumley called him "an original—funny, weird and wonderful." Carl Hiaasen, whose first wacky Florida crime thriller, *Tourist Season,* was published two years after *Miami Blues,* told me that Willeford was "a wonderful, crusty guy" who was "among the first to figure out that this is a pretty phenomenal setting for a novel."

Willeford himself once commented about his books, "Just tell the truth, and they'll accuse you of writing black humor."

☼

Charles Ray Willeford III was born in 1919 in Little Rock, Arkansas. His father died of tuberculosis in 1922, so he and his mother moved to Los Angeles. She died of TB in 1927, leaving him in the care of his grandmother. After the Great Depression hit, Willeford became concerned that his grandmother couldn't afford to feed him as well as herself, so at 13 he dropped out of school and hit the road as a hobo.

After riding the rails for a year, he lied about his age and enlisted in the military, beginning what would become a lengthy career in two different branches of the service. Initially he was an Army grunt, working with horses in a cavalry unit and later serving as a truck driver and a cook. When World War II came along, he was shipped out to Europe as a tank commander. He was wounded in the Battle of the Bulge and earned a Purple Heart, a Bronze Star and a Silver Star for heroism.

What did he do to earn those medals? He never wanted to talk about his war experiences, Betsy Willeford told me.

"I think he had what we would now call post-traumatic stress disorder," she said. "He had some bad dreams even 40 years later."

His first book, *Proletarian Laughter,* came out in 1948. It's a collection of poems, but in between were short pieces that he called "Schematics." They recounted, in a matter-of-fact way, some bits of what he'd witnessed, including one horrific story about a fellow tank commander who committed a rape and a double-murder. Betsy once asked him if the "Schematics"

Charles Willeford savors a cup of café con leche. He spent three decades cranking out books of every kind before penning his hit, *Miami Blues,* which encapsulated all the weirdness of 1980s-era South Florida. Photo copyright David Poller, all rights reserved.

were non-fiction. He said yes, but in a way that indicated he didn't want any more questions, she said.

A year after his book came out, he left the Army and moved to Peru. He convinced the teachers at the Universitarias de Belles Artes to admit him as an art student by telling them he had studied at "Woodrow Wilson" in California. When they finally figured out that "Woodrow Wilson" was the name of the middle school he'd dropped out of and not a college, they kicked him out.

Willeford returned to the military, this time enlisting in the U.S. Air Force. While still in uniform he wrote his first pulp novel, *The High Priest of California,* featuring a ruthless and fairly despicable San Francisco used-car salesman named Russell Haxby. He's obsessed with manipulating and bedding married women, especially one in particular. The writing is crisp, the dialogue crackles, but Haxby's such a nasty customer that it turned off some readers.

He soon followed that up with more short, sharp stories of detestable people, including *Pick-Up* (1955), which concerns a pair of down-and-out alcoholics in San Francisco who can't even commit suicide properly, and *The Black Mass of Brother Springer* (1958), about a phony White preacher who takes charge of an African-American church in Florida and later runs off with a deacon's wife. (*Pick-Up* was later included in the Library of America series on '50s American noir, where it's described as "hardboiled writing at its nihilistic best.") More followed, with titles like *Wild Wives* and *Whip Hand*.

His publishers tended to be third-rate sleaze merchants who paid him poorly and would change his titles to make them sound even pulpier. *Black Mass*, for instance, became *Honey Gal*, and *Made in Miami* became *Lust Is a Woman*. One publisher misspelled Willeford's name on the cover as "Williford." His lone Western, which he called *The Difference*, hit bookshelves as *The Hombre from Sonora*. Still, he kept plugging away. In addition to his fiction he wrote a memoir (*I Was Looking for a Street*) and a raucous remembrance of a painful operation, which he called *A Guide for the Unhemorrhoided*.

He once told a fan that the key to cranking out all those books was quite simple: "Never allow yourself to take a leak in the morning until you've written a page. That way you're guaranteed a page a day, and at the end of a year you have a novel."

The Air Force stationed him in Palm Beach for a while, his first taste of Florida living. After retiring from the military, he studied painting in France, worked as a boxer, horse trainer and radio announcer, then returned to Florida to stay. He wanted to get the college education he'd missed. He earned a master's degree in English literature from the University of Miami. This led to him teaching, first at the University of Miami, and later at Miami-Dade Community College.

At Miami-Dade he taught at the southern campus, while the same classes were being taught at the northern campus by another would-be writer named James Lee Burke, still years away from launching his Dave Robicheaux mystery series. The pair became friends and often got together to discuss their work and how to make it better. When Willeford read the first chapters of the first Robicheaux novel, *The Neon Rain*, he encouraged Burke to keep going.

As a teacher, Willeford was determined to get a reaction out of his students, if only to make sure they were listening. He once told a class that scientists had developed a way of determining someone's personality by examining the person's armpit hair. The gasps he heard in response told him he'd succeeded.

Willeford was willing to say just about anything, to pull any prank. He once asked Lawrence Block if he'd ever eaten cat, then assured him that he'd read of a worldwide association of men devoted to that practice. Another time, his wife Betsy recalled, they were sitting in a Miami restaurant surrounded by prosperous young men smoking big cigars, so when a well-dressed couple walked in, Willeford shouted, "NARCS!" just to see everyone else scramble.

"He was always lighting these little fires and then walking away," she said.

❀

Although he was writing fiction, Willeford believed in doing his homework to make the story believable. He spent two years learning everything he could about the sport of cockfighting before he wrote his 1962 novel *Cockfighter*. Hard-boiled fiction is known for its terse heroes, but the hero of *Cockfighter*, Frank Mansfield, tops them all. He vows not to speak to anyone until he wins the big championship.

Cockfighter was going to be Willeford's big breakthrough novel. But shortly after it was published, his publisher died and the publishing house went bankrupt. As a result, most of the print run, more than 20,000 copies, never reached bookstores.

Later, in 1974, Roger Corman produced a movie version directed by Monte Hellman and starring a masterful Warren Oates as Mansfield and Harry Dean Stanton as his nemesis. Willeford wrote the screenplay and had a cameo as a ring official. Corman said that it was his only film that lost money, despite the movie's legendary tagline: "He came to town with his cock in his hand, and what he did with it was illegal in 49 states."

The reason Corman found *Cockfighter* at all was because it had been republished. That happened thanks to the success of Willeford's next novel, *The Burnt Orange Heresy*, which leans more toward satire than noir. The narrator is an egotistical art critic named James Figueras who hopes to become the greatest art critic in the world. In Palm Beach he meets an art collector who gives him the chance to interview a reclusive but widely acclaimed artist named Jacques Debierue, an interview which Figueras is sure will cement his reputation. In exchange, though, he has to steal one of the artist's paintings for the collector. The reader soon learns that the only art on display here is the art of the con. Violence follows, of course.

Although some critics consider *Heresy* his masterpiece, Willeford followed it with a fallow period. He tried a novel about a game show, and another about life on a military base, but they didn't work. He wrote a sort of non-fiction novel about the Son of Sam case but it didn't sell. He wrote one of his bleakest novels, *The Shark-Infested Custard*, but it wasn't published until after his death.

Then came *Miami Blues*.

When Betsy Willeford met her future husband, he was twice divorced and headed for a heart attack. They were both working for a magazine based in the artsy Miami enclave known as Coconut Grove. They soon discovered they shared a twisted sense of humor. For instance, back then Florida law required people to list an occupation on their driver's licenses. Willeford's said, "Typewriter Repairman."

They moved in together, and later wed in the backyard. The groom's side consisted of his poker buddies. Soon he started on a new book, a most unusual police procedural that would change both his fortunes and the shape of crime literature, and he dedicated it to his new bride.

Willeford had reviewed mysteries for the *Miami Herald* and had served for a time as an editor for *Alfred Hitchcock's Mystery Magazine,* so he knew how to write a proper mystery. Of course, what he wrote wasn't like any other mystery in print.

Take the opening line: "Frederick J. Frenger, Jr., a blithe psychopath from California, asked the flight attendant in first class for another glass of champagne and some writing materials." Freddy has recently been released from San Quentin and plans to start fresh in Florida—with help from the credit cards in some wallets he stole. While practicing forging the signatures on the credit cards, he pauses to examine what else is in the wallets. Upon spotting photos of some kids, he wonders, "Why would any man want to carry around pictures of such ugly children in his wallet?"

Then there's the murder. When Freddy steps off the plane at the Miami airport, he encounters a Hare Krishna who pins something to Freddy's brand new leather jacket, then asks him for money. Outraged that there's now a pinprick in his new jacket, Freddy promptly breaks the Hare Krishna's middle finger and goes on his merry way. The Krishna, meanwhile, goes into shock and dies—which is what brings Hoke Moseley into the plot, as he's assigned to find out who killed the Krishna. And Hoke is just as unusual as the murder he's investigating.

"I wanted to show that Hoke is not a cop 24 hours a day," Willeford told a Florida newspaper reporter in 1988. "Most cops are fairly normal people. I wanted to write a novel with police procedural elements, but concentrating on character and on reflecting the times."

Moseley is an amazing creation: A cheapskate who gets his dentures made for free by the medical examiner, a divorced dad who wants little to do with his daughters, a loner who lives in one of the rundown hotels on Miami Beach. He has opinions about a lot of things, many of them wrong. Physically he's no match for the younger, more muscular Freddy, who ambushes him and steals his identity. Nevertheless Hoke stumbles along and eventually comes out on top—thanks, in part, to Miami itself, which proves much tougher for Freddy to deal with than anything he's encountered before.

"Willeford flipped the script on the rugged, tough-talking cop/private eye, instead showing readers a sloppy, messed-up, clunky, but still very relatable hero in Hoke," explained Alex Segura, a Willeford fan and the author of *Miami Midnight* and four other novels about South Florida private eye Pete Fernandez.

The third player in this novel is a young prostitute named Susan who begins hanging out with Freddy in what becomes a spoof of wedded bliss. Neither Freddy nor Hoke thinks she's very smart but by the end of the book she's outfoxed them both.

The book concludes after fewer than 200 pages. Even the ending is unusual—the last page has a recipe on it.

Mitchell Kaplan, who befriended Willeford not long after opening his Books and Books store in Coral Gables, well remembers how a lot of people didn't get what Willeford was up to with *Miami Blues*—including the publisher, which failed to promote it properly.

"My impression was that the publisher did not really completely understand that they had just published a classic American author," said Kaplan, who would go on to launch the Miami Book Fair International. Even worse, he said, "the *Miami Herald* critic panned it."

But the *New Yorker* raved that the book was "extraordinarily winning," and the *New York Times Book Review* said, "If you are looking for a master's insight into the humid decadence of South Florida and its polyglot tribes, nobody does it better than Mr. Willeford." Suddenly, Willeford had a bestseller on his hands.

The setting, and his sharp-eyed observations about it, were the key to the book's success. Willeford had written it as a way to talk about an extraordinary time in South Florida's history. In the 1980s violent crime soared. Drug dealers had a shoot-out on Interstate 95, the medical examiner brought in refrigerator trucks to handle the overflow of bodies, and the FBI declared the entire Key West police department to be so corrupt that it was a criminal enterprise. Meanwhile the Mariel boatlift had brought in thousands of refugees from Castro's jails. Some were political prisoners, but plenty were not, and they didn't mix well with the elderly Jewish retirees eking out their last days in the old South Beach hotels.

"It was a hell of a time to be a writer, a spectacular time," Hiaasen told me. In the Hoke Mosely novels, Willeford perfectly captured that, he said. "There was no other place you could set those books—the stories wouldn't work."

All of the elements of '80s Miami—the random violence, the refrigerator truck morgue, the drug gang overkill, the police corruption, the Marielitos and the Jewish retirees—shows up in *Miami Blues*. The novel serves as a wicked funhouse mirror of the TV show *Miami Vice*, which premiered that same year.

"He'd clearly staked out his own unique territory with the absurd, prickly, anti-heroic Hoke," his friend James W. Hall, whose first novel about Key West private eye Thorn, *Under Cover of Daylight*, was published three years after *Miami Blues*. "There was something almost pornographic about the novel, lurid, extreme. And for me it was liberating to see someone taking material that I was very familiar with and find a unique and engaging voice."

For the first time in his life, Willeford was a success. His old out-of-print books became collectibles. Kaplan said one man moved to Miami just to meet Willeford and cut a deal to print special signed and numbered editions of his work, including *New Forms of Ugly*, which was drawn from Willeford's 1964 master's thesis.

But Willeford soon learned there was a downside to success. His agent and publisher were clamoring for a sequel. The one thing Willeford had never done as a writer was repeat himself. He viewed writing a series of books about one character as the equivalent of paint-by-numbers art, Betsy Willeford told me.

Finally he gave in to their demands—sort of. Willeford sat down and wrote the nastiest, foulest novel of his career. He called it "Grimhaven," with the emphasis on that first syllable. In it, Hoke murders his daughters so he won't have to deal with them anymore, and gladly goes off to prison to pay for his crime.

His agent read it and immediately rejected it, telling him to stop screwing around and write a real sequel. His spleen vented, Willeford did just that, producing *New Hope for the Dead*, in which Hoke takes on a pile of cold-case files while trying to find a new place to live. That was followed by *Sideswipe* and *The Way We Die Now*. While each one had Hoke in it, each one took a very different tack from the one before it.

"Willeford knew how to strike the perfect balance between the noir ingredients of Miami—weird, deadly, funny," Segura said. "The Hoke novels

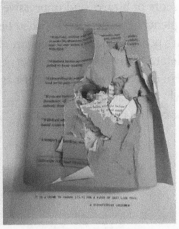

Shortly after Charles Willeford's novel *Sideswipe* was published, someone mailed him a copy that had been shot six times. An enclosed note said, "It's a crime to charge $15.95 for shit like this." It was signed, "A Dissatisfied Customer." Photo by Erin Purdy, Broward County Public Library.

are sublime, and I find myself reading them over and over again as time passes, just to learn more."

The fourth book in the series brought him the biggest payday of his career, a $225,000 advance. He told the Fort Lauderdale newspaper, "I've made more money writing since 1981 than I did in 16 years of teaching."

Meanwhile *Miami Blues* had been optioned by Hollywood. It would eventually become a zippy 1990 comedy starring a grizzled Fred Ward as Hoke, Jennifer Jason Leigh as Susan and a young and dangerous Alec Baldwin as Freddy.

By the time *The Way We Die Now* hit stores, Willeford was already at work on the fifth book in the series, Betsy told me. In this one, the inveterate rule-bender Hoke finds himself assigned to work in Internal Affairs, a set-up that offered plenty of comic possibilities.

One day, the couple strolled by the front window at Kaplan's bookstore and Willeford took great pleasure in seeing *The Way We Die Now* prominently displayed, Betsy said.

A week later—before he could spend much of the advance, or see the movie, or write that fifth book—he was dead of a heart attack. It was just the kind of punchline that Willeford himself might have written, one touched with cosmic irony. He left behind a mourning widow, lots of friends, a score of bizarre and impressive books of nearly every possible kind, and plenty of readers who wished he'd written more.

While it's possible the movie version of *The Burnt Orange Heresy* will bring Willeford a wave of new fans, Betsy isn't counting on it. That pitch-black tone in everything he wrote is just as likely to repel new readers as it did back when he was alive.

"He's for certain people," she told me. "They've already found him."

part III

WILD, WILD LIFE

27

THE FASTEST GOPHER IN FLORIDA

Tampa Bay Times, December 15, 2016

Only in Florida could a long-term science project nearly get derailed by someone's dinner plans.

It started when a couple driving through Central Florida last month made a mistake. They drove into the Archbold Biological Station in Venus because they thought they could buy plants there. It's not a nursery, though. It's a research facility.

As they cruised along in a silver Nissan Murano, the driver noticed something by the roadside—a gopher tortoise nearly a foot long. On its shell was painted "1721" in white numbers 2 inches high. A radio transmitter had been glued on there, too.

"I'm going to get that on the way back," the driver, a 40-year-old man from Port Orange, said. According to his passenger, he had plans for the tortoise: "We are going to eat it for dinner."

Sure enough, while driving back out of Archbold, the driver stopped, hopped out, grabbed the tortoise and wrestled it into the Murano's hatchback.

At some point, someone used a long blade like a machete to chop the radio transmitter off the shell.

As the couple cruised east toward home, though, they got into an argument. The passenger called 911 on her cellphone to report that the driver had hit her. A Florida Highway Patrol trooper pulled the Nissan over at a RaceTrac gas station in Palm Bay.

That's when the passenger, Pamela Hampton, informed the trooper that they had a live tortoise in the back. The trooper called in a state Fish and Wildlife Conservation Commission officer.

The wildlife officer, Joshua Horst, questioned the Murano's driver. The man said he'd seen another car hit the tortoise and he had picked up the injured animal out of compassion. He planned to take it to a neighbor in

The man who stole gopher tortoise 1721 from Archbold Biological Station didn't intend to upset a science experiment—he just wanted to grab something quick for dinner. Photo courtesy of Hilary Swain, Archbold Biological Station.

Port Orange who is a wildlife rehabilitation expert. He said he had no idea what happened to its tracking device.

"He admitted making a comment that 'they used to eat them back in the day,'" Horst wrote in his report. (During the Great Depression, hungry Floridians ate gopher tortoises, which they dubbed "Hoover chickens," after President Herbert Hoover's promise of a chicken in every pot.)

Horst examined the abducted animal and found "no scrapes, fractures or drag marks" showing it had been run over. The only mark on its shell was a "straight slice/cut" about an inch from where the tracking device had been, suggesting the first swing of the blade had missed the target.

Horst handed the driver a citation for illegal possession of a gopher tortoise, which is classified as a threatened species in Florida. The tortoise, a female, was handed back over to the biologists at Archbold, who hadn't realized it was gone, much less that it was traveling faster than any other tortoise in Florida. At best they check the tortoises' radio signals every couple of weeks, explained biologist Betsie Rothermel.

Rothermel said Wednesday that they returned 1721 to its burrow, where it has gone back to its humdrum tortoise life without any apparent ill effects from its Nov. 8 adventure.

Scientists first marked No. 1721 back in the 1980s as part of a tortoise study that's been going on for nearly 50 years now.

"She is at least 45-years-old and has been living in this part of the station for decades," Archbold director Hilary Swain wrote on the Archbold blog this week. "In the past five years, we have recorded 23 observations of her grazing along the driveway, or in a few cases, scuffling with her apparent rival, a similar-sized female #795."

To the folks at Archbold, good old 1721 (sorry, no cute nickname) is more than just a number. It is "a valuable study animal and beloved by visiting children and adults alike," Swain noted.

So they're glad that it escaped a stew pot. The best part of the story, according to Swain, was the driver's name: Stewart Butcher.

28

A NASTY BATHROOM SURPRISE

Tampa Bay Times, December 24, 2017

Iguanas are commonly found in Mexico, Central America, South America and the Caribbean. In 2017, you could add "Florida toilets" to that list.

So far this year, news stories reported that iguanas have turned up in Florida commodes at least five times—although there's reason to believe it's happened more often than that.

What are they doing in the toilet? Besides the backstroke, that is?

Trying to get out.

Although other animals have been known to intrude into toilets—rats, for instance—iguanas are perfectly adapted for plumbing infiltration. The voracious little Godzillas, which can grow to be 6 feet long from snout to tail, frequently climb trees and also tend to be good swimmers, able to hold their breath for an extended time period.

From the trees "they come down from the vent pipe in the roof," explained veteran Boca Grande iguana trapper George Cera, who has written a cookbook called *Save Florida, Eat an Iguana.* "Even if your vent pipe is closed, that doesn't mean your neighbors' is."

Once an iguana gets into someone's plumbing, it can quickly wind up swimming in the sewer system, he explained. Then it's looking for a way to escape.

"It's the luck of the draw where they come out," he said. "The next place to pop out is your 3-inch toilet pipe."

In other words, while New York's sewers may not be filled with alligators, as the legend has it, Florida's sewers do apparently team with toothy green iguanas that frequently pop up in the pooper.

Among the many perils that Floridians regularly confront—the state gets more hurricanes, lightning strikes, sinkholes and shark bites than anywhere else in the United States—finding an iguana in the toilet is unique. Not only does it happen more in Florida, but a LexisNexis search of news stories from around the nation reveals that it happens *only* in Florida.

This year isn't the first time an iguana has turned up in a Florida toilet. In 2015, for instance, a woman in Fort Lauderdale called Roto-Rooter to clear a clogged commode, only to hear the plumber scream upon yanking out an iguana. It died—the iguana, that is, not the plumber.

But this is the year when reports of iguanas in toilets repeatedly hit the news.

The most recent toilet iguana to make news happened Nov. 30 in Hialeah. A man named Giovanni Profera told Telemundo, "I sat down, I felt pressure, I jumped and saw a lizard." The iguana scrambled out of the bowl and fled, no one knows where.

The video went viral after it was broadcast on the Spanish language channel. But the *New York Times* subsequently reported that the incident was actually a hoax perpetrated by a performance artist named Zardulu, who titled the piece "The Usurpation of Ouranos."

The newspaper noted that the hoax seemed plausible only because so many real cases of iguanas popping out of toilets occurred in Florida.

Among those real cases was another one last month. A woman in Palmetto was going to clean her toilet but freaked out when she discovered an iguana swimming in the bowl. She has been afraid of lizards since she was 5.

"I didn't know what it was at first, so I instantly screamed and my 9-year-old daughter come running in and she said, 'Mommy what is it?' and I said, 'I don't know,'" Dani Craven told WFLA-TV. "All I could see were scaly, like a scaly tail. I couldn't tell if it was an alligator or a lizard. I didn't know."

Her husband wasn't home and she wasn't about to tackle it alone. She put out a cry for help on Facebook and a neighbor came over armed with rubber gloves, a net and a cooler. The neighbor caught the creature, even though it kept hissing at her. She took it to a wildlife rehabilitation facility.

In August, a man in the South Florida community of Medley was trying to unclog a toilet when he looked down the drainpipe and saw an iguana peering up at him. The man's uncle calmly caught it with a loop of rope, then walked it outside as if it were on a leash and turned it loose, which means it can go invade someone else's toilet.

In July, Univision reporter David Adams, who lives in Key Biscayne, donned ski gloves, a gas mask and a bulletproof vest to remove an iguana from his toilet. He captured it by wrapping it in a beach towel. He, too, chose to release the lizard back into the wild.

Iguanas are commonly found in Mexico, Central America, South America and the Caribbean—and, in recent years, Florida toilets. Photo courtesy of the Fort Lauderdale Fire Department.

"He hissed at me and had a couple of jaw snaps, but then scampered away to rejoin the reptilian hordes in our neighborhood," Adams wrote in a Facebook post about the encounter.

In May something similar happened in the Miami suburb of Kendall. A woman lifted the lid of her commode, spotted the iguana, closed the lid and dialed 911. Miami-Dade Fire Rescue's Venom Unit—which routinely handles calls involving pythons and other snakes—captured the critter, and said it was a first for them. They took it to a wildlife rescue center.

Florida is infested with more exotic and invasive species than any other state, with the roster ranging from feral hogs originally imported by Spanish conquistadors to giant African land snails smuggled in a few years ago by a religious cult.

Pythons are the best known, though they're largely confined to the Everglades, but iguanas are among those that have spread the most widely across the state.

The earliest official report of iguanas roaming the Florida wild dates back to Miami-Dade County in 1965, according to Sarah Lessard, spokeswoman for the state Fish and Wildlife Conservation Commission. Now they're found all along the Atlantic coast from Martin County down to the Keys and in isolated instances have been found on the state's west coast as well.

The next official sighting, from 1979, came from the island community of Boca Grande, near Fort Myers. Local legend says a Boca Grande resident brought a pair back from Mexico as pets, then either turned them loose or lost them, and they became the Adam and Eve of a huge Florida iguana colony.

By 2007 the island was overrun by thousands of the lively lizards. Finally Lee County assessed a tax to pay for a trapper, making it the only place in America with an iguana tax. In just his first two years on the job, George Cera, the trapper, caught 16,000 iguanas. As of last year he was still averaging about 2,000 captures a year.

A similar drop has occurred in reports of iguanas in Boca Grande's toilets, Cera said—but it has never entirely stopped.

"Back when the population on the island was larger, it would happen two or three times a month," he said. "Now it's maybe one or two times a year." None of those incidents made the news, suggesting that there are some iguanas that, like a politician facing indictment, manage to find a way to slip past reporters.

Cera, whose cookbook includes recipes for such delicacies as iguana tacos, said the frequency of iguana toilet sightings has made him wonder what sort of animals routinely pop up at Florida's sewer plants.

Bill Logan, spokesman for St. Petersburg's public works department, said city officials are unaware of any iguanas appearing in the city's sewer system. But two years ago, he said, workers shutting down the old Albert Whitted sewer plant caught an 18-inch-long Australian catfish swimming in the aerators. They figured someone had flushed the fish when it was smaller and it just kept growing.

Nobody, he said, was brave enough to eat it.

29

SWAMP THING

Tampa Bay Times, January 2, 2019

For years, it was just a Florida myth, a legend no one took seriously. Panhandle residents called it "the leopard eel," a 2-foot-long, slimy creature with nubs where its front legs should be, spots all over its body and what appeared to be a set of wings on either side of its head.

Only a few people claimed to have seen one. The most intriguing story came from an Alabama biologist who said that on one rainy night in 1994, while driving near the Florida-Alabama border, he'd come across hundreds writhing in a flooded road. It was, he told fellow scientists, the most incredible natural event he'd ever witnessed.

And then, in 2009, a biologist named David Steen accidentally caught one. He had set out wire mesh traps in the swamps around Eglin Air Force Base near Fort Walton Beach, looking for turtles. While checking one trap he discovered it contained one of the legendary creatures curled up in the bottom, apparently just waiting for him. He quickly stuck it back in the water so it wouldn't escape.

Over the next nine years, Steen and a colleague, Sean Graham, worked on their own time and with no official funding to verify their suspicion that this was a new species, previously undescribed by any scientist. They published their findings in December, announcing that it wasn't an eel after all, but a rare type of spotted salamander known as a siren.

"We name this species the Reticulated Siren, *Siren reticulate*," they wrote.

Their publication in the journal *PLOS ONE* set off a round of excited reports about this odd-looking swamp thing in the *New York Times,* the *Washington Post* and on CNN and NPR's *Science Friday. Scientific American* called their discovery "a highly unusual animal—and one of the largest vertebrates described in the United States or Canada in the past few decades."

David Steen (*left*) and Sean Graham (*right*) found and identified a supposedly mythical creature in the Florida Panhandle—thus raising the question of what other undiscovered species might be out there in the piney woods. Photo courtesy of David Steen.

Graham, in a blog post, wrote that "a bird with comparable uniqueness to this animal would have looked something like an ostrich with polka dots."

The notion that such a big and bizarre-looking creature had existed mostly unnoticed in the Florida swamps for so long raises questions about what else might be out there that no one has officially identified.

For Steen, a research ecologist with the Georgia Sea Turtle Center, this is vindication for an obsession that dates back more than a decade.

When he was a graduate student at Auburn University, his adviser was showing him around the university's museum of natural history and rapped his knuckles on a large glass specimen jar labeled as a salamander species called "the greater siren." The adviser said he didn't think the specimen was identified correctly, and added, "It's probably a new species just waiting for someone to describe it."

Steen and Graham, also an Auburn grad student who is now with Sul Ross State University in Texas, became fascinated by the possibility of finding that new species of siren in an age when most people think there's nothing new under the sun. It was, Graham wrote, "the stuff of lore. It may as well have been Bigfoot."

But they didn't strike pay dirt until Steen's accidental catch at Eglin. Steen said when he pulled up the trap and saw what he had, he reacted with "stunned silence. I'd been primed for this for years, waiting for just this moment, just to see this salamander that my friends thought was a legend."

When he regained the power to move, he transferred his find into a bucket and then into a big Tupperware container. When he showed what he'd caught to Graham, his colleague screamed hysterically and shouted, "Oh, my God!"

The animal's physical attributes were unusual, to say the least. Those wings on its head, for instance, were actually intricately branched, tree-like external gills. While technically an amphibian, the reticulated siren spends almost its entire life underwater—another reason why it had been so hard to find.

To officially identify a new species, though, Steen and Graham, needed more examples to study. In their spare time they hunted around Eglin, but found no more. They tried Conecuh National Forest in Alabama, where the Auburn jar creature had been caught, and around an Alabama lake near where the biologist had seen so many in a road. Still no luck.

Then, in 2014, while searching a marsh in northern Okaloosa County that's adjacent to the state-line lake, they caught three of the salamanders, enabling them to do the genetic testing and other studies required to prove it is a new species.

"I wish I could convey to you our excitement," Graham wrote. "The rush of lifting up our traps from the swirling, black murk, and seeing the serpentine bodies of huge salamanders unknown to the world."

Steen said he's hopeful now that they have named the creature, the state wildlife and environmental agencies in Alabama and Florida will be interested in learning more about them and whether they deserve endangered species protection.

No matter what happens next, Graham wrote, he and Steen have the satisfaction of making a bizarre scientific discovery that nobody else ever did: "We found a giant salamander under everyone's noses and described it as a new species."

~~~~~~

Note: After this story ran, I got a sternly worded letter from a New York patent attorney about using the word "Tupperware" if the resealable plastic container involved was not a true Tupperware product. Here's the reply I sent, which satisfied the attorney's query:

"*Thanks for your note. To answer your question: I used the word 'Tupperware' because that's the word that the scientist I interviewed for the story, Dr. David A. Steen, used. He specifically said he put the reticulated siren in a Tupperware container—not a plastic container. He was very clear about it.*

"*As you know, journalists value accuracy above all things, and we find that using specific rather than generic terms on details such as this can be important to conveying to readers the accuracy of a story. That's why I used the brand name mentioned in the interview. I think this makes the story more relatable for the readers who frequently use their Tupperware for more mundane storage tasks.*

"*I am a big fan of Tupperware, as I am a big fan of so many things with Florida roots. I am friends with the author who wrote the definitive biography of Brownie Wise, who started Tupperware home parties (Bob Kealing, Life of the Party). I would not intentionally do anything to harm Kissimmee's greatest export. But I think you're viewing this the wrong way. Rather than regarding its mention in this story as a detriment to its product line, perhaps your client could regard it as an endorsement. Think how it would boost sales if the company were to include it in their advertising for the product: 'Used by real scientists to contain previously unknown swamp creatures!'*

"*Cordially, Craig Pittman*"

30

CUKES FOR COUPLES

Tampa Bay Times, February 17, 2014

This is a story about sex, supply and demand, global trade, corruption, government regulation and one of the ugliest sea creatures in Florida.

Among the marine animals that live in the Florida Keys is the sea cucumber. It is animal, not vegetable—a long and lumpy invertebrate that looks like a cross between a diseased zucchini and an overinflated éclair.

For decades, divers who strapped on scuba gear to collect saltwater fish for aquariums have also scooped up the occasional sea cucumber. In 2012, they collected about 14,000 of them in the Keys, according to Melissa Recks of the Florida Fish and Wildlife Conservation Commission. Nobody got rich off of them—they were going for about $1 each.

Then, last year, Florida's sea cucumber catch more than tripled, hitting 54,000, Recks said.

The reason for that astonishing jump lies in the Asian market, where they are eaten, not displayed in aquariums. In China in particular, the sea cucumber is used to treat joint pain—and, more importantly, as an aphrodisiac.

As a result, demand is heavy there for sea cucumbers, also known as "trepang" and "b'che-de-mer" and "the vacuum cleaners of the sea." The demand is so heavy that worldwide 20 percent of sea cucumber fisheries have been fully depleted.

That's bad news. Despite their alleged ability to boost human sexual performance, sea cucumbers suffer from a major disadvantage in their own reproduction because they are "broadcast spawners," Recks said.

That means they eject their sperm and eggs out into the water in the expectation that enough other sea cucumbers are close by doing the same thing so that they will mix. If there aren't any others, no spawning occurs. If too many sea cucumbers are harvested, they may never bounce back.

So many sea cucumbers were harvested in Costa Rica, Ecuador, India and eight other countries that the population collapsed, prompting those

The sea cucumber found in the Florida Keys is a long and lumpy invertebrate that looks like a cross between a diseased zucchini and an overinflated éclair. In China, it's considered an aphrodisiac. Photo by Carli Segelson, courtesy of the Florida Fish and Wildlife Conservation Commission.

countries to ban further harvesting, Recks said. Even in areas that are supposed to be protected, such as the Great Barrier Reef and Galapagos Islands National Park, so many sea cucumbers were snatched up that their population crashed.

Except for requiring a license to collect live sea creatures, Florida does not regulate sea cucumber collectors. Fearing disaster will occur in the Keys as it has elsewhere, the group that represents people collecting sea creatures there, the Florida Marine Life Association, asked state wildlife officials to create new regulations to protect sea cucumbers—a rare move.

Because the association requested a limit of 200 sea cucumbers per person per trip, that's the limit Recks recommended to wildlife commissioners.

"We're taking the advice of the industry here because we don't have anything better," she said during a meeting in Tampa this month.

To Eric Lee, a limit that small would be a disaster: "I would definitely be out of business."

Lee spent nine years working in the oil and coal industries in China, leaving because the pollution got too bad. He now runs Florida's only sea cucumber processing plant on Ramrod Key.

Lee said he spent a year and a half getting the plant started, including obtaining permits from the state and federal governments, with an eye toward selling Florida sea cucumbers to the Asian market.

At first, all went well. In communist China, sea cucumber is often handed out in expensive gift boxes to family, friends or—nudge nudge, wink wink—to government officials who might be inclined to do favors. That was a major part of Lee's expected market.

But then the Chinese government cracked down on government corruption "and now government officials are terrified to take gifts," Lee said.

Thus Lee is now concentrating on the retail market, he said. But to make it work he needs the wildlife commission to set a higher limit—say 500 to 800 sea cucumbers per person per trip.

For the wildlife commission meeting, Lee brought along a bag of dried sea cucumbers and handed them around to the commissioners.

"I guess the question is whether the commissioners should view them or eat them," quipped commission chairman Richard Corbett, a Tampa mall developer.

The commissioners initially voted to limit the take to 200, but then reconsidered and said they would give their staff time to work out a compromise prior to their next meeting, which is in April in Tallahassee.

Until then, it's still open season on sea cucumbers in the Keys, although it seems unlikely they will show up on any Florida seafood menus. One diner quoted by the *Independent,* a British newspaper, described their taste as "slightly lower than phlegm, the texture of which it closely resembles."

Note: In April 2014, the state wildlife commission voted to limit the sea cucumber harvest to 400 per person per trip, which Lee predicted would drive him out of business. A month after that, though, Lee's company was featured on an episode of the Travel Channel show Bizarre Foods. *When I checked five years later, the company's website was still offering sea cucumbers for sale.*

31

MONKEYS AMOK

Tampa Bay Times, February 27, 2018

Here's a regulation you won't find anywhere but Florida. The Florida Fish and Wildlife Conservation Commission recently decreed that it is now illegal to feed wild monkeys.

Wild monkeys are not, of course, native to Florida. Yet about a hundred of them live in Silver Springs State Park. The story of how they got there is a classic Florida tale of a plan gone awry.

Back in the 1930s, when Silver Springs was just another roadside attraction, the captain of its version of the Disney Jungle Cruise, Col. Tooey, put six monkeys on a small island in the Silver River. He thought seeing them would spice up the ride for tourists. He thought the monkeys would stay on the island. He didn't think they could swim.

Boy, was he wrong.

At first, as the rhesus macaques spread into the forest around Silver Springs, they were just a local oddity. But for the past 30 years, as suburbia has sprawled closer to the spring, state wildlife officials began warning that the monkeys posed a threat to humans.

In 1984 the *New York Times* reported that "stray monkeys have been found in . . . the nearby city of Ocala foraging in garbage cans. . . . Male monkeys ranging up to 30 pounds have also been spotted on thoroughbred horse farms in the area, and some were shot and killed while stealing fruit in citrus groves."

That story, incidentally, included this great quote from a University of Florida professor who was studying the monkeys: "The trouble with the monkeys at Silver Springs is that they don't know they are in Florida. They think they're somewhere in Southern Asia and they go looking for other monkeys."

The state game commission produced a report back then that said one monkey bit a 3-year-old boy in the neck. Some jumped into a boat as frightened passengers dove into the river. A wildlife officer killed a male

The story of how rhesus macaques like this one got loose in what's now Silver Springs State Park is a classic Florida tale of a tourist attraction plan gone awry. Photo courtesy of Robert Gottschalk.

monkey that had "approached him in a threat display" and then an angry mob "of approximately 50 macaques advanced on First Sergeant Jones, forcing him to leave the area."

For a while the park employed a professional trapper to thin out the macaque menagerie, until an animal welfare group noted that the trapper was selling what he caught to be used by a scientific specimens company. The state then yanked his permit.

State officials have repeatedly noted that they're worried about diseases. Many rhesus monkeys carry herpes-B, a virus that is fatal to humans. The trapper warned about potential diseases spread by contact with "rhesus feces," which is surely the worst proposed candy flavor ever.

That potential threat is what's behind the new regulation against feeding them. That threat always garners a lot of hysterical tabloid headlines, such as "Florida monkeys could pass killer herpes to people."

However, only a quarter of the Silver Springs monkeys carry the virus, and experts say there are exactly zero cases of humans contracting herpes-B from macaques in the wild. The most recent study, the one that prompted the state's action, notes: "All documented cases of human contraction of and death . . . have been associated with captive animals within laboratory settings."

Still, if you feed wild monkeys, or any other wild animal, they get used to begging for food, and that is never good.

Despite the official hostility, the monkeys remain a popular (if accidental) park attraction. Tourists love snapping pictures of them. They've been spotted by hikers on the Cross-Florida Greenway. Not every monkey encounter is a good one, though. Last year a whole family of monkeys chased away a whole family of human tourists.

A few years ago, one of the Silver Springs macaques wandered our way to become the elusive Mystery Monkey of Tampa Bay. The Mystery Monkey, in case you've forgotten, showed up in backyards all over the Tampa and St. Petersburg area, repeatedly eluding capture for three years, and in the process became such a media star that, ahead of the 2008 Republican National Convention in Tampa, the *New York Times* ran a profile of the monkey.

No wonder Florida gets such a rep for monkey business.

32

WE'RE GOING ON A BEAR HUNT

Tampa Bay Times, October 25, 2015

Note: I covered Florida's first bear hunt since 1994 from a check-in station at Rock Creek Park in Central Florida. My colleague Michael Auslen contributed to the coverage from another check station up in the Panhandle. I wrote this story on the first day of the hunt.

Florida's first bear hunt in 21 years began Saturday, bringing camouflage-clad hunters flocking to the forests for a shot at going down in history. By day's end they had killed 207, according to state wildlife officials—so many that two regions would not be allowed to kill any more.

"I've been waiting 20 some-odd years to kill a bear in Florida," said Rick Sajko, 48, a pool enclosure contractor who has killed bears in his native Pennsylvania and in Canada. His Florida prize, he said, he shot at 60 yards.

"One shot and down it went," said Sajko, of Valrico.

He said he expected to process and eat the meat from his 178-pound bear, turn the pelt into a rug, and apply the oil to his snakeskin boots. As for the fat, "it makes excellent pies," he said.

Meanwhile, monitors such as Astevia Willett of Largo kept careful track of the number of bears killed, vowing to make sure the state wildlife agency did not allow more bears to be killed than 320, the limit set for the entire state.

Willett, who drove two hours to serve as a monitor in Central Florida, said she'd never seen a bear before outside a zoo. By the end of Saturday she'd seen more than 20, all dead, some of them already gutted but still bleeding.

Hunters in two regions of the state, Central Florida and the eastern Panhandle, shot so many bears on the first day of the weeklong hunt that they won't get a second day. The Panhandle hunters killed 81, which was

In 2015, Florida held its first bear hunt in 21 years. At the Rock Springs Run Wildlife Management Area, hunter Richard Sajko of Valrico talked about how he killed one of the two bears on the back of his pickup truck. Photo by Luis Santana, used by permission of the *Tampa Bay Times*.

more than double their quota of 40. The Central Florida limit was 100, and as of late Saturday the number of dead bears had hit 99.

Florida Fish and Wildlife Conservation Commission executive director Nick Wiley shied away from calling the hunt a success, though.

"This has not been an easy thing to do for our agency," he said.

Among the Panhandle hunters were Andrew Rapuzzi and his daughter Julie, who shot a bear in their yard. They knew when it might come by—the bear has made a habit of spending the morning in their yard.

Andrew grabbed his crossbow and shot the bear from 40 yards away. Because the family has Apache heritage, he and his daughter then performed a sacred ceremony, putting sage and tobacco in the bear's mouth "to help his spirit go to the Creator," he said.

No protesters showed up to disrupt the proceedings until the sun went down. Then, at the Rock Springs Run Wildlife Management Area's hunter check-in station near Sanford, a vegan veterinarian from Orlando, Randall Cannon, switched on a large flat-screen TV on the back of his truck. It began flashing bright images of bears along with quotes from serial killer Ted Bundy, to whom he compared the hunters.

"None of these bears died peacefully," Cannon said as his message blared through the deepening shadows.

Florida's black bears were last hunted in 1994. Until 2012 they were considered an imperiled species, deserving state protection like panthers and scrub jays. Some activists tried in vain to get the federal government to add them to the national endangered species list.

Instead, three years ago the state took them off its protected list. That's when a movement began to bring back bear hunting—a movement that has proven to be unpopular with the general public, but widely supported by hunters. The wildlife commission voted this summer to proceed with the hunt, despite not knowing how many bears there are. A statewide census is supposed to be complete in 2016.

Fueling the push for the hunt was a series of incidents in which bears attacked and mauled five people—four women and, on the eve of Saturday's hunt, a 65-year-old man who was attacked near a Panhandle motel. His injuries were considered minor and wildlife officials were still trying to capture the bear as of late Saturday.

Opponents of the hunt tried to stop it with a lawsuit but lost. The group Speak Up Wekiva appealed, but a court ruling that came down at 7:37 p.m. on Friday cleared the hunt to proceed as scheduled, starting just before sunup. By then 3,778 licenses had been sold.

Rock Creek Springs is a state-owned natural area thick with bears, turkey and deer that's become surrounded by suburban development. It's also just a stone's throw from where one of the bear attacks occurred.

Before 5 a.m. Saturday, trucks lined up for a quarter mile down State Road 46 as hunters waited for Rock Springs' gates to open so they could settle into their tree stands before the time when it would be legal to start shooting.

Among them sat Billy Girard, ready to take out either a deer or a bear using his muzzle-loading rifle. He bought his $100 bear hunt permit Friday at 11 p.m., just before the sales closed.

"It's the first time Florida's done it in what, 20 years? So I figured why not?" the Oviedo resident said. He was going deer hunting anyway, "so if a buck comes out, I'll shoot it, and if a bear comes out, I'll shoot that." A bear, he said, "would be a nice thing to have."

Just before 10 a.m., a pickup truck pulled in at Rock Springs Run and a team of state biologists climbed in the back to unload a dead female bear, still lactating from where it had nursed cubs recently. A biologist said the cubs, at nine months, were old enough to survive despite being orphaned.

The biologists wanted to weigh the carcass, take a hair sample for DNA testing, even pull out one its teeth to check its age. They shoved it forward and a winch hoisted it in the air as a scale registered a weight of 298 pounds. The bear's tongue lolled out of its mouth, and a gush of saliva the color of strawberry jam spilled across the tailgate.

The hunter who shot it stood at a green table in the shade answering questions for a survey, a tight smile on her face, a pink cellphone shoved into the back pocket of her jeans.

Amanda Holmes, 23, said she spotted the bear 200 yards from her tree stand, and brought it down with her Remington. She and her brother Caleb had spent weeks scouting the right place to get her quarry—one of the first, if not the first, shot dead in the state.

"I'm sure we'll find a use for everything," she said, her hand wrapped around one of the wooden rails, showing off a set of scarlet nails.

Note: The Florida bear hunt proved to be all too successful, with so many bears killed in such a short time that the wildlife commission's executive director shut it down after two days. The hunt proved unpopular with the general public, and as of 2020 the state has not scheduled a second one.

33

LOVED TO DEATH

Sarasota, April 2013

The two Sarasota County deputies from the marine patrol division got the word about 5 p.m. on Friday, Sept. 12. A dead dolphin was floating near marker 15 north of the Albee Road Bridge. They had to go retrieve it.

After a 20-minute search, the deputies found the carcass. They put a rope on it and towed it to the boat ramp at Nokomis Beach. The dolphin had been dead for some time. That much was obvious. The body was bloated and sloughing off skin.

When dolphins wash up dead or injured along the coast, volunteers who are part of a network working with stranded marine mammals are called to collect them. Three members of Mote Marine Laboratory's stranding investigations team arrived at the Nokomis Beach boat ramp about 6:15 p.m.

They immediately recognized that the deputies had found Florida's most famous bottlenose dolphin since Flipper the television star.

The dead dolphin's name was Beggar. That was its claim to fame, too. Over more than two decades, Beggar had become widely known for panhandling the boats passing by in the Intracoastal Waterway.

Tourists and locals alike knew that if they rapped on the side of their boats, Beggar would swim up, thrust a smiling snout out of the water and beg for food. Pictures and videos of Beggar circulated widely on the Internet—jumping, snatching a tossed fish from the air, shooting through the water in hot pursuit of a speeding boat, swimming mere inches from the spinning propellers, risking life and fin in hopes of earning handouts.

Many boaters threw fish to Beggar, but some tossed more exotic fare. "Researchers have spotted people feeding him potato chips, macadamia nuts, oranges and apples as well as rotting shrimp, squid and other fishing bait that reek with bacteria," an official Mote report noted.

The stranding team members trucked the carcass back to the Mote Marine laboratory on City Island. They wanted to figure out what had killed the celebrity dolphin. As humans undergo an autopsy, so animals are cut open for what's known as a necropsy. The necropsy for Beggar began about 7 p.m. and ended eight hours later.

In one way, the necropsy results were inconclusive. Biologists found nothing they could call the cause of Beggar's death. But in another way, the necropsy confirmed every suspicion that dolphin experts ever had about Beggar, and about the people enthralled by his antics.

They found multiple broken bones and vertebrae, as well as several healed wounds on his fins and skin—signs that Beggar had gotten a little too close to the boats of all those admiring fans and suffered the consequences.

And inside, in Beggar's three stomachs, they found something even more disturbing: three fishing hooks, small bits of line and two squid beaks. Sarasota-area dolphins don't normally eat squid, so it was clear that Beggar had been stealing the bait from local anglers, along with the hooks and line that went with it.

The biologists could see that Beggar was markedly dehydrated—a remarkable finding for an animal spending its whole life in the water. And instead of a normal weight of nearly 500 pounds, he weighed in at just 300 pounds, probably a result of not pursuing and eating the fish that constitute a normal dolphin diet, and in a quantity that normal dolphins consume.

To the biologists studying the marine mammal's emaciated remains, the evidence was clear as could be about who killed Beggar: all those fans who tossed food to the star. Said Stacey Horstman, bottlenose dolphin conservation coordinator for the National Oceanic and Atmospheric Administration: "Every time a hand reached out to Beggar, it contributed to his death."

Randy Wells has spent three decades studying the dolphins that swim around Sarasota. The first time he saw Beggar was Aug. 10, 1990. The young dolphin had already perfected its performing routine.

The encounter, as with nearly all encounters with Beggar, occurred in the Intracoastal Waterway just north of Albee Bridge. The waterway narrows here between Casey Key and the mainland, funneling boaters down into something like single file. There's a drawbridge to negotiate, too. And because the area is designated as a manatee habitat, boaters are supposed to slow down to idle speed.

On that late summer day, Wells recalled, he and other dolphin researchers from Mote were cruising along slowly when a young dolphin swam up next to their boat and popped open its mouth, precisely imitating a baby bird asking to be fed by its mama. They had never seen anything quite like it in the wild.

"We were surprised," Wells, director of the Sarasota Dolphin Research Program at Mote, says. "We thought he was more of an anomaly than he turned out to be."

Wells and his colleagues jotted down the obvious name for this newly identified dolphin, then set about trying to figure out where it had learned to panhandle.

They concluded this youngster had either escaped or been released from captivity somewhere along the Gulf coast. It must have come from a place that copied the SeaWorld formula of entertaining ticket buyers with a choreographed dolphin show. But when they contacted the places that featured performing dolphins, no one admitted to having one missing, Wells says.

Ultimately, they concluded that Beggar was not trained as a performer. Instead, Wells explains, Beggar was a wild dolphin that had learned how to coax people to toss out food. In a way, Beggar had trained the humans, not the other way around.

The young dolphin's primary range included an area where lots of boats passed by that contained generous humans. They saw the smiling young dolphin and tossed him some fish, a tribute to his cuteness. Soon enough, Wells says, Beggar "figured out that food from people was easier to come by" than chasing it down and catching it, the way most dolphins do.

Soon, Beggar had picked up a companion. Beginning in 1993, Beggar was paired up with another begging male that the scientists named "Mooch." They worked together for about three years, and then Mooch moved on or died, no one knows for sure. But Beggar stayed put, still working the same stretch of waterway.

From time to time, Beggar popped up with a female companion named Bardot. Bardot had also learned to solicit food from passing boats, probably from watching Beggar at work. Bardot had a calf that also picked up the begging habit. When it died in 2000, at four years old, the calf was emaciated. A necropsy found the calf had fish hooks in its stomach, line entanglement scars on all of its fins, a shark bite scar, and fresh, deep, boat propeller wounds on its tail stalk. Bardot's calf "was a poster child for all that could go wrong from interactions with humans," the Mote report on Beggar noted.

In 2005, when red tide devastated the fish population in Sarasota Bay, more dolphins turned to taking handouts or seizing the bait from anglers' lines. Meanwhile, the more biologists looked, the more begging behavior they had begun seeing among wild dolphins—and not just around Sarasota.

From North Carolina down to the Keys and all along the Gulf coast, Horstman said, "Wherever we have dolphins and people there, we're seeing increased reports of human interactions with dolphins—feeding them, trying to touch them, swimming with them."

Such behavior hasn't been confined to the United States, either. In Australia biologists spent a decade studying bottlenose dolphins in the bay off Perth and watched the number that begged for food go from one to 14. The dolphins, which live amid a complex social structure, taught each other how to beg. The ones that begged for food tended to be the ones that wound up being hit by boats.

That's the thing about these handouts. They draw wild animals in close enough to humans for them to get hurt or killed.

✿

All around the Florida coast are well-meaning waterfront homeowners who stand on their docks and use a hose to spray water into the mouths of manatees. They think they are doing something nice for the manatees. They never consider whether it's wise to get manatees in the habit of congregating around docks where boats also tend to congregate.

What's true on the water is true on land. In the Florida Keys is a colony of about 700 deer that are the size of big dogs. This species has been on the endangered list since 1967. The Key deer are so petite and appealing that tourists driving through the National Key Deer Refuge can't resist rolling down their windows and offering them treats.

The Key deer now associate cars with food. Whenever they see a car they run up looking for a handout. As a result, the leading cause of death for Key deer is being run over by vehicles.

Dolphins and manatees and Key deer are the victims of their own appealing looks. The dolphin's smile hides so much about them. People see that smile and think the dolphin is always friendly, always eager to please a human.

The problem is, some people can't just watch a wild animal being wild. Like the woman in St. Petersburg who spotted a passing manatee at the beach and tried to ride it, they want to be more than passive observers. They have to put themselves into the picture somehow, make themselves the star of this nature show.

"People just can't resist feeding the dolphin or petting the dolphin," one

Sarasota-area tour boat operator told the *Tampa Bay Times* after Beggar's death. "You don't go hiking in the Rockies and see a grizzly bear and walk up and try to feed it. But dolphins are characterized so differently in movies, people think it's going to be just like a puppy. So they just go up and try to pet it."

Just as Beggar got in the habit of taking handouts, people have been conditioned to think that way by repetition. They've seen the dolphins at SeaWorld leaping on command and being tossed their rewards by human handlers. They've been to the dolphin feeding areas at the theme parks. They've seen Flipper on TV. They think they know what dolphins want and how to react to them.

Until the teeth clamp down on their skin, that is.

"In Beggar's defense," Wells says, "he only used the teeth when people weren't feeding him."

For three months in 2011, from March to June, Mote Marine's Dr. Katie McHugh spent 100 hours watching Beggar's behavior. In that time, she documented 3,600 times that Beggar had some sort of interaction with humans. Mostly she saw people trying to attract Beggar's attention, then tossing fish and other food.

But 121 times, people wanted to do something more intimate. They wanted to touch Beggar, to pat the dolphin's head the way they would a dog's, to stroke its skin as if it were a cat.

Nine times, that ended with Beggar biting the human. The dolphin wanted food, not affection, and exhibited little patience with those who showed up empty-handed.

"People see that smile and they assume it indicates friendship," Wells says. Instead all a dolphin's smile indicates is that dolphins have 100 or so teeth.

A bottlenose dolphin's teeth are not razor sharp. Their teeth are cone-shaped and wear down over the years. The dolphins use them for grasping their prey, not for chewing them up or ripping them apart, Wells explains.

"Once they grab a fish, they typically maneuver it to be able to swallow it, intact, head first," he says. "If they catch a fish that is too large to swallow, they may drag it along the bottom or shake their heads to try to tear the fish into smaller pieces." Still, he says, if someone whose hand wound up trapped in a dolphin's mouth were to try to snatch it back, "they would be lacerated."

Over 20 years, Beggar bit plenty of would-be admirers, administering a stiff penalty to anyone who failed to pay tribute. But nobody got it worse than Kim Foy.

In July 1992, she was boating with her family in the Intracoastal Waterway, tossing bait to a dolphin that Wells believes was Beggar.

Then she and her eight-year-old son jumped into the water to cool off. Meanwhile the occupants of another boat "started teasing the dolphin by holding a shoe above the water as if it were food," the *Sarasota Herald-Tribune* later reported.

Suddenly Foy felt the dolphin's teeth chomp down on her knee. She broke free, but then the dolphin clamped down on her son. Foy's husband, Edward, was able to lean out of the boat, yank the boy loose and haul him to safety.

Still on the attack, the dolphin grabbed Foy's leg again. This time, no matter how she struggled, she could not get loose. Her husband jumped into the water and kicked the dolphin in the face, forcing it to let go, and then helped her climb back aboard the boat, blood welling from her leg.

Foy's wound took 20 stitches to close. The next day, her leg swelled up. She had contracted a cholera infection. Doctors said they couldn't tell if it was caused by pollution in the water or contamination from the dolphin's bite. She spent a week in the hospital recovering.

Before the attack, Foy regarded swimming with the dolphins as "neat," she told CBS News in 2009.

She remembered thinking, "This is just like Flipper on TV."

Not anymore, she said. Even 17 years later, "I still think about the pressure of the jaws around my leg and pulling me down," she told the TV camera. "It was a horrible experience."

For about a year in the late 1990s, Wells and a team of researchers from Mote spent hours on end watching how passing boaters behaved when they encountered Beggar. They saw more than 8,000 boats. They watched 68 boaters toss food to the dolphin and saw 80 try to touch or pet it. They saw 18 get bitten and heard about 10 more bites.

As part of their research, the Mote crew approached 173 boaters to tell them that what they were doing was illegal. Under the federal Marine Mammal Protection Act, feeding and teasing a dolphin constitute harassment. Violations can bring a fine of up to $20,000 per incident, plus a year behind bars.

Of the 146 boaters who agreed to talk to them, they found that 61 percent knew that feeding dolphins was wrong and yet they did it anyway.

Even having a state wildlife officer on patrol nearby didn't discourage them.

"While the officer was talking to the occupants of one boat about the dangers of feeding wild marine mammals, other boats engaged in feeding interactions with the dolphin," the study reported.

That should come as no surprise. Panama City has been the capital of the tours that allow paying customers to swim with the dolphins. Tour operators who wanted to make sure their customers got a good show would regularly toss fish to the dolphins. Two of the tour operators in Panama City and one in Cape Coral were hit with $5,000 fines by the National Oceanic and Atmospheric Administration last summer.

Yet when federal officials surveyed Panama City tourists, residents and businesses in 2011, they found that the people who already knew about the law against feeding dolphins also didn't take it seriously. They didn't see any harm in what they were doing.

To biologists the harm is obvious: Feed a dolphin and you alter its behavior. Mothers compete with their own calves for food instead of showing them how to hunt. Animals that should shy away from boats swim up under spinning propellers. Wild creatures lose their healthy fear of humans. The result is predictable. So far this year six dolphins along the Gulf coast have been killed violently. One was shot. One was stabbed with a screwdriver. One had had its lower jaw ripped off.

So to Wells and the other biologists who studied Beggar's death, there was no real mystery about what had killed Florida's most famous dolphin since Flipper. The real mystery was why the people who say they adore dolphins so much were the ones most at fault.

"They just love these animals so much," Horstman says, "and they don't recognize how feeding a wild animal can kill an animal."

34

WHERE THE BUFFALO ROAM

Tampa Bay Times, November 27, 2011

Florida's state parks are a haven for all sorts of wildlife—roseate spoonbills, bats and black bears, to name a few. But only Paynes Prairie Preserve State Park can claim to have a herd of bison.

Being known as the home of buffalo that roam has been a big tourist draw for the park south of Gainesville. But the herd has also become a headache for state park officials.

The bison break through fences, cross highways and wander in the suburbs. They've blocked hiking paths, charged rangers, scared tourists. One woman reported being trapped in a felled tree, where she feared being trampled. Instead she wound up "covered with—as politely as I can put this—buffalo snot."

State park officials want to thin the herd this winter, removing all the adult males. They have asked contractors to put in proposals for how they would do the job and how much it might cost—and where they might move up to 35 males that have already shown some attitude.

"Our wish is that they remain safe and live out the rest of their lives," said Florida Park Service director Donald Forgione. But when asked where the bison could be moved so they won't wind up being shot for sport or turned into burgers, he said, "We're not really sure."

The park service plan has stirred up strong feelings among the bison's many fans. Some have picketed. Others have organized a petition drive. The Florida Wildlife Federation has joined in calls to preserve the herd intact, led by President Manley Fuller, who says of the big animals, "I see them and my heart just starts going. They're one of the cool things about living in Florida."

Florida used to have native bison herds. Naturalist William Bartram reported seeing them in the vicinity of Paynes Prairie when he hiked through the region in 1774. Settlers and Seminoles wiped them out.

So 200 years after Bartram's sighting, state park officials decided that they needed to make the prairie look the way it did in his day. That meant bringing back the animals he saw.

"Some of our fellows got the bright idea to restore the bison," recalled Ney Landrum, then the head of the park service. "So I said, 'Have at it.'" In 1975 Landrum got permission from federal officials to move about 10 buffalo from the Wichita Mountains National Wildlife Refuge in Oklahoma to Paynes Prairie.

Except for a brucellosis outbreak that nearly wiped them out, the bison have adapted well to their new home. The herd doubles every four years, and now numbers 50 to 70, Forgione said. The park just isn't equipped to manage 140 bison in 2015, he said, especially given some of the incidents of the past two years.

Twice last year males escaped from the park, and when rangers and local deputies tried to catch them, the animals charged. The pursuers, now being pursued, fired shotguns and rifles repeatedly, eventually killing the big beasts. In one case, a neighbor later complained about the stench.

"We love the bison and we love the visitors loving the bison," Forgione said. But given incidents like that one, removing all the males "is just responsible herd management."

Some opponents have suggested the park should instead beef up its fences. Forgione pointed out two problems: Stronger fences would keep out the deer that now cross back and forth over the park boundary, and a fence hasn't been built that can contain a determined bison.

"A fence, for a bison, is just a suggested boundary," Forgione said.

Fuller said the park should instead make it easier for visitors to view the bison safely, by offering, say, elevated viewing stands. Among the supporters of that plan is the woman who wound up smeared with mucus from one head-swinging female buffalo.

Tonja Walker, who lives in Ocala, said that despite her ordeal, she doesn't want the herd thinned. The whole time she was surrounded by smelly beasts and being painted with mucus, she said, her one thought was, "I am going to die today, but isn't this awesome?"

Walker compared the bison to the alligators that also populate the prairie—one of which almost landed on her foot once. "Does that mean they're going to remove all the alligators from the prairie because they represent a physical threat?" she asked.

The bottom line, she said, is that the bison belong on the prairie.

"It's their property," she said. "We're just sharing it with them."

Note: There are still about 50 bison at Paynes Prairie, and they still like to roam like the line in the song. In 2018, a Gainesville man shot video of several escaped bison crossing U.S. 441 and interrupting everyone's commute, which he posted on social media with the comment "Just a casual morning in Micanopy." The video went viral, of course.

35

LAST LOOK

Sarasota, July 2010

The red warning flags in the Perdido Key State Park beach parking lot in Pensacola were flapping so hard it sounded like they were trying to take flight. I stepped out of my car and the wind blasted me with spray. I inhaled sharply, savoring the salty tang. It smelled clean.

A big storm out in the Gulf of Mexico was driving huge, dark waves onto the beach, crashing them into the sand and creating dangerous rip currents—hence the warning flags. I figured on a day like this I would have this beach all to myself.

I was wrong.

At the end of the boardwalk stood two middle-aged women, dressed for a day at the office. They were leaning against the wooden railing with their arms crossed, talking quietly and looking out at the beach, dotted here and there with a bluish bubble of a Portuguese man-of-war washed ashore by the storm.

They told me their names and that they had both lived in Pensacola for more than 30 years. I asked what they were doing out here on such a blustery day, but I knew what their answer would be as soon as the words left my mouth.

"We wanted to take one last look at it," Candy Mosko said. "It's such a gift, to have it here. And now to think it could be gone . . ."

The two women said they used to visit the beach a lot when they first moved to Pensacola—not the crowded, hectic Pensacola Beach, home to lots of spring break bars and T-shirt shops, but this 247-acre slice of sugar-white sand, the westernmost state park in Florida, where the only structures are a few picnic pavilions. It's a popular place for swimming and surf-fishing.

Over the years, the ladies said, their visits had tapered off. Still, they enjoyed knowing the beach was there. They had assumed it would remain the same forever.

And now, maybe, it wouldn't.

Just a week before, the BP rig blew up 50 miles off the coast of Louisiana; and now it was gushing more than 200,000 gallons of oil a day into the Gulf. An oil slick was bearing down on the Florida coast. That's why I was back in my hometown, writing about all the fear and anger bubbling up across the Panhandle.

"I never thought I'd see this day," said Capt. J. R. Hinojosa, who runs the Blue Marlin Water Taxi on Pensacola Beach. He shook his head. "I would have thought that there were better safety measures on the rigs."

Hinojosa was one of about 40 people who showed up at the hulking Pensacola Civic Center on a Sunday afternoon to take a four-hour course in how to clean up any oil that washes onto the beach. The work, warned teacher Steve Fruchtman of Beck Disaster Recovery, would require protective suits covering the volunteers from head to toe, even when the temperature topped 90 degrees. Fruchtman said he would teach the volunteers how to deal with "potential exposure to hazardous substances." He warned that even the air at the beach could become toxic. "If anything happens where a supervisor determines conditions have changed and it's unsafe, they're going to ask you to leave," he said.

The toxic nature of the spill worried everyone, and no one could really answer their questions about it. A community meeting in Pensacola Beach drew some 400 people, including college professor Richard Sjolander, who pointed out that hurricane season is less than a month away.

When Hurricane Ivan made landfall in 2004, it swept waves across the top of the fishing pier and into streets and houses, he reminded everyone. If some similar storm crosses the Gulf next month, it might push the oil ahead of it into those same areas.

Since the oil is considered toxic, Sjolander asked, "Will it require demolition of everything on the beach?"

Ironies gushed out like the oil. It turned out that, at the time of the explosion, BP executives had been visiting the rig, celebrating its safety record. And after the accident, the U.S. Minerals Management Service announced it was postponing its annual oil industry safety awards ceremony.

In the wake of the spill, all the politicians who had been claiming drilling was safe were suddenly backpedaling. Meanwhile, pundit Rush Limbaugh, a Palm Beach County resident, questioned whether tree-hugging terrorists had set off the blast at the rig for Earth Day. He also declared that nature would clean up the Gulf just the way it had cleaned up Prince William Sound after the *Exxon Valdez* spill in 1989. The only problem: Scientists say there's still oil polluting Prince William Sound 21 years later.

All along the Florida coast, all eyes were on that spreading stain on the Gulf, and efforts, so far futile, by BP to stop it. Although BP was paying to put out thousands of feet of booms to protect the coast, the only boom I saw on Perdido Key was one that had broken loose and was floating in the surf behind the Flora-Bama Lounge, famous for its annual Mullet Toss.

As I learned while growing up there, Pensacola is a city built on making the best of a bad situation. It touts its sun-drenched beaches even though it gets more annual rainfall than Seattle. For years the mayor bragged about the comparatively small population, proclaiming that Pensacola is the place "where thousands live the way millions wish they could."

Everybody figured the worst thing that could ever happen was Hurricane Ivan, which flattened the city six years ago. But they had bounced back from that—only to face this new threat.

Everyone I talked to around Pensacola feared this was the end, the oilpocalypse, the catastrophe that would at last drive away the tourists, kill the seafood business and deliver the *coup de grace* to an already ailing real estate industry.

"First we had the hurricane, and then the economy tanked, and now this oil spill," longtime seafood dealer Larry Nix told me while his son fixed me a shrimp po-boy. "If it hits us, there ain't gonna be enough people left here to start a fight."

The thing is, Pensacola is not alone. Most of the coast is in the same boat, dependent on the clean beaches and azure waters to keep the economy afloat. And like the ladies at Perdido Key, everyone has taken it for granted that the beach would always stay the same. But it won't. No matter where the oil comes ashore in Florida, it is likely to wreak havoc on us all.

So I thanked the ladies on the beach and walked out onto the sand a ways, to where the sandpipers were scurrying along the edge of the surging waves. I reached down and picked up a small shell and tucked it in my pocket—a memento for my kids of the way things used to look, back when the beach was clean.

~~~~~~

Note: Before BP could shut off the flow, gooey chunks of weathered oil washed ashore on the beaches of eight Florida Panhandle counties. Ten years later, scientists have found signs that it's still in the gulf and still harming marine life. Meanwhile a massive public health study found that the people who helped with cleanup suffered more respiratory problems than the general public. Offshore oil drilling remains politically unpopular in Florida, despite the efforts of oil industry spokesmen to convince everyone that Deepwater Horizon wasn't as bad as everyone remembers.

36

CAT FIGHT IN THE LAP OF LUXURY

St. Petersburg Times, June 15, 2003

NORTH KEY LARGO—The cats are waiting.

Hidden in the hibiscus, they twitch their tails and watch the road. Then a golf cart rolls up, and a woman in shorts and a polo shirt steps out. She fills one bowl with water and another with Kit & Kaboodle cat food.

At last the denizens of Florida's largest feral cat colony come into the open. They eat their fill and slink back into the shrubbery.

The world they occupy is not some grungy back alley but the Ocean Reef Club, an exclusive island community 18 miles south of Miami that boasts some of South Florida's wealthiest residents. Club membership costs at least $185,000, and waterfront homes can go for more than $5 million.

About 500 stray cats live amid Ocean Reef's 2,000 acres: tough old toms, scruffy kittens, wary females adept at avoiding people. They are the beneficiaries of a program called ORCAT, set up by Ocean Reef's homeowners, which spends more than $75,000 a year on their care and feeding. The initials stand for "Ocean Reef Community Association Trap-Neuter-Release."

To Ocean Reef residents, ORCAT is a huge success. To state and federal wildlife experts, it's a threat. The dispute has turned into quite a cat fight.

But if the wildlife experts are right, then Ocean Reef's cats have become a pain in the pocketbook for the federal taxpayers.

Blame geography. Next door to Ocean Reef is the Dagny Johnson Key Largo Hammocks Botanical State Park. Across a road is the Crocodile Lake National Wildlife Refuge. Together they cover more than 8,000 acres.

Among the endangered species protected on that land is the Key Largo wood rat, a small rodent with cinnamon fur and bulging black eyes. The wood rat builds stick nests from tropical hardwoods such as mahogany, wild tamarind, black ironwood and pigeon plum.

Because the hardwoods have been cleared from most of Key Largo for development, the Key Largo wood rat was classified as endangered in 1984, as was a relative, the Key Largo cotton mouse. Despite the protection provided by 8,000 acres of preserved habitat, over the last decade the rats and mice have nearly disappeared.

ORCAT's cats may be responsible.

"It's a very serious problem for Key Largo wood rats," said University of Florida wildlife scientist Frank Mazzotti. "Releasing a feral cat in a natural area is like releasing a serial murderer in a maternity ward."

Two weeks ago, the state wildlife commission approved a controversial new policy to "minimize or eliminate the impacts of cats where they pose significant threat to local wildlife populations." State officials cited what has happened to the Key Largo wood rat and Key Largo cotton mouse as two reasons for trying to halt the spread of feral cats.

That didn't sway the cat advocates who packed the meeting. They accused state officials of being cat-killers. State officials denied the charge and promised killing would only be a last resort.

Biologists say the state had to do something. The plight of the wood rat has become so dire that experts estimate less than 50 remain.

Last year federal officials decided the only hope was captive breeding. Four Key Largo rats were trapped and trucked to Lowry Park Zoo in Tampa. U.S. Fish and Wildlife Service officials figure to spend $12,000 a year on the wood rat breeding program.

Yes, the taxpayers are paying to breed rats.

The first ones were born last month, on Mother's Day weekend.

Ocean Reef officials don't buy it. Ocean Reef's cats have no reason to invade the parks and kill the rats, said David Ritz, community administrator for the homeowners' association.

"In our 10-year experience, we're completely satisfied that our cats are fat and happy and don't stray from our feeding stations," Ritz said.

But biologists and environmental activists insist that even fat cats are driven to kill, hungry or not. It's part of their genetic makeup as predators.

In fact, Ocean Reef's cats were first brought there in the 1950s to knock off the rats overrunning the club.

"They thought the way to fix the rat problem was to bring in a bunch of cats," Ritz said. "Then in the 1960s we found out we had a cat problem. So they rounded them all up and killed them. Then in the 1970s, we discovered we had a rat problem. So they went around to all the pounds and rounded up a bunch of cats again."

Soon the rats were gone, but by the late 1980s Ocean Reef's cat population had ballooned to 2,000.

"The cats were out of control," Ritz said. They yowled all night, fought and made messes—all very bad for Ocean Reef's image.

"They were such an emaciated-looking group," recalled ORCAT president John Storm, who feeds nearly a dozen strays by his own back door. "It was a real black eye for this place."

Ocean Reef's woes were not unique. There are an estimated 60 million feral cats prowling the highways and hedges of America. Abandoned pets and their offspring, they survive on the scraps of civilization and any small animals they can catch.

In 1989, Ocean Reef's owners were plotting another round of cat slaughtering when Alan Litman intervened. Litman, an eccentric nature lover from Pittsburgh, lived part-time at Ocean Reef and helped found Crocodile Lake National Wildlife Refuge.

"His two passions were crocodiles and cats," said Mazzotti, the UF scientist and a friend. At his home in Pittsburgh, Mazzotti said, Litman kept a 13-foot crocodile named Ernst in the basement, and he devoted a wing to feral cats.

Litman, who died in March, saved Ocean Reef's cats by launching ORCAT. He subscribed to a theory called trap-neuter-release. Females would be caught in humane traps and neutered, then turned loose. Since they could no longer reproduce, the feral cat colony would dwindle and disappear.

ORCAT is staffed by three veterinary techs. Once a week a veterinarian visits ORCAT's small office by Ocean Reef's sewer plant to perform surgeries and provide other medical care.

Such trap-neuter-release programs became popular in the United States in the 1990s. Advocates from national groups such as Alley Cat Allies, which has filed a legal challenge to the new state policy, contend that this approach is more effective and less expensive than killing the strays.

But wildlife experts decry the "release" part as bad news for birds and mice. Florida Wildlife Federation president Manley Fuller contends releasing even neutered cats back into the wild constitutes "animal pollution," and warned that Ocean Reef's cats may be violating the Endangered Species Act.

Ritz, who likes to call ORCAT's office a "cathouse," said park officials complain to him at least once a year about ORCAT's cats poaching wildlife.

"Every time one of these guys comes here, we tell them, 'Hey, we've reduced our cat population by 75 percent. What have you done?'" Ritz said.

David Ritz, community administrator at the Ocean Reef Club at Key Largo, with one of the club's hundreds of feral cats. He referred to the office of the club's feral cat program as "the cathouse." Photo by Bill Cooke, used by permission of the *Tampa Bay Times*.

Still, ORCAT has been unable to whittle that number down to zero. Some females learn to avoid the traps but not pregnancy. Meanwhile, the guardhouse that keeps uninvited humans out of Ocean Reef has not barred an influx of abandoned pets, perhaps brought in by workers from outside.

So seven days a week, rain or shine, vet techs like Dana MacDonald cruise the club's grounds putting out food and water. MacDonald knows every cat. She knows they're waiting for her.

"They're generally always there," she said. "They don't venture far from the feeding stations."

But if they did choose to wander off in search of wilder fare, nothing would stop them—yet.

In the 1960s, when Ocean Reef was undergoing its first cat crisis, Crocodile Lake belonged to the Army. Soldiers stationed there guarded nuclear-tipped Nike missiles, awaiting war with Castro while fighting off hordes of bloodthirsty mosquitoes.

The missiles are gone but the buildings that housed them remain, now guarded only by turkey vultures. Federal officials hope to tear them down, just as they already have razed an elaborate cockfighting ring and a police target range that somehow occupied the property simultaneously.

Their goal is to restore Crocodile Lake to something close to its natural state, in hopes it will revive endangered animals from the American crocodile to the Key Largo wood rat.

Captive breeding is a desperate last step in saving a species, and breeding rare rats is not as easy as it sounds. To prevent them from killing each other, a zoo staffer has to observe each mating attempt, said Deborah Pierce of the U.S. Fish and Wildlife Service.

Why breed rats?

"They're an integral part of the environment," she said. "The wood rats have a niche. They're seed dispersers. They belong here. They should be here. Besides, they're cute."

Federal officials hope to eventually have 24 rats producing offspring, which they would then release back into the wild, she said.

But before turning any captive-bred rats loose, wildlife officials want to ensure they don't fall prey to whatever pushed them near extinction.

"We don't know what's causing their demise but a likely cause could be the feral cats," said Britta Muiznieks, who is in charge of what's left of the wood rat population at Crocodile Lake. "I guess we'll see when we start trapping."

The plan is to put traps around the outside of Ocean Reef and see what shows up. Cats with no owner tags will go to the nearest animal shelter. If they are ORCAT cats—identifiable by a notch the veterinarian cuts in one ear—the shelter will be instructed to notify ORCAT.

But Ritz says he's not worried: "My guess is they're going to catch a bunch of raccoons."

Note: I will forever remember this reporting trip. Our Crocodile Lake guide got us lost in the woods. The mosquitoes were so bad that the photographer and I tried to coat ourselves all over in bug spray but wound up getting it in our eyes. As for the rats, we never saw them. When we went over to Ocean Reef, everyone looked askance at our sweat-soaked clothing, muddy footwear and reddened eyes. I wrote several follow-up stories to this one. Here's the gist: With help from Disney's Animal Kingdom, scientists succeeded in breeding a lot more Key Largo wood rats, but when they were released back into the wild wearing tiny transmitters for tracking, predators found them easy pickings. Soon there was only one left, his little transmitter still beep-beep-beeping. A biologist went to track him down, hoping to learn how he'd survived when all the others had been eaten—only to come face to face with a large Burmese python that had apparently swallowed the rat, transmitter and all. This marked the first sighting of a python in the Keys, confirmation they could swim over from the mainland.

37

SO LONG, SNOOTY

Tampa Bay Times, July 30, 2017

New York City has the Statue of Liberty. San Francisco has the Golden Gate Bridge. St. Louis has the Arch.

And for 68 years, Bradenton had Snooty.

Then tragedy struck last weekend. The most famous manatee in Florida, the longtime star attraction of Bradenton's South Florida Museum, the official mascot of Manatee County, drowned in his tank on Sunday, a day after the celebration of his 69th birthday.

His influence was immense.

"He reached millions of people who now have a better understanding of manatees," said Pat Rose, executive director of the Save the Manatee Club.

Yet Snooty's birth and life were so different from every other manatee's that it marked him as a breed apart. Bradenton became his home because of a bureaucratic problem, and there was similar confusion over his gender and his name.

Even in death, Snooty will forever swim apart from his fellow manatees.

He was born aboard one boat in Miami after another one ran over his mother. Some men spotted the injured female manatee in Biscayne Bay, caught her in a net and hauled her aboard a floating museum, the Miami Aquarium and Tackle Shop.

The crew carried the wounded manatee below deck, putting her in their largest tank, recalled Alice Walters Wallace, the daughter of aquarium owner R. J. Walters, in a 2008 interview.

Someone concocted an ointment for the manatee's injuries, she said, "and I would get in the tank and rub it on her back. She liked that . . . We'd get in the tank and hug her. For a manatee, she was a beautiful manatee."

They dubbed her "Lady." Then they discovered Lady was pregnant. The aquarium had already had one captive manatee give birth, only to lose the calf. The staff was determined to keep this one alive.

On July 21, 1948, Walters recalled, "my dad called and told us the little one was on the way . . . We came down because we wanted to see this new baby. He was such a little fellow in comparison to his mom."

They named the calf "Baby." The newborn was just as affectionate as Lady. When Walters and her sister climbed into the tank—something none of the tourists could do, of course—"both (manatees) liked to be loved and petted. They liked to give kisses."

To entertain tourists, the girls would ride on Lady's back—but never Baby's.

The aquarium's operator, a former women's wear manufacturer named Sam Stout, taught both manatees a few tricks. They learned to come when summoned, and to roll over in order to get a treat and hoist themselves out of the water. Biologists later pointed to those performances as evidence that manatees are smarter than they might appear.

✳

In 1949, Manatee County planned a festival to celebrate the landing of conquistador Hernando de Soto four centuries earlier. Someone came up with the idea of exhibiting a manatee. But nobody could find any manatees in Manatee County.

"Our name will be MUD without the Manatee," wrote one festival organizer in a letter.

Stout bailed them out. He drove Baby across the state and displayed the 9-month-old in a tank for a few days. The calf "gave pleasure to thousands of people who had a chance for the first time to see the animal this county was named for," a local official wrote. "It was a great favorite with children and hundreds of them petted it, fed it lettuce, and watched it roll over . . ."

The publicity backfired for Stout. State officials noted that he had a permit for one manatee, not two. He was ordered to let Baby go. Stout was horrified. Baby would die, he said.

His solution: donate Baby to Manatee County. The state said yes.

But no one asked Manatee County officials if they wanted a full-time manatee mascot.

"Bradenton learned with some consternation today that it owns a sea cow," the *Bradenton Herald* reported on April 1, 1949. Eventually city officials embraced their new manatee, installing a tank in a building that became the South Florida Museum.

The Miami Herald, writing about Baby's imminent departure, joked that "the youngster probably has an inferiority complex by now, the way she has been treated in recent months."

New York City has the Statue of Liberty, San Francisco has the Golden Gate Bridge, and for 68 years, Bradenton had Snooty the manatee, shown here nibbling a carrot held by a student on a school field trip. Photo by Karl E. Holland of the Florida Park Service, courtesy of the Florida State Archives.

Note the pronoun. Stout and everyone else assumed Baby was female. At some point in later years, someone figured out he was a he. The name changed too, going from "Baby" to "Baby Snoots"—apparently a corruption of Baby Snooks, a popular radio character.

Finally around 1970, when he was in his 20s, he became "Snooty."

☼

As the years rolled on, Snooty became a treasured institution.

In 1973, a clumsy tourist dropped a mechanical pencil in Snooty's tank. Snooty swallowed it and became badly constipated for more than a week. News reports warned that he might die, and "if he dies, the museum will have lost its main attraction. Manatee County will have lost the embodiment of its name . . ."

Snooty survived the Great Pencil Scare. He also survived being raised in a too-small tank, which biologists said stunted his growth before he was finally moved to a larger facility.

The greater concern was solitude. While Snooty was spared the fate of many manatees—being clobbered by boats or poisoned by red tide—the price he paid for his perfect hide was celibacy and isolation.

In 1991, when Snooty turned 43, the Save the Manatee Club and the Humane Society demanded he be moved two hours north to Homosassa Springs State Wildlife Park. There he could meet, and perhaps mate with, seven breeding-age females.

Snooty's solitary captivity is "the most depressing manatee story around," the club's then-president, Judith Vallee, told this newspaper, then known as the St. Petersburg Times. But Snooty's chief keeper, Carol Audette, warned that moving Snooty in with other manatees might be bad for him.

"He's so acclimated to people," she said. "That's all he knows."

Bradenton was bombarded with angry letters from around the country. But Snooty's captivity predated the Endangered Species Act, leaving no legal grounds to challenge it.

In 1998, he started getting roommates, manatees that had been injured in the wild and needed time to recuperate. Snooty, according to Rose, showed them how to behave. Meanwhile, the manatee menagerie drew more and more people, who bought Snooty T-shirts, postcards and plush toys.

☼

As a vegetarian who got lots of exercise, Snooty was in good health for a geriatric. His most recent physical was July 17, a few days before more than 4,000 well-wishers celebrated his 69th birthday last Saturday. Grandparents who had visited Snooty in their young years were now bringing toddlers who were astonished to be so close to such a natural wonder.

Then he was gone, dying in the dark of night under circumstances that are still under investigation.

As with all manatees that die in Florida, Snooty underwent a necropsy. But Martine de Wit, who oversees the state's marine mammal pathology laboratory in St. Petersburg, said that, even in death, Snooty won't be like other manatees.

"He won't go into our database" of manatee deaths, she said, "because he wasn't part of the wild population."

Note: An investigation concluded that Snooty's death was a preventable accident. Manatee County's favorite manatee swam through a loose underwater panel in the tank and became trapped, and thus was unable to surface for air. Maintenance workers had been aware of the malfunctioning panel for more than a week. Once these findings became public, the museum ousted its aquarium director.

38

SNAKES ALIVE!

Tampa Bay Times, August 17, 2019

ON A LEVEE IN THE EVERGLADES—Beth Koehler stood on the Jeep's console, her boots braced against the two front seats, half her body thrust through the sunroof. As the Jeep crept along a narrow gravel road atop a levee 60 miles west of Miami, Koehler's eyes swept the landscape. Lights atop the car turned the darkness ahead as bright as day.

She had been at this for more than two hours Monday, and now it was nearly midnight. The humid night air was filled with a subdued chorus of hoots and ribbets.

Suddenly Koehler, 60, shouted, "Go forward!" Behind the wheel, Peggy Van Gorder, 53, co-owner with Koehler of the Hair of the Dog dog-grooming salon in St. Petersburg, hit the gas. The Jeep jumped toward a dark figure sliding across the road.

When they got closer, though, the women could see it was just a three-foot Florida cottonmouth, its head lifted like a submarine's periscope. They watched the venomous snake scoot to the other side of the levee and slide down into a canal, then the Jeep moved on.

Koehler and Van Gorder were hunting for snakes, but they were seeking the non-native kind—Burmese pythons. The bigger, the better.

☼

Earlier this month, Gov. Ron DeSantis announced the state was going to double down on its efforts to eradicate the pythons, but he was short on specifics. State officials say they're still working those out.

For now, though, the most cost-effective method for catching pythons is to do what Koehler and Van Gorder have been doing: Drive around all night looking for them.

Avid bass anglers, the pair got hooked on python-hunting when, on a lark, they competed as amateurs in the state's 2016 python roundup. They didn't win any prizes, but they found they liked the work enough to get licensed as professionals. Two years into this side-gig, they figure they have found about 70 pythons, the longest about 12 feet. Their state paycheck last month, Van Gorder said, basically amounted to minimum wage.

But they said they're not doing it for the money—$8.25 an hour plus a $50-per-snake bonus, another $25 per foot beyond 4 feet. They're doing it to try to make a difference for Florida's environment.

"I grew up down here," Koehler, a Pembroke Pines native, said from her lookout perch. "I've seen the changes that have taken place."

She pointed out that the pythons—powerful constrictors that squeeze the life out of their prey—have eaten plenty of birds and deer, and nearly all the foxes, raccoons, squirrels and other small mammals that once made the Everglades region special. "And now," she said, "all you're going to see are rats, gators and pythons. . . . That's why they have to be taken out."

Besides, Van Gorder said, they relish the adrenaline rush of wrestling with a big, hissing snake, even though she once got bitten by a python and the snake's tooth remained lodged in her finger for months.

"We want to get our adventure in now," she said cheerfully. "I can sit on a cruise ship when I'm an old lady."

❈

Experts have estimated there are 10,000 to 100,000 pythons infesting Everglades National Park, Big Cypress National Preserve and the thousands of acres of marshy public land surrounding them. Koehler and Van Gorder are two of the 41 licensed snake hunters—28 male, 13 female—whom the state Fish and Wildlife Conservation Commission has dispatched to thin this reptile army. The pair received some acclaim earlier this summer for catching the program's 500th python.

The wildlife agency is spending $581,000 a year battling pythons. It has done background checks on its hunters, spent hours training them and handed them global positioning units so they can record where, when and under what conditions they catch each snake.

The two women don't call what they're doing "hunting." They call it "surveying." They're searching for a snake that's incredibly hard to find despite their numbers. Pythons are ambush hunters, highly skilled at holding still and hiding until their prey is near enough to grab.

Generally, if the women's survey leads to a python, they catch it but don't kill it. They put it in a white cotton bag, stuff it into a padlocked box with airholes and take it to the state's laboratory in Davie. There the lab

Beth Koehler (*left*) and Peggy Van Gorder (*right*) run a dog-grooming salon in St. Petersburg, but on weekends they work for the state hunting pythons in the Everglades. Photo courtesy of Beth Koehler and Peggy Van Gorder.

staff kills it with a bolt to the brain, then takes measurements and performs a necropsy that includes an examination of what it's been eating.

Meanwhile the South Florida Water Management District has taken a different approach to solving the snake problem. The water agency, with a python-fighting budget of $225,000 a year, has hired 26 contractors, trained them on how to handle pythons and sent them out to find and kill them.

As Van Gorder sees it, the district simply "hired hunters and told them to go kill snakes. We'll see which approach is better."

☼

Koehler kept the Jeep inching forward at about 6 mph. They spotted the occasional owl, several enormous rats and more than a few toothy alligators, but so far no pythons.

As a cloud passed over the gibbous moon Monday night, Van Gorder noticed a pair of headlights facing them in the distance. She knew who they likely belonged to: a wild man.

Dustin "Wildman" Crum is the most famous python hunter employed by the water management district. A Venice orchid dealer, he stars in the Discovery Channel show *Guardians of the Glades*.

On the show, the thick-bearded Crum runs through the swamp barefoot, with little apparent regard for the gators, feral hogs and venomous native snakes that also occupy this soggy terrain. He once caught a python that measured 16-feet, 11-inches long.

Koehler and Van Gorder knew Crum was working the same levee. They even timed their search so they wouldn't run up behind him. They said they like Crum personally, but once clashed with his camera crew.

They believe what's depicted on his TV show is, as Van Gorder said, "absolutely everything you shouldn't do to catch a python." She and Koehler blame the show for inspiring a rash of would-be poachers to show up in rural areas of South Florida looking to blow the head off any big snake, regardless of whether they are trained and licensed to do it.

"Everybody wants to be a snake hunter now," Crum conceded in a phone interview.

Crum, 39, says he started hunting pythons back in 2012 by riding a bike around the levees at night, grabbing any snakes he saw, then getting a few hours of restless sleep in a tent during the heat of the day. Back then, he said, nobody seemed to take the python threat seriously, but he could foresee what kind of damage they could do.

Now Crum spends his daylight hours snoozing in an air-conditioned camper next to a roadside attraction called the Skunk Ape Research Headquarters in Ochopee.

The Skunk Ape, a smelly cousin of Bigfoot that allegedly roams the Everglades wilderness, exists primarily on souvenir T-shirts, bumper stickers and several selfie-ready statues out front. Inside, there's a glass case containing Goldie, a 24-foot python—a reticulated one, not a Burmese. Although the Skunk Ape campground is popular with many members of the snake-seeker brigade, Koehler and Van Gorder prefer to park their camper at a different campground, where they stay with their little Papillon dogs, Kate and Esabelle.

On Monday night, the drivers of the two trucks paced their vehicles so that they would intersect at a spot in the road wide enough for them to pass. Crum, without his camera crew, was perched in a camp chair in the back of his truck as Koehler and Van Gorder pulled alongside.

"Any luck?" Van Gorder called out.

"No," Crum replied, sounding bored. "We must have already caught 'em all."

The following night, Crum posted a video to Facebook showing him wrangling a 12-footer into a bag. "Wooo!" he said when he was done. "That'll get your blood pumping!"

☼

Forty years have passed since the first Burmese python turned up in the Everglades.

In October 1979, the owner of an airboat tour operation called Everglades Safari notified park rangers that he had found a python on U.S. 41 that measured 11-foot-9. Someone had run over and killed it, he said. Park biologists jotted the information down on a notecard but that was all they did.

In 1992, when Hurricane Andrew blasted through South Florida, it blew apart a reptile breeding facility near the park, releasing an unknown number of captive snakes. Other exotic animal facilities were damaged as well, setting free hundreds of monkeys and other creatures. The owners scurried around trying to recapture what they could, but experts say at least some of the pythons got away.

Still, no one was worried yet even as pythons grew in popularity among reptile aficionados. Federal records show that between 1999 and 2006, importers brought more than 99,000 Burmese pythons into the U.S. No one knows how many were later set free in the Everglades.

A National Park Service biologist named Ray "Skip" Snow began sounding the alarm about the invading snakes in the late 1990s, but no one took his warnings seriously because he had no proof that pythons were mating in the wild. Then, in 2003, he finally found hatchlings, incontrovertible evidence of breeding—only to be told by the people in charge that it was now too late to stop the pythons from spreading across the park.

In 2005, Snow and a park helicopter pilot named Michael Baron stumbled on a gruesome scene: A python had tried to swallow an alligator, and in the struggle both the animals wound up dead. A photo of the grisly aftermath went viral, and suddenly pythons became the poster child for invasive species in Florida, which has more non-native animals and plants than any other state.

Yet officials were reluctant to take steps to halt imports of more pythons, a move that the pet industry strongly opposed. In 2010, during a congressional subcommittee hearing on possibly banning python imports, the state Wildlife Commission's top invasive species expert, Scott Hardin, said Florida was on top of the python problem. Instead of an immediate ban, he urged "flexible legal and operational solutions."

"He certainly made it sound like the state could deal with it" with no help from the federal government, said invasive species expert Daniel Simberloff, a University of Tennessee-Knoxville environmental science professor who also testified at that hearing. No legislation passed. Instead, then-President Barack Obama issued an executive decision banning further Burmese python imports, although domestic breeding is still allowed.

Larry Perez, a former Everglades National Park ranger who wrote a book called *Snake in the Grass: An Everglades Invasion,* said Hardin always reminded him of a police officer telling everyone, "Move along, nothing to see here."

Two years later, Hardin—credited with creating the state's first python-hunting program—retired from the wildlife agency. He immediately got hired as a consultant for the pet industry. An industry website noted that Hardin owns a ball python named Ricky.

"His change of careers speaks volumes," Perez said.

Hardin, in an interview with the *Tampa Bay Times,* said the government moved slowly in confronting the python invasion because "it was not a problem for which we had a lot of experience." He defended his job switch by saying that "I saw no conflict between the Wildlife Commission's position and that of the pet industry, which was to encourage responsible pet ownership."

☼

From kudzu vines swallowing barns across the South to feral camels gobbling up native plants across Australia, invasive species are a problem the world over. But the python invasion, and the way they have eaten everything in their path, tops all other cases, according to Simberloff.

The pythons have expanded their range to the north, west and even south to the Keys. When a cold snap in January 2010 killed hundreds of them, a study later found that the survivors had adapted to the change in temperature, so future generations of pythons would be less likely to die from a blast of cold air.

The only case that's comparable to the pythons, Simberloff said, involves the brown tree snakes that invaded Guam, wiping out the island's songbirds. Federal officials have been attempting to combat these invaders by air-dropping dead rats attached to little parachutes. The rats are stuffed with the pain reliever acetaminophen, which kills the snakes.

Florida has not yet become that desperate, but it too has tried innovative techniques for tracking down pythons. Snake-sniffing dogs found their quarry but had a hard time handling the heat. Traps didn't catch the elusive reptiles. A pair of python rodeos, while attracting hundreds of wannabe snake wranglers, resulted in such a small number of captures that they could be replaced with a couple of females laying a single clutch of eggs.

Scientists have tried attaching transmitters to captured female pythons and releasing them, then tracking them to a group of males ready to mate. But that's expensive and time-consuming.

State officials have high hopes for altering the snakes' DNA to make them sterile, or adapting the snake's own pheromones—the scent that enables one python to find another for mating—as a method of detecting them. But so far those are goals, not tactics. Thus the only practical way to get the pythons is to send hunters like Koehler, Van Gorder and Crum out to the levees, armed with sheath knives, sharp eyes and nerves of steel.

"Boots on the ground is still the best way to catch them," the barefoot Crum said.

☼

During Monday's python search near Big Cypress National Preserve, Van Gorder kept going by munching on a bag of mixed nuts and playing Taylor Swift songs. Occasionally she found a wide spot and pulled over so she could stand up and Koehler could sit down. Then they'd get back in position and start rolling again.

This is their routine: If Koehler spots a python, she shouts that word. Even before Van Gorder hits the brake she's moving, sliding down from the sunroof and scooting out the passenger door to run toward the snake. Koehler is slender, with glasses, yet more than once she's made a flying, face-first leap at a python to pin it down before it could slide away.

If Koehler has pinned the snake's head, then Van Gorder, who is the stronger of the two, will grab its flailing body.

"It's important not to let them coil up around your hands, because they will try to pop them off," Van Gorder said. "They're one giant tube of muscle." But sometimes, she said, "I like to let it coil around my leg so I can walk it back up the levee."

The way they nabbed the 500th snake—a female nearly 10 feet long—was by grabbing it and then just lying on top of it for a half-hour or so.

"We tuckered it out," Koehler said.

On Monday night, they talked about some of the other things they've spotted during python surveys, like meteor showers. Once, they said, they encountered a panther, the sight so stunning they couldn't react before it was gone.

However, they could do without the bugs—mosquitoes galore, moths attracted by the lights, beetles that fly into Koehler's hair. Despite the hunters' fearlessness when tackling pythons, on one night they found a praying mantis in the Jeep and both bailed out.

Monday night's search continued until 3 a.m., when they gave up on finding any pythons. Before heading back to camp, though, they showed off the Jeep's hidden passenger: A live 8-foot python they'd captured the night before. They had been keeping it in a cotton bag inside a locked box, stuck behind the back seat.

On Tuesday night they went back out surveying again. This time, all they caught was a 2-foot python, a little hatchling that Koehler grabbed one-handed. Three nights of effort, 24 hours of relentless searching, had yielded just two pythons, one a juvenile.

The fight that hatchling put up, Van Gorder said, would seem like nothing on Thursday, when they got back to their dog-grooming business and encountered "the first shih tzu . . . with a bad attitude."

part IV

THE STATE YOU'RE IN

39

DON'T OKAHUMPKA MY WEWAHITCHKA!

Tampa Bay Times, April 24, 2018

Because I grew up in Florida—a rare experience these days, as about two-thirds of the people who live in Florida hail from somewhere else—I have seen a lot of rapid change in the state's landscape. A forest becomes an orange grove and then an apartment building and then that's torn down for a shopping mall, which is flattened for a parking lot and then that's torn up to become storage units and so on.

But some things in Florida never change. One of them is how odd some of our place names sound. Florida has some of the greatest place names ever. The Native American tribes that once inhabited Florida left behind some wonderfully mellifluous names, such as Wewahitchka, Umatilla and Sopchoppy. Some of them sound like euphemisms for your naughty bits, like Yalaha and Okahumpka. Not all of them roll off the tongue so beautifully. A friend of mine claims "Palatka" sounds like "horse poop hitting the ground."

The early settlers threw in some colorful names, too: Tate's Hell Swamp and Zephyrhills, for instance, and, in the Panhandle, Two Egg, best known as the birthplace of Faye Dunaway.

My family claims that one of my ancestors named that one. He was the storekeeper there, letting his customers trade chickens and other livestock for clothing and cookware and other goods. One day, though, he was feeling down about the future prospects of the small community and said, "This town ain't even worth two eggs."

A lot of Florida place names have intriguing little stories behind them. El Jobean was named by its developer, Joel Bean. You see what he did there, right? Nalcrest is where members of the National Association of Letter Carriers, or NALC for short, go to retire.

Some names signal that the settlers felt a little homesick. Dunedin, for instance, was founded by Scotsmen who named it after the Gaelic name for Scotland's capital city of Edinburgh—Dùn Èideann.

Yeehaw Junction was originally known as Jackass Junction, which I think we can all agree would be more appropriate for our state capital. State officials changed the name when the Florida Turnpike cut through there in the 1950s because they thought "Yeehaw" sounded more sophisticated.

Incidentally, the current name has nothing to do with the fact that the historic Desert Inn that's been standing there since 1898 used to house a bordello. More recently a developer tried to change the name to "Destiny," but apparently he was destined to fail.

Because nothing in Florida is ever quite what it seems, it should not surprise you to learn that a lot of Florida place names are fraudulent. The town of Frostproof has gotten quite a few freezes. Hernando Beach has no beach, although they are thinking of building one. Gulfport—previously known as "Disston City," "Veterans City" and even, believe it or not, "Bonafacio"—has no port, and it's not on the Gulf, either, but rather Boca Ciega Bay.

My favorite Florida place name is the one most likely to make Beavis and Butthead laugh. It's in Seminole County, and it's called "the Village of Taintsville." The name, officially sanctioned by the county in 1991, comes from its location between two somewhat larger communities. Local residents explain the origin this way: "Tain't Oviedo and "tain't Chuluota."

A friend of mine who lives near there told me he visited it once and, as he put it, "Tain't that exciting."

Note: I'm sorry to report that in 2020 an 18-wheeler ran into the Desert Inn in Yeehaw Junction and virtually demolished it. I drove by and saw the wreckage and it was a sad sight indeed. On the other hand, on that same trip I was lucky enough to sneak in a side trip to Nalcrest, where residents told me that there are two things not allowed in city limits: dogs and home delivery of mail. In other words, no letter carrier delivers the mail to all those retired letter carriers. They have to hoof it to their post office to pick it up in person.

40

FAREWELL TO SOME CLASSIC FLORIDA KITSCH

Tampa Bay Times, February 28, 2017

I know I wasn't the only one bummed out last month by the news that Florida's version of Stonehenge, the Airstream Ranch, was being torn down.

Now the only cool stuff left to look at when you're stuck in a massive traffic jam on Interstate 4 are Dinosaur World and the Mickey Mouse power pole. Oh, and whatever crazy thing is happening in the car next to you—drivers shaving, flossing, loading their guns; you know, the usual.

The Airstream Ranch, a line of shiny silver travel trailers buried nose down in the dirt like the famed Cadillac Ranch out west, was one of those classically kitschy Florida attractions.

"It was a whimsical thing for me to do at the time," recalled Frank Bates, who built it in 2007.

Now, Matt Strollo of RV Superstores, which owns the property, says it's time to replace the Airstream Ranch with a 17,000-square-foot Airstream dealership. The dealership's footprint, says Strollo, made saving the display impossible.

He thinks we should all be happy about this. Anyone who's upset "should turn the frowns upside down and be excited about what's going to come just on the horizon," Strollo told my colleague Tony Marrero. "A brand-new dealership for people to enjoy instead of just taking pictures as passers-by of broken-down Airstreams."

Oh, yes, an RV dealership on I-4, where there are already about a dozen. That's a lovely new tourist attraction. Make sure you get an E-Z Pass before the lines get too long!

Back before Walt Disney showed up, Florida was chock-full of nutty attractions like the Airstream Ranch. Those of us who grew up here remember the delightful old tourist traps, like the Tragedy in U.S. History

The Airstream Ranch, off Interstate 4, was Florida's kitschy version of Stonehenge—until a new owner deemed it to be a little too kitschy. Photo by Skip O'Rourke, used by permission of the *Tampa Bay Times*.

Museum and the Atomic Tunnel. We had the House of Mystery near Haines City, the Snell Peacock Farm in Clearwater and, of course, the St. Petersburg Alligator Farm.

Florida was cosplay central back then. You could visit jungle gardens with employees dressed as Tarzan and Jane, pirate coves where the staff all said, "Arrrrr!" and Western towns with regular Main Street shootouts—anything to drag in the tourists and get them to open their wallets.

A few of the old classics are still around, like the Monkey Jungle in Miami and Everglades Wonder Gardens in Bonita Springs. Some became state parks, such as Weeki Wachee Springs, which makes Florida the only state where the list of government jobs includes "mermaid."

With the price of Disney tickets skyrocketing, maybe we'll get some of the old ones back soon.

All these tourist attractions are here, by the way, because of a writer named Harriet Beecher Stowe. You may recall that her novel *Uncle Tom's Cabin* helped touch off the Civil War. After that was over, she moved to a home on the St. Johns River and fell in love with Florida.

Stowe wrote stories for Northern newspapers urging people to visit, and sure enough, they did. She basically invented the Florida tourism industry. Her home became one of our first tourist attractions. She'd stand on her porch and wave at the boats full of gawkers as they floated past (no doubt with their turn signals blinking for miles).

What Stowe set in motion has forever altered the state she loved so much. People began pouring in, and they haven't stopped. That human tsunami has been the justification for rapid and unsettling alterations in the Florida landscape, some good, some not so.

My friend Claire was telling me the other day about how different the state seems from the one she grew up in in the '50s and '60s: "I remember . . . when we'd see wild hogs and black bears, and the islands had vast stretches of pure, empty sand. You could scoop up live coquinas by the handful, and sand dollars, and the water table was so healthy, you could dig a hole for a tomato plant, and water would bubble up, and we'd see flocks—huge flocks—of roseate spoonbills."

This is the burden of being a longtime Floridian: You remember the way things used to be and what was lost. You remember the fun times you had before all the changes came. The blessing of Florida, though, is that we get to see these odd and unusual things before they're gone, buried in the ground like the Airstream Ranch. Now if you'll excuse me, I have to go turn off my blinker.

41

HAUNTED HIGHWAY

Tampa Bay Times, October 26, 2017

Let me tell you a ghost story.

No, I'm not talking about some ectoplasmic special effect from Disney's Haunted Mansion. I'm talking about a real ghost story. A Florida ghost story.

You wouldn't think a place that's this bright and sunny would be a hangout for sinister shades, but it is. You find them all over Florida, from the haunted Pensacola Lighthouse up in the Panhandle to the infamous "Robert the Doll" on display in Key West, also known as "the original Chucky."

Spooky stuff pops up in Florida news all the time. We had a wannabe vampire who sank her teeth into a senior citizen at a vacant Hooters in St. Petersburg, and a zombie cat that clawed its way out of an early grave in Tampa.

Meanwhile, down in South Florida, they've got ghost ships washing up on the beaches, monster pythons crawling all over the place gobbling up everything in their path and so many people sacrificing chickens to influence cases at the Miami-Dade courthouse that the janitors have formed what they call "the Voodoo Squad" to clean them up every morning.

Pretty scary, huh, kids?

But the ghost story I want to talk about is the one on Interstate 4.

You know I-4, the 132-mile road that doesn't really run from town to town but just connects one highway (I-275) to another (I-95). This is the one thoroughfare in Florida where the drivers are *supposed* to be thoroughly distracted. It takes you past not just Disney World but also Universal, SeaWorld, Dinosaur World (which is, yes, full of dinosaurs) and the Holy Land Experience, the Bible-themed park where you can see Jesus re-crucified six days a week.

Everyone who lives in Florida or visits it frequently has traveled on I-4, usually all at the same time. The I-4 traffic tie-ups are the stuff of legends, the most epic clogs this side of California's Car-mageddon.

But what few people know is that I-4 is under a ghostly curse.

For the proper effect, read this next part with a flashlight under your chin:

The story goes that in 1886, a family of four German immigrants died of yellow fever at a small settlement near present-day Sanford. Their priest, who was visiting Tampa, couldn't make it back in time to administer the last rites because he, too, fell dead from the fever.

So the unblessed quartet were duly buried in a farmer's field, and there they apparently rested in peace—until around 1961, when I-4 was built through that area.

The state Department of Transportation paved right over their graves, rolling a slab of pavement across their final resting place just the way it rolls over thousands of acres of wetlands and forest and farmland every chance it gets.

Now that spot where the dead were paved over—it's on the approach to a bridge over the St. Johns River—is known as the "I-4 Dead Zone." It's supposedly cursed by frequent wrecks and other signs of bad luck. Those vindictive ghosts have declared war on the motorists who dare cross their desecrated graves—although apparently not on the DOT that actually did the desecrating.

The thing is, all of I-4 is like that, not just the "Dead Zone." That road is a death trap. Last year I-4 was declared the most dangerous road in America, with 1.41 fatalities per mile. We could blame this on poor land-use decisions, poor traffic design and control and lax law enforcement— or we could blame the I-4 ghosts!

In fact, maybe we could even blame the I-4 Curse for the fact that Florida's elected leaders rejected the idea of building a high-speed rail line parallel to it, even though it would have taken a lot of motorists off that hellish highway. The ghosts clouded their brains so they'd believe we would all rather be stuck in massive, coronary-inducing traffic jams than ride a fast train.

Yes, that makes sense. Let's not blame the people making the decisions. Let's blame those darn immigrants.

42

STATUES WE'D SALUTE

Tampa Bay Times, August 25, 2017

I grew up in Pensacola, maybe the most Southern of North Florida's cities, or at least the one close enough to the state line to be dubbed "Lower Alabama."

I ate grits. I said "y'all" and "ain't." I still do.

When I was a kid, my parents would take me downtown to see the latest Disney movie (because that's where you went to see movies before the malls were built), and I always knew we were getting close when I could see the 50-foot-tall Confederate memorial. We'd be driving along the city's main street, and the weathered gray monument would suddenly loom up like a ghost.

Unveiled in 1891, three sides of the monument salute Confederate Secretary of the Navy Stephen R. Mallory, Confederate General Edward Aylesworth Perry—both from Pensacola—and Confederate President Jefferson Davis. The fourth side is dedicated to "The Uncrowned Heroes of the Southern Confederacy, whose joy was to suffer and die for a cause they believed to be just. Their unchallenged devotion and matchless heroism shall continue to be the wonder and inspiration of the ages."

The current mayor of Pensacola has a name straight out of *Gone with the Wind:* Ashton Hayward. Days after the tragic events in Charlottesville, Mayor Hayward announced that he wants to tear down that Confederate monument.

All I can say is: Good!

Being put on a statue is an honor. The people named on that statue committed treason against the United States, and they did so in defense of slavery. They don't deserve the honor they've been granted.

This same discussion is going on all over the South right now, including Manatee County, where the commission just voted to remove their statue. A lot of people signed a petition to replace it with a statue of Snooty, the late, lamented manatee that lived for more than 60 years at the South Florida Museum.

What a great idea! Instead of just tearing down old monuments, let's replace them with new ones that will bring people together. Salute things that everyone can enjoy. Salute people who fought for America, not people who fought against it.

For instance, why not replace Pensacola's monument with a statue of someone from Pensacola who achieved something great? Reubin Askew, the governor so widely praised that his nickname was "Reubin the Good," would fit that bill. So would Emmitt Smith, who set the NFL's all-time rushing record.

Hillsborough County could replace theirs with a star from Tampa's history, such as jazz giant Cannonball Adderley, actress Butterfly McQueen or TV pitchman Billy Mays—maybe holding a ShamWow. I bet ShamWow would even help pay for it, or at least keep it clean.

People in Polk County now debating the fate of their statue could replace it with one of computer inventor John Atanasoff, Red Lobster founder Bill Darden, or Gov. "Walkin'" Lawton Chiles. My preference for that one would be a pose from his second inaugural, when he showed up wearing a coonskin cap and toting a potato gun with which he fired several spuds toward the governor's mansion.

And up in St. Augustine, their Confederate monument could be replaced by one of Pulitzer-winning author Marjorie Kinnan Rawlings (she ran a hotel there that's now a Ripley's Believe It or Not museum, believe it or not) or musical genius Ray Charles, who learned to play the piano there at the Florida School for the Deaf and Blind. Picture that monument with a speaker that plays Brother Ray's greatest hits at the push of a button. Now picture all the tourist traffic for that!

There are plenty of Florida people more deserving of a statue than any Johnny Reb. For instance, the first soldier to earn a Medal of Honor in World War II was Lt. Alexander "Sandy" Nininger Jr. of Fort Lauderdale. Where's his statue?

Or we could go the Snooty route and put up statues to all the animals that have made Florida great. The mighty tarpon, for instance, did a lot more to build up the tourist trade in Lee County than Robert E. Lee ever did. Yet Lee gets the county named for him and the fish gets no recognition.

More people come to Florida to see our wildlife than to see those old monuments. Yet where are our alligator statues? Our roseate spoonbill monuments? Where's the memorial to the leaping (and delicious) mullet?

The greatest Florida statue of them all, I think, is the Possum Monument in the Panhandle community of Wausau. Every August, Wausau throws a festival to honor the humble possum for providing everyone in town with food during the Great Depression. They even name a Possum Queen. Now 'fess up, y'all, ain't that better for Florida than a statue of a traitor?

Enough said. Now let's all go eat a big ol' bowl of grits.

Note: In July 2020, after a five-hour public hearing at which 150 people spoke, the Pensacola City Council voted 6–1 to dismantle its Confederate monument.

43

THE BRIDGE TO NOWHERE

Tampa Bay Times, July 11, 2011

Even in a state known for political boondoggles like a Taj Mahal court-house and an unneeded aircraft hangar, the Garcon Point Bridge stands out.

Nicknamed "Bo's Bridge" for its biggest backer, former House Speaker Bolley "Bo" Johnson, the bridge over eastern Pensacola Bay was built us-ing bogus traffic projections, faulty financing and shoddy construction practices. The day it opened in 1999, it had already incurred hefty fines for environmental destruction. Now Bo's Bridge is broke, and the taxpayers are likely to be stuck with millions of dollars in debt.

The bridge's owner, the Santa Rosa Bay Bridge Authority, owes its bondholders $90 million. It owes the state Department of Transportation more than $24 million. The amount in its bank account: $4 million.

State officials have said the bridge authority is so broke that it couldn't afford to mail out notices of its meetings. But that's not a problem because the board hasn't met in nearly a year. Once federal investigators began poking around, all but one member quit.

"People laugh and point fingers at me and say, 'He's the last remaining idiot there,'" joked Morgan Lamb, the sole board member of the authority.

What happened to Bo's Bridge is a cautionary tale about how bending the rules for a politician's pet project can ruin everyone who touches it.

"This thing is so upside down, it's really embarrassing," said state Rep. Doug Broxson, R-Gulf Breeze. "We all feel kind of powerless to do anything."

When the bridge was built, its backers contended it would cost the tax-payers nothing. It was financed by selling bonds that would be paid back using tolls—tolls that now are the highest in Florida: $3.75 to cross its 3½ mile, two-lane span.

Why so much? Because so few drivers use it. Fewer than ever as the toll keeps climbing.

"It's really a goofy way to run a bridge," conceded Lamb, who is also president of the Santa Rosa County Republican Club.

Critics have even launched a Facebook page, "I Won't Use the Garcon Point Bridge." More than 900 have joined, some posting items like a clip of Elvis Presley singing "Bridge Over Troubled Waters."

On July 1, the authority failed to make a $5 million payment to a New York bank, which is now demanding the entire amount it is owed: $90 million.

State officials quickly announced that they would not bail out the bridge authority. They said that if it declared bankruptcy, that would not affect Florida's ability to borrow money.

But Joe Mooney, who was ousted as the bridge authority's financial adviser when he warned board members that their borrowing plan didn't make sense, says the state is liable.

"The fact of the matter is, the state directed that project, the state signed off on every decision the board made . . . the state's hands are all over this thing," Mooney said.

❋

Bo's Bridge would have never been built if not for Johnson, a real estate wheeler-dealer who grew up amid the rough-and-tumble of Panhandle politics. His father, a former Santa Rosa County commissioner, was once accused of trying to hire a hit man to rub out someone who'd crossed him.

In the late 1980s Garcon (pronounced GAR-sohn) Point was an isolated, rural area, as was the stretch of peninsula across the bay from it. But Johnson could foresee development erupting there if only a bridge could connect the two spots for easy access to Interstate 10 and U.S. 98.

Environmental groups warned that such a bridge would harm the bay and never attract enough motorists to justify its expense.

But Johnson, a Milton Democrat, had an interest in the land on one side of the bridge route. As House speaker he had the clout to push the project along. He even waived state rules to get the authority an $8.5 million startup loan when the limit was supposed to be $500,000.

The builders put the bridge together in just 29 months, setting a speed record and collecting a big bonus. Then they set another record: the largest financial penalty in Panhandle history for an environmental crime.

The secret to the bridge's rapid construction was that the company, Odebrecht-Metric, dumped concrete and other waste into the bay, sometimes barely missing fishermen's heads. Odebrecht-Metric paid $4 million in fines and restitution.

House Speaker Bolley "Bo" Johnson toys with an oversized gavel. He used his clout to get approval for a toll bridge at Garcon Point, one that was built using bogus traffic projections, faulty financing and shoddy construction practices. Photo by Donn Dughi, courtesy of the Florida State Archives.

Then the authority had to borrow millions of dollars more to pay for the builders' destruction of wetlands.

The week the bridge opened, Johnson was convicted in an unrelated case of taking "consulting fees" from road builders, casinos and other companies while speaker and not reporting it on his taxes. He spent two years in federal prison.

☼

The worst was yet to come.

The bridge's financing was based on traffic estimates from URS Greiner Woodward Clyde of San Francisco. URS predicted the bridge would quickly attract 7,500 motorists a day, enough to pay for itself.

Mooney, the financial adviser and a longtime Panhandle resident, knew that was wrong and said so. The bridge authority got another financial adviser.

Two years after it opened, the bridge was drawing an average of just 4,000 motorists a day paying the $2 toll. Two months ago the average was 3,844 cars a day. URS based its projections on another bridge that leads to the popular beach resort of Destin. There is no Destin at the end of the Garcon Point Bridge.

"We now know that," Arthur Goldberg, the URS vice president who wrote the estimates for Garcon Point Bridge, said in 2000.

URS also provided off-base traffic predictions for the Veterans Expressway in Tampa and the Suncoast Parkway in Pasco and Hernando counties. URS vice president Hugh Miller told the Times in 2000 they "were basically guessing."

Yet URS is still the bridge authority's traffic adviser. When collections fell short, URS recommended raising tolls, and the authority did it "like a bunch of zombies," said Lamb, the lone board member.

State legislators agreed to a $1 million bailout in 2001, but then-Gov. Jeb Bush vetoed it. So the authority started dipping into reserves to make payments to bondholders. After a decade, the account is all but empty.

The authority failed to post official notices about its woes, an apparent violation of U.S. Securities and Exchange Commission rules. Last fall, SEC officials summoned the authority's chairman and vice chairman to testify and turn over two crates of documents. No charges have been filed.

What happens next is anyone's guess.

There's talk the bondholders might take possession of the bridge and try to sell it, or sue the state demanding their money. But the state is a creditor, too. The DOT operated the bridge for 12 years for $1 million a year—another debt the authority has yet to pay.

DOT officials say they will keep it open for the drivers who might still want to cross that bridge when they come to it.

Note: The last remaining bridge authority board member resigned in 2014. Repeated attempts to get the state to take ownership of the bridge have failed. In 2019, a judge ruled the bondholders could force the toll to go up to $5 per car to recoup their lost investment.

44

THE LAST BOOKSTORE

Tampa Bay Times, January 11, 2013

KEY WEST—Like a lot of island communities, Key West must import meat, vegetables and a lot of other goods that its residents need. It does, however, export a few local products: tacky T-shirts, lurid tattoos and great literature.

Ernest Hemingway wrote *A Farewell to Arms, For Whom the Bell Tolls* and *The Snows of Kilimanjaro* while living here. Tennessee Williams penned *Summer and Smoke* and *Night of the Iguana* in Key West. Robert Frost, Thornton Wilder, Ralph Ellison, Annie Dillard and Thomas Mc-Guane, among others, also put in serious writing time in Florida's southernmost city.

But the number of stores in Key West selling these authors' books has dwindled to just one. The sole survivor, Key West Island Books, has managed to keep its doors open for 35 years despite sometimes not having a living owner. The secret to its longevity is simple.

"It's a darn good bookstore," said Boston University professor William McKeen, the author of a book on Key West's literary legacy called *Mile Marker Zero: The Moveable Feast of Key West.*

In a town that offers 400 places to buy alcohol in its 7.4-square-mile area, how did Key West wind up with just one bookstore? It happened slowly, like a sandcastle gradually washed away by the tide.

Once there were plenty of places to buy books in Key West. There was a gay bookstore, Flaming Maggie's (so named because it stood at the corner of Fleming and Margaret streets). There was even a store devoted to mysteries, run by noted thriller maven Dilys Winn, recalled Tom Corcoran, a onetime Key West resident who writes mysteries set there.

But they all closed because of rising rents and disappearing customers, he said. By 2011 all that was left were Key West Island, a Borders Express and two other independents, Voltaire Books and Bargain Books. Borders Express closed that summer as part of the chain's collapse.

Voltaire had an enviable cachet. It supplied books for the annual Key West Literary Seminar, held every January, which features talks by capital-W Writers such as Jonathan Lethem, Margaret Atwood and Joyce Carol Oates. But it wasn't enough.

"We haven't had the community support we had hoped for," Voltaire co-owner Peter Rogers told the *Key West Citizen* when he closed his doors in July 2011. Six months later, in January, the other remaining independent, Bargain Books, closed because of its owner's declining health.

A potential competitor to Key West Island Books, Miami's famed Books & Books, "has looked at opening a branch in Key West," said owner Mitchell Kaplan, but "we're not close to anything right now."

To McKeen, Key West's transformation from an island of creative misfits to a tourism mecca is partly to blame for the declining number of bookstores: "People who go down there on vacation take their Kindles or a dog-eared paperback they don't mind getting suntan oil on."

But poet Arlo Haskell, who is associate director of the Key West Literary Seminar, said what has happened here reflects what has happened across the country: "You don't have to go down the street to buy books anymore when you can just order them on your phone."

To walk into Key West Island Books is to see what most bookstores used to be like. There are no comfy chairs tempting patrons to sit a spell. There's no coffee shop with free Wi-Fi. There are a few racks of used DVDs, but mostly there are books of every shape, size and subject matter—and clerks who know all about them.

"That's the secret to that store," Corcoran said. "There are people there who care about books."

"We've got very capable employees who are literature nuts," agreed the store's owner, Scott Shaffer, who bought it in 2010. One clerk, Chip Phillips, said, "I've worked here for a year but I've been a customer for 20."

Amid a hodge-podge of shelving is a section of books by and about Hemingway, and near it are works by Thomas McGuane and the rest of Key West's luminaries. There are also heavy leather-bound collectors' editions shelved near the register, and large sections on pirates and Cuban history.

There's now a small section of the latest bestsellers from Gillian Flynn and Dennis Lehane. Stretching back to the rear is a wide range of second-hand books, from well-thumbed copies of Ayn Rand's *Atlas Shrugged* to a cross-dressing paper doll cut-out book called *Drag Dolls*.

The mashup of offerings reflects the store's past. The first owner was an aficionado of antique books and reserved the back room for his fellow collectors, Corcoran said. The second had worked with remaindered books—the ones sent back to the publisher—and he stocked the store with so many that cardboard boxes of them jammed every aisle, Shaffer said.

When that owner died, though, the store was left in the lurch. The store's longtime manager ran it for the attorneys overseeing the estate, who hunted for a year for a buyer. Finally the landlord stepped in to take charge, along with son-in-law Shaffer.

"We didn't want to see the business go away," said Shaffer, an Ohio transplant. "We agreed to step in and keep it as part of the community that it's served for 35 years."

Shaffer's background is in real estate, not book sales. He says he thought of the store "as a property that needed to be rehabbed." He set to work getting rid of the cardboard boxes of remainders and then began updating the inventory—a move required by the loss of his competition.

"This store's niche was secondhand books," Shaffer said. "But now we have people coming in who want the bestsellers."

To deal with the lack of easy parking, he is considering creating an Internet-based bestseller delivery service for condominium residents—sort of like a localized Amazon.

He's not done with the changes yet—and he's not convinced he'll be the only game in town for long, either. "I think you're going to see more local, independent bookstores pop up," he predicted. Not because Key West has been home to a lot of authors, he said, but because "we've got some good readers here."

Note: I stumbled across this story while I was in the Keys to promote my book The Scent of Scandal *at a meeting of the Key West Garden Club. Three years later, a new bookstore opened in Key West, calling itself "Books & Books at the Studios of Key West." It was started by George Cooper, founder of the Tropic Cinema, and his wife, the beloved author Judy Blume, and affiliated with Kaplan's Miami chain. The next time I was in the Keys, I stopped in and had the distinct pleasure of having Judy Blume both autograph and ring up my purchase.*

45

LET US NOW PRAISE FLORIDA LOVEBUGS

Tampa Bay Times, April 28, 2016

Florida has a lot of symbols: a state animal (the panther), a state reptile (the alligator), even a state sand (Myakka fine) and a state pie (key lime, of course). I've got no complaints about those.

We've also got a familiar-sounding state slogan: "In God We Trust." It was adopted in 1868 after legislators copied it off the back of a silver dollar. Apparently there wasn't room on the state seal for the rest of it: "All Others Pay Cash."

I have long believed we could come up with a better slogan, one that is more distinctly Florida.

Just last month, a Plant City man looked out his window, dialed 911 and announced, "I live in a mobile home and I've got an alligator at my door!"

The minute I read that line, I thought, "Okay, that would make a great state slogan!"

The alligator showed up on the man's doorstep because it's spring, a time when male gators emerge from their winter hibernation and go looking for love in all the wrong places. They waddle into your driveway and bite your bumper, interrupt your golf game by wrestling on the green, crash your picnic and gobble up your burgers.

Those wandering gators make me think Florida should steal away Virginia's slogan, because really, Florida is for lovers.

I know you might think I'm kidding. Florida is better known for being a state full of strangers. So many of us just recently moved here. We often don't know our neighbors until we get into an argument with them over hedge-trimming and start pulling out machetes. The only bond many Floridians feel is for the place they left, not the place where they now live. But just look at how often lovers make the news in Florida—although, admittedly, it's often in the police log.

There was that couple in The Villages caught in flagrante delicto in the middle of the town square. And the Jacksonville couple in a police

When lovebugs are mating on Florida's highways, love is literally in the air—and then smeared across your bumper, windshield and fenders. Photo by Tim Donovan, courtesy of the Florida Fish and Wildlife Conservation Commission

standoff who refused to surrender until they had one last love connection. And the man in Casselberry who got naked to propose to his girlfriend, only to show up at the wrong house and get Tasered. ("Don't Tase me, bro!" a line first shouted by a University of Florida student in 2007, also would make a fine state slogan.)

This month, love is literally in the air in Florida as lovebugs begin their mating season. The little buggers pair up and flutter blissfully along our highways by the bajillions, oblivious to all the oncoming cars and trucks that are about to give them the ickiest interruptus imaginable. The bugs get their revenge, though, corroding your car's finish unless you wash them off quick.

Some people think lovebugs were created in a University of Florida lab, just like Gatorade. Actually they are a South American species that invaded our air space in 1949 and decided to stick around.

Many Floridians regard them as among the worst pests ever, but they are officially classified as harmless. They don't bite, sting, transmit diseases or exude a poison, which is pretty unusual for a Florida insect.

"You can even swallow them if you're on a motorcycle," said Norman Leppla, a University of Florida scientist who knows more about lovebugs than anyone else.

They do carry one human health hazard. I know several parents who have twisted themselves into knots trying to explain to their kids what the two bugs were doing in midair. ("Well, honey, he's uh, er, um, giving a friend a piggyback ride!")

Leppla thinks we've got the lovebugs all wrong. "If they were bigger, you could see the males and you could see their eyes," he told me. "They're as cute as can be."

If they didn't swarm over roads so much, he said, people might see them in a different light.

"Lovebugs sail from flower to flower much like butterflies and in smaller numbers could be perceived as beautiful," he once wrote.

Yes, he called them "beautiful."

They're not that different from a lot of us Floridians. They came from elsewhere but made a home here. They find themselves on the road for a far larger percentage of their lives than they would probably prefer. Their huge numbers and tendency to swarm can give people the wrong impression.

Meanwhile, they're doing their best to connect to someone else here, however fleeting that connection may be. That's more than I can say for some of us.

Leppla, by the way, does not defend all Florida insects.

"You want ugly," he told me, "how about a great big ugly palmetto bug?"

Maybe that should be our state slogan.

DYING EVERY NIGHT AT THE RODEO

St. Petersburg Times, July 3, 1992

Note: This story, which ran on 1A, is one of my favorites because I was able to cover a century of history. However, this story contains a quote that, even in 1992, sounded ugly. In 2021 it sounds far, far worse. At the time that I was reporting the story, I couldn't find anyone who would corroborate the anecdote of lassoing with intent to humiliate. As a result, I just put it in the story without comment and let it speak for itself, trusting the readers would catch the full nastiness of what was being described. Looking back now, I wish I had dug a lot harder for details on this, and maybe even made it into a separate story.

ARCADIA—Greg Albritton will die tonight.

He knows how it will happen. A shot will ring out and he'll fall to the ground, dead.

After a while, though, he'll get up, dust himself off and sign autographs. And on Saturday and Sunday he'll get killed all over again.

Usually the 28-year-old Albritton, who describes himself as "your typical Florida Cracker," works as a welder. But when it's rodeo time in his hometown of Arcadia, he straps on a six-shooter, saddles his horse and joins up with the Tater Hill Bluff Gang.

Every year the outlaw band rides into the rodeo arena, and, in front of a crowd of cheering tourists, they shoot up a bar and rob a bank. And every year the bad guys are killed by the brave sheriff and his deputies—sometimes shot, sometimes hanged.

"Good always wins," Albritton says. "That's the way it works, and that's the way we want it."

All the events in Arcadia's venerable All-Florida Championship Rodeo, founded in 1929, are supposed to celebrate the city's pioneer heritage. But the cartoon violence of the shootout gives the rodeo's spectators the clearest picture of what life was really like in Arcadia a century ago.

In the 1890s, Arcadia was a muddy cowtown on the edge of the frontier. Outlaws ruled the range and disputes were settled with fists, knives and guns. Death hung over the town like a storm cloud over the palmetto prairie.

"It was a wide open and woolly place," says lawyer turned historian Canter Brown Jr., author of *Florida's Peace River Frontier.* "Murder was epidemic."

Tonight, when Albritton and the other actors ride into Fenton Arena, they'll be shooting blanks and playing the script for laughs. But every gunshot will carry an echo of Arcadia's history of violence, a legacy that still haunts the town.

❖

Driving the 40 miles of two-lane blacktop from I-75 into Arcadia is like swimming upstream in the river of time. You leave behind the modern-day Florida of beachfront condominiums and cookie-cutter subdivisions.

Cross the DeSoto County line, and you gaze out across acres of pasture as flat and green as God's own pool table. Cattle in shades of white, black and brown hide from the noonday sun beneath shady oaks at the edge of the field.

Nowadays cattle and cowboys are at best curiosities in most of Florida. But a century ago, cattle were the biggest business around, and the cattlemen were kings.

"My two granddads owned everything from here to Lake Okeechobee," says Dick Welles, 71, a rancher and former president of the Arcadia rodeo.

The ranchers let their cows wander through the forests and swamps until round-up time, then drove them to ports on the Gulf of Mexico to ship them to Cuba for sale. The Cubans paid with heavy sacks of Spanish gold.

The cattle kings had clout. They brought the railroad to Arcadia, turning what had been a tiny settlement known as Tater Hill Bluff into a bustling city.

But for every cattle king, there were dozens of poor cowboys tending the herds—rough and rowdy men prone to drinking and fighting, with one often leading to the other.

The best known Florida cowboy was an Arcadian named Bone Mizell, famed for his sense of humor and capacity for alcohol.

One night when Mizell rode into camp too drunk to stay on his horse, cowboy writer Jim Bob Tinsley says, the other ranch hands waited until he passed out. Then they built a small fire around where he'd fallen.

Gov. Doyle Carlton Sr. (*third from left*) attended this 1930s DeSoto County Rodeo in Arcadia. The rodeo then featured local cowboys competing for prizes, but in 1962 professional rodeo riders took over. Photo courtesy of the Florida State Archives.

When the dazed Mizell woke up, he looked at the ring of fire around him and said, "Dead and gone to hell. No more 'n I expected."

    ✕

According to artist Frederic Remington, though, the real hell was the Florida frontier.

Remington's paintings and sculptures of Western cowboys stamped a romantic image of the West in the minds of Americans. But when he visited Arcadia in 1895, he saw no romance at all.

In *Harper's New Monthly Magazine,* he describes Florida cowboys as "wild-looking individuals, whose hanging hair and drooping hats and generally bedraggled appearance would remind you at once of Spanish moss."

Remington was especially annoyed that these "low-browed cow-folks" often bushwhacked their enemies rather than facing them down in the open.

The artist's visit came at the height of the DeSoto County Range Wars, a time when, as Remington put it, "desperate men armed to the teeth" battled for control of the cattle business.

Across the unfenced ranges outside Arcadia, cattle were spread out by the thousands, easy pickings for a cowboy like Mizell who knew how to change a brand. The loss of a few cows here and there didn't bother the ranchers or surprise them.

But when gangs of rustlers began stealing whole herds, the ranchers formed posses to track down the outlaws. The chase usually ended with dozens of men "going at each other with guns blazing," Brown says.

The thieves who didn't escape or get shot usually were strung up on the spot. But a lot of them slipped away into the swamps, where a man won't leave a trail.

Rustling became so widespread that the cattle kings started stealing from each other, leading to further bloodshed. Remington recounted the tale of two cowboys from rival ranches who saw each other on the range and started shooting.

"Both were found stretched out dying under the palmettoes, one calling deliriously the name of his boss," he wrote. And all this killing, he wrote, was over "the possession of scrawny creatures not fit for a pointer-dog to mess on."

By 1896, DeSoto's cattlemen had grown sick of the carnage and signed a peace treaty. It was an uneasy truce. Twenty years later, Tinsley says, ranchers still kept away from windows at night to avoid being shot by snipers.

Remington suggested that Florida cowboys were a different breed than their Western counterparts because, instead of living in the open spaces out West, they spent their time hunting cows and each other through dark and treacherous swamps. It was "not a country for . . . moral giants."

But Brown says Arcadians were typical of all American pioneers: Far from civilization, facing a harsh and unforgiving wilderness, they lived by their own rules and depended only on themselves. They could indulge their worst instincts, so they fought and stole and killed.

Rugged individualism has been a valuable legacy of the American frontier, Brown says. "But there are unfortunate legacies too, and violence is one of them."

※

Arcadia's violence did differ from Dodge City in one respect: It was complicated by the racial tensions of the post–Civil War South.

Black families began settling in Arcadia in the 1890s, drawn by jobs in the first phosphate mines along the Peace River. The Crackers didn't take to their new neighbors, Brown said. Arcadia's first lynching occurred in 1892.

Sometimes, though, the Black men and women were more than just neighbors to the White families, even powerful ones like the Parkers.

Capt. John Parker was a Seminole War veteran who once served as sheriff in Hillsborough County. He launched the Parker cattle dynasty, but died after someone poisoned the liquor he was drinking at a revival meeting.

He left behind four sons he fathered with his wife and another three he fathered with Rachel Davis, his former slave.

The White sons formed the Parker Brothers Ranch, which for decades remained the largest outfit in DeSoto County. And one of Parker's Black sons, Lloyd Davis, worked for his White half-brothers.

"He was sort of like their foreman," says historian Kyle Van Landingham, a descendant of the Parker family who lives in Tampa. "He also did some of their dirty work."

In short, he says, Davis was their hit man.

Davis carried out at least one very public assassination. One of the White Parker brothers' daughters was married to a prominent Arcadia lawyer who frequently beat her. So the family, led then by Zeb Parker, told Davis to take care of the problem.

On June 5, 1908, Davis gunned down the lawyer while he was dining at the Arcadia House, a popular hotel. Davis got away clean, thanks to the Parkers.

"Zeb was a very formidable figure," Van Landingham says. "His word was law in DeSoto County in the early part of this century."

These days, though, Zeb Parker is remembered for helping get Arcadia's first rodeo started.

☼

The tourists driving through Arcadia this weekend on their way to the rodeo won't see the cowtown of the 1890s. The Arcadia House, for instance, was torn down in the 1960s to make room for a hamburger stand.

But Arcadia isn't like the more populous parts of Florida, where the past is swept away so fast it seems the state is ruled by amnesiacs. Parts of the town look much as they did in the 1920s. More than 370 homes and businesses are on the National Registry of Historic Places, including Zeb Parker's old bungalow.

If the tourists stray across the railroad tracks from the white-columned homes of the historic district, they'll see some other ancient dwellings: the tumbledown shacks of the poorer Black residents, who have repeatedly sued the city contending Arcadia is just a few steps away from apartheid.

Still, some things have changed. Eugene Hickson Sr., whose funeral home is the oldest Black-owned business in DeSoto County, is Arcadia's vice mayor.

Modern Arcadia faces a lot of the same problems confronting every small town: empty storefronts downtown, local business owners who say they can't compete with Walmart. Anyone searching for nightlife usually has to hit the road for Sarasota or Fort Myers, an hour away.

When Arcadia's young people go looking for work, they find few opportunities beyond the area's three largest employers: a state mental hospital, a state prison and a transformer factory.

"The ones who finish high school and college go off somewhere else because there's not much here for them," Hickson says.

Orange groves now cover much of the rural landscape, but cattle remain a big business. On the edge of town stands the Arcadia State Livestock Market, where men in Stetsons sit in rocking chairs and bid on steers with a languid wave of the hand. Occasionally, while the auctioneer rattles on, a buyer will lean over and spit tobacco juice into a bucket of sand.

Rustlers are still around, too. Just last month, deputies rounded up five Arcadia men and charged them with stealing cattle and hogs from area ranches.

But those fenced-in ranches are so small now they seem like mere grass patches, says Runt Smith, 67, whose leathery skin and stiff walk attest to a life spent on horseback.

Smith started working as a ranch hand in the early 1940s, camping out on the range, rising before dawn to ride for miles out to the herds. He figures the cowboys of today have it easy.

"We worked a sight harder," he says. "Today they start at 7 or 8 a.m. and at 5 o'clock they got to be home."

Cowboys today aren't as rowdy as the old-timers either, according to longtime Arcadia resident Eugene Taylor Jr., a sandy-haired man with a handshake like a sprung trap, whose real estate agency specializes in ranchland.

"They were good, honest working people, but when they played, they played hard," Turner says. "Back before we had all these racial problems, it was a tradition of the Fourth of July parade that the cowboys would give (Black people) a hard time. They would ride their horses into bars and drink, and then they might rope one or two people and drag them around."

Nowadays, Turner says, Arcadia and its rodeo are "more laid-back."

But one thing remains the same as it was in the 1890s: Arcadia's reputation.

☼

The DeSoto County Chamber of Commerce boasts about how Arcadians always say "Howdy" on the street. But let a stranger ask about their hometown and they turn shy. They're still smarting over the newspaper headline that dubbed it "the town without pity."

"There are some real good people in Arcadia," says Kaye Mercer, whose clothing store sells jeans, boots and hats to DeSoto's cowboys. "But it seems like we only ever get bad publicity, because that's what makes the news."

In recent years tiny Arcadia, population 6,488, has drawn an astounding amount of national attention. At one point, so many television trucks surrounded its stately redbrick courthouse with satellite dishes that it looked like a beleaguered outpost in *The War of the Worlds*.

That was the day in 1989 a judge decided James Richardson, an illiterate Black fruit picker, had been wrongfully imprisoned for 21 years on charges he had poisoned his seven children.

When Richardson's children were murdered, reporters from around the country descended on Arcadia to cover what everyone called the most heinous crime in Florida history.

Richardson was convicted by an all-White jury in Fort Myers. But for years, rumors floated around Arcadia that he had been framed, and the White sheriff had protected another Black suspect because he was sleeping with the suspect's daughter, a rumor both parties denied.

Two decades later, newspaper reports raised strong doubts about Richardson's conviction. But it took a rustler to see justice done.

Remus Griffin, a trucker and convicted pig thief, took the law into his own hands to help Richardson, breaking into a former prosecutor's office to steal his case files. The files eventually landed on Gov. Bob Martinez's desk, prompting him to order the investigation that eventually freed Richardson.

Once again, reporters descended on Arcadia. Plenty of Arcadians cheered Richardson's release, but some said the case should have come to a different end. One White man, still arguing that Richardson was guilty,

Arcadia fruit-picker James Richardson, seen here at Tomoka Correctional Institution, spent 21 years in prison after being convicted of poisoning his seven children, a crime he did not commit. A rustler helped free him.
Photo by Charles Flowers, courtesy of Tanman Films.

told a reporter, "Somebody ought to take a .30-06 and blow his head off."

The revelations of the Richardson investigation came hard on the heels of another nationally publicized brouhaha in Arcadia: the Ray case.

The DeSoto County School Board barred the three sons of Clifford and Louise Ray from attending classes because the boys, all hemophiliacs, had contracted the AIDS virus through blood transfusions.

The Rays sued and won, but it was a hollow victory. Anonymous callers threatened to bomb their children's school. The Rays became the focus of protests by fearful parents, gay rights groups and the Ku Klux Klan.

Then, one night, someone set fire to the Rays' house. The family left town. The arsonist got away clean, just like Lloyd Davis. But Arcadia didn't.

Even then-President Reagan joined the crowd booing Arcadia. Like Remington, they painted it as a village full of yahoos, out of step with the ideals of civilized behavior.

Since the furor over the Rays and Richardson, Arcadia has quieted down again, but its residents are well aware of the image outsiders have of their city.

"You know Arcadia's got a bad reputation," says Hickson, the funeral home owner. But not everyone in Arcadia deserves the blame for killing the Richardson children, framing Richardson and burning out the Rays.

"I'll say this: It happened," Hickson says. "There's all kinds of people in a town, and some of them cause more disturbances than others."

But the wilder the story, the wider it circulates. In the 1890s Arcadia had a temperance society and a literary club, but the national publicity went to those hard-drinking, gun-toting cowboys.

Yet now Arcadia looks to the cowboys to salvage its reputation.

☼

In March and again in July, the rodeo brings thousands of tourists to a part of Florida they probably wouldn't visit otherwise, to spend thousands of dollars at Arcadia's restaurants and motels.

"For a little bitty town, we get a lot of people here," says Duane Bachtold, who plays the chief outlaw in the shootout.

Out West, rodeos started as a way for cowboys to show off their skills after a roundup. But Arcadia's rodeo always has been designed as a money-making gimmick. The first one, set up to help the American Legion pay off its debts, took place just two weeks after the stock market crash that launched the Great Depression.

"Times was hard," recalls Welles, who proudly displays a reproduction of one of Remington's cowboy sculptures on his desk.

The first Arcadia rodeo was influenced as much by the romantic cowboys in popular Western movies as by the real cowboys who worked around Arcadia. But there would have been no rodeo without those local cowboys competing in it, and cattlemen like Zeb Parker serving as judges.

For decades, the rodeo was a homegrown product. Welles won the bull-riding competition in the 1930s. Runt Smith parlayed his experience riding the Florida range into a career as a rodeo cowboy, becoming an all-around champion in the early '50s.

But in 1962 the Arcadia rodeo turned pro. That meant only someone belonging to the Professional Rodeo Cowboys Association could compete. Now the contestants are professional athletes who follow the rodeo circuit around the country and may make $100,000 a year, not local cowboys like Smith and Welles.

"It's changed the character of rodeo," Welles says. "It took it away from the local people."

The one event that local residents still dominate is the shootout, begun in the mid-'70s by Welles's nephew Terry.

Originally it took place in downtown Arcadia, drawing the tourists there. The shootout was a gory play, with every gunshot "wound" spurting a sticky mix of molasses and red dye. The "corpses" tended to attract a lot of flies.

But the crowds grew so large that the shootout moved to the more spacious rodeo arena. In that less intimate setting, the shootout became a bloodless affair, because the special effects were too hard to see.

Like the cowboys of the 1890s, though, the Tater Hill Bluff Gang still faces trouble when they go for their guns. Although they're just shooting blanks, Bachtold once fired his gun too close to his leg, producing a real gunshot wound the kind that Arcadians of a century ago saw too many times. The actors understand why.

"You get to shooting," says Albritton, "and sometimes you get caught up in it."

Note: In 2015, producer-director Ty Flowers and Tanman Films released a documentary called Time Simply Passes *recounting the story of James Richardson's unjust incarceration, his exoneration and his subsequent quest to get the state to compensate him for his stolen life (the Legislature finally awarded him $2.1 million). Tanman showed the film in Arcadia at two churches—one White, one Black—on the 50th anniversary of the Richardson children's deaths. Both viewing events, Flowers said, "were solemn and kind of beautiful."*

47

HURRICANE CENTRAL

Tampa Bay Times, September 22, 2017

I don't want to make light of the misery and death that Hurricane Irma inflicted on Florida this month. A lot of it was ugly, and some of it was downright criminal. We saw greed and pettiness on display, and it brought illness and death.

We also saw heartwarming images of courage and kindness. We saw a nun with a chainsaw cutting up downed trees after learning about chainsaws on Google, and a man who gave up the last generator so that someone who needed it more could have it.

This being Florida, of course, we saw some very Florida things happen too:

- A sign language interpreter in Manatee County who didn't really know how to do sign language flashed a bunch of gibberish during a televised pre-Irma news conference, including this sterling sentence: "Help you at that time too use bear big."
- Two shirtless guys in Jacksonville tried to steal a metal power pole, and even managed to get it tied to the top of their SUV and attach a little safety rag to the end of it before the cops showed up.
- A Fort Myers woman who'd recently undergone a double-organ transplant painted a sign that said, "HOT SINGLE FEMALE SEEKS SEXY LINEMAN TO ELECTRIFY HER LIFE" and sure enough, she got her power turned back on.

What was interesting to me, though, is that even before Irma made landfall in the Keys, all the Smart People had already begun dropping their weighty opinions about Florida on our heads.

TV commentators pontificated on how Irma might at last be the Big One sent to chastise Floridians for our hubris and wash away our ignorance and corruption. (If Hurricane Andrew couldn't do that 25 years ago, then Irma sure couldn't.)

Then came the think pieces and the hot takes. "Florida is impossible!" they said. "Nobody in their right mind lives there! Good Lord, they have hurricanes!"

Does anyone write that kind of thing about California after earthquakes, or Kansas after tornadoes or Wisconsin after snowstorms? No, only Florida gets depicted as an uninhabitable hellhole.

This is, of course, Grade-A baloney. People have been living in Florida for thousands of years. The original Floridians—the Calusa, the Tequesta, the Timucua, the Apalachee and the Tocobaga—made a comfortable home here long before the first tin-hatted Spanish conquistador showed up.

They knew how to live in harmony with the landscape. They ate lots of seafood, dressed to keep cool in a hot climate and didn't build anything on the coast that couldn't survive a storm surge. They also never wore sandals with socks.

If we want to keep living in Florida, we need to follow their example. Instead of trying to conquer nature, we need to figure out how to fit into it.

We know hurricanes are going to keep hitting us. We know the sea level is rising. We need to stop ignoring those factors and instead adapt to them.

If we want to keep our lights and air-conditioning on, then we need to figure out how to make our power grid stronger or find ways to better back it up. If we want to keep flushing our toilets during a storm, then we need to fix our sewer systems so they don't overflow into our bays and rivers every time there's a little rain. If we want to keep our population growing, then we need to figure out how to avoid creating bottlenecks during evacuations. If we want our houses to stand up to big storms, then the building codes that worked in South Florida should probably become requirements all over the state.

If you think all that will cost too much, then we need to find a way to pay for it, because that's what it's going to take to keep on living in Florida. Hurricane preparedness is not cheap.

In the past, Florida's reaction to hurricanes always reminded me of a story that Sam Spade tells in Dashiell Hammett's novel *The Maltese Falcon*. Spade says he was hired to find a man named Flitcraft. The man had led a fairly humdrum life until one day he simply vanished "like a fist when you open your hand," Spade says.

Turns out he had moved to a different town and started leading the exact same life as before, just under a different name.

Flitcraft explains his disappearance by saying that one day he'd been walking down a city street and a steel beam fell 10 stories from a construction site to land smack in front of him. One more step and he'd have been killed. Seeing that made him feel "like somebody had taken the lid off his life and let him look at the works," Spade says.

That's why he changed his life—but then he settled back into the same rut he was in before. As Spade puts it, "He adjusted himself to beams falling, and then no more of them fell, and he adjusted himself to them not falling."

Florida, we're Flitcraft, and Irma is the beam. Let's not pretend there won't be more.

48

ANDREW, PLUS 10

St. Petersburg Times, August 18, 2002

Note: When Hurricane Andrew struck South Florida in 1992, an editor named Susan Taylor Martin dispatched me to cover the aftermath. She specifically told me to find one neighborhood that had been hit hard and report on what happened there—and then plan on going back at three month intervals to see how they bounced back over the course of a year. A decade later, I went back to see how everyone was doing.

HOMESTEAD—When Dan Sanabria walks through Publix, he automatically looks for shelter. If he sees an enclosed space away from the windows, he thinks, "That would be a good place to hide."

For years Mary Herzog, didn't hang a picture on her walls because she feared losing everything again.

"That's how whacked out I became," she says, shaking her head. "Every time there's thunder and wind, it brings it all back."

George Brown's daily reminder towers over his front yard: two mahogany trees, one alive, one nearly dead. On Aug. 24, 1992, Hurricane Andrew knocked them both over, killing one. Brown wanted to save the survivor but he couldn't cut them apart.

"The roots were intertwined, and I thought if I tried to separate them it would kill them both," he said. "So I stuck them in together."

For Sanabria, Herzog, Brown and their neighbors on SW 294th Terrace, 10 years after Hurricane Andrew tore through their tiny cul-de-sac, the nation's worst natural disaster still haunts them.

Hundreds of thousands of people fled South Florida for higher ground, some of them permanently. But for those who stayed, who slowly rebuilt their homes and their lives, the memories of the devastation Andrew wrought are intertwined with those of better days.

They can't cut away one without losing the other.

＊

Ten houses line SW 294th Terrace, tucked between U.S. 1 and Homestead Air Force Base. Among the first residents were Air Force veteran Charles Wilson and his wife, Dora. They bought a house there in the 1970s because it was 10 minutes from the base and stuck around after he retired.

The base once employed 6,500 military personnel and 1,000 civilians, making it the mainstay of the local economy.

Homestead was home to more than 26,000 people, with another 9,000 in nearby Florida City. Thousands more filled surrounding unincorporated areas like Naranja and Leisure City. There were sprawling mobile home parks where neighbors gathered Friday nights for potluck suppers, and migrant camps of Haitians, Salvadorans, Guatemalans and Mexicans hired to cultivate Dade County's vegetable crops.

The daily routines—eat, sleep, work, watch TV—seemed as fixed as the stars. Twenty-seven quiet summers had passed since the last deadly hurricane, Betsy, hit South Florida in 1965.

So on Aug. 16, 1992, when the National Weather Service reported a tropical depression forming 3,500 miles away near Africa, few paid attention.

But by Sunday, Aug. 23, Hurricane Andrew was closing in on South Florida. Panicked shoppers jammed grocery and hardware stores. The highways clogged. More than 700,000 people evacuated, though many went only a few miles. Thousands more decided to stick it out.

Wilson didn't evacuate because for years storms had roared toward South Florida and then swerved. He was convinced Andrew would do the same.

"We were in for a big surprise," he said.

Dan Sanabria had no clue a storm was coming. He spent all weekend moving from the Princetonian Mobile Home Park to the new house he would share with his elderly parents on SW 294th Terrace.

He finished late Sunday. Exhausted, Sanabria fell sleep. Before dawn on Monday, Aug. 24, 1992, odd noises jolted him awake.

"The shed in the back yard was going up and down. The sliding glass door started to move in and out," he said. Then came "something horrendous. That sound is one thing I'll never forget."

＊

Many survivors groped for the right words to describe Andrew's howl. They compared it to a freight train in the living room, a fighter jet on the roof. To George Brown, it sounded like his house was being blasted away by a giant shotgun.

Andrew was compact, just 60 miles across, but so ferocious its winds blew away the instruments that were supposed to measure them.

Top gusts hit 175 mph, making Andrew a Category 4 hurricane, not quite the strongest on the scale. Researchers are still debating whether it should be reclassified as a Category 5.

Sanabria and his parents crowded into their new bathroom and braced themselves against the door.

"When the eye passed over I went out for a look and we had no roof," Sanabria said. "Three minutes after we left the bathroom, the ceiling collapsed."

Across the street, Mary Herzog just hunkered down when her windows blew out. "I was staying with my home and was going to die where I was," she said.

She survived. Others did not. Fifteen people were killed during the storm and another 25 later died of indirect causes. Andrew demolished more than 25,000 homes and damaged another 100,000. It flattened the air base. Of the 1,176 mobile homes in Homestead, all but nine were destroyed.

Right after Andrew, Sanabria drove by the mobile home he had just left. All he found was the toilet.

☼

Five days after the storm, Maj. Gen. Richard B. Griffits landed in Homestead with 23,000 troops, the biggest peacetime domestic military operation in U.S. history. The devastation stunned him.

"I had never seen a place completely leveled in all directions," Griffits later recalled. "There was a smell to it. A smell of utter destruction."

On SW 294th, every home was damaged, but the change went deeper. Andrew had plunged the survivors into a primitive world with no air-conditioning, no microwaves, no TV to show them what was going on in the other neighborhoods smashed by the storm.

Gwendolyn Sherman, now 23, has vivid memories of those jittery, pitch-black nights. With no way to cool the house, "we left the doors open, so I was nervous with all the looting that was going on."

When George Brown spotted some thieves, he chased them away at gunpoint. "They didn't want to talk to Mr. Twelve Gauge," he said.

Sunrise brought the rumble of portable generators, the pounding of

Homestead resident Carmen Rivera surveys the damage left by Hurricane Andrew, which in 1992 demolished more than 25,000 homes and damaged another 100,000. Photo by John Luke, courtesy of the Florida State Archives.

hammers and the constant whir of helicopters that scared the migrant workers who thought they were about to be strafed.

From above, the battered cul-de-sac seemed to blend in with all the other battered neighborhoods. Andrew caused an estimated $30 billion in damage and left a quarter-million people homeless.

In the first few days, no rescue agency sprang to action fast enough to help the storm's victims. People went days without water. Hungry residents queued up for hours for food that never arrived.

By the time donations began pouring in from around the country, the survivors were ready to snap. As Mary Herzog stood in a line for free clothing, people around her started fighting. Weary, she lay down in a pile of clothes.

"I said the hell with it, I'm just going to take a nap," she said.

For some victims the prospect of the long struggle ahead was too much to bear.

Before the storm, five condominiums made up Naranja Lakes, population 3,500, mostly retirees. Three of them died during Andrew. Hurricane experts say it was ground zero for the storm's impact.

Afterward, four condo associations reviewed the damage and voted themselves out of existence. The fifth decided to rebuild. Reconstruction took more than a year and cost half the property's value, said association president Len Anthony, 73. Had the 200 residents known that in advance, he said, they would have given up, too.

Today their condo still stands alone, surrounded by the weed-covered slabs of the others. People call it "The Dead Zone." In retrospect, Anthony said, "the county should've condemned the property and forced everybody to move."

More than 100,000 South Dade residents moved away. The migration altered the area's racial makeup, according to a Florida International University study.

Most White evacuees "found they liked where they moved better, so they sold their houses for cheap," said Lilia Cunningham, an FIU researcher. Blacks and Hispanics were more likely to rebuild or move into areas the Whites had left, FIU found.

The cul-de-sac lost several families, including the Wilsons.

For years Charles Wilson's wife, Dora, a Texas native, had tried to talk him into moving there. Wilson resisted because of his strong ties to Homestead.

But now the base was gone. The Sears where he worked was damaged. The 7-Eleven, where he had a second job, was blown to bits. And every room of his house had a quarter-inch of standing water.

"I went to bed with two jobs and a home," Wilson said. "I woke up with no jobs and a piece of a home."

Two months after the storm the Wilsons sold their $46,000 home for $15,000 and moved to El Paso.

The new residents, the Shropshire family, toiled for months to repair the house while living in a backyard trailer. They were happy to have something with walls still standing, after what Andrew did to the Leisure City home where they used to live.

During the storm "I just prayed and I prayed and I prayed and I prayed," said Pearlie Shropshire. When it was over, recalled her son Travis, "the only thing left up was the bed we was under."

✴

Rebuilding brought its own frustrations. Mary Herzog caught her contractor using debris to repair her roof instead of new lumber. The Shermans' contractor took their $15,000 and disappeared.

When then-Gov. Lawton Chiles toured South Dade a year after Andrew, one woman told him, "My contractor was on *America's Most Wanted* last night."

Contractor fraud made a long recovery even longer for some victims, said B. J. Behnken, vice president for Project Teamwork, one Andrew relief agency still at work.

"Even three or four years after the storm we still had people living in trailers behind their homes, living in sheds, living in half a home," Behnken said.

Project Teamwork has 10 houses left. "Most of them are elderly people or people with mental problems," Behnken said. "It's just a nightmare."

Some storm survivors are still battling psychological problems, the FIU study found. One boy who was 7 at the time was so traumatized that he refuses as a 17-year-old to go more than five blocks from his house, Cunningham said.

In Andrew's wake, domestic violence complaints in Dade County shot up 50 percent, divorce rates by 30 percent. FIU researchers found that many of the couples who split after the storm did so because of money— not too little, but too much.

"These marriages already were in trouble and all of a sudden they had $60,000 or $80,000," Cunningham said. "It was easier to split the money in half than to fix the marriage."

☼

Homestead's population has since rebounded to its 1992 level. Because the city had so much vacant land, developers who have run out of room elsewhere in Dade have gobbled up the cheap acreage there, even buying Naranja Lakes' empty slabs.

City officials plan to observe the 10th anniversary of Andrew's rampage with a "Celebrate Our Second Wind Music and Arts Festival," with bands, a motorcycle show and the flying of 100 kites. Some survivors wonder if it's right to celebrate such a tragedy.

"It's not really a celebration of the hurricane, but a celebration of our progress," said city spokesman Charles LaPradd. "One of the main things is to say thank you to everybody who helped us: the Salvation Army, the Red Cross, the little fire departments from the middle of nowhere that helped us rebuild."

Many of Homestead's new residents are recent arrivals in Florida who missed Andrew's fury. But some are Andrew victims at last returning home.

Charles Wilson is one. Now a widower, he moved back from Texas five months ago to a condo not far from the cul-de-sac. Yet he is still surrounded by reminders of the storm that drove him away.

"You see the water marks on all the furniture?" he asked, pointing around the room at the couch and chairs he has owned for more than 10 years.

He knows now he was wrong to try to ride out a hurricane at home. If a storm like Andrew ever returned, he said, "I'd just shut up the house, lock the doors and go."

Note: In 2004, Andrew was officially reclassified as a Category 5 storm.

49

SPRINGS OF LOVE

Tampa Bay Times, November 27, 2013

To see a Florida spring that looks the way Florida springs used to look, travel to Gilchrist County, pay $10 and walk to the end of a wooden diving dock. Then, in the words of artist Margaret Tolbert, you just "jump off into wonderland."

At Blue Springs, the water is so clear that the hundreds of turtles that call it home appear to be swimming through air. The white sand on the bottom shines like a beacon, and the current blasts up from the limestone caverns as if it were squirting from the world's biggest fire hose.

Other Florida springs are suffering from pollution, toxic algae blooms and a loss of flow, but Blue Springs has largely been spared from those woes.

Since 1958, the same family has operated Blue Springs as a private park, open to anyone with a few bucks and a swimsuit. But now they're putting it up for sale. The spring—and the 400 acres around it—can be yours for a cool $10 million.

The decision to sell Blue Springs Park wasn't an easy one, said Kim Davis and Harry "Matt" Barr, the sister and brother who inherited it earlier this year when their parents died.

After all, the spring was a gift of love—a secret love.

In the 1950s, Blue Springs belonged to a St. Petersburg business mogul named Ed C. Wright, who owned some 20,000 acres in 20 counties.

Wright, a short and solid man, had made a fortune investing in municipal bonds, railroad stock and radio stations. One newspaper story described his profession as "capitalist." He preferred "speculator." In Pinellas County alone, Wright owned the north end of Sand Key, St. Petersburg's Gateway area, half of Weedon Island and the Belleview Biltmore Hotel.

Wright's longtime secretary was a petite, reserved woman named Ruth Kirby. Around 1931, soon after Kirby's family moved down from Alabama,

At Gilchrist Blue Spring, the water is so clear that the hundreds of turtles that call it home appear to be swimming through air, and the white sand on the bottom shines like a beacon. Photo courtesy of John Moran.

Wright hired her from a secretarial pool for a day of filing papers. Then he asked the teenage girl to take a letter.

"I was scared to death," she recalled years later. But Wright was impressed by how quickly she worked and how meticulous she was. "He said he could use a girl full time, and he hired me for $9 a week."

At the time, Wright's St. Petersburg office was filled with a constant clatter: Teletype machines spitting out stock prices, Western Union machines clackety-clacking with the latest financial news, phones ringing so much that his phone bill ran to $1,000 a month.

Kirby's duties included listening in on all those calls and taking notes. Soon she was trading bonds and buying land too, and she proved to be as savvy an investor as her boss.

When a stumble on some stairs in 1969 left Wright with a serious head injury, Kirby kept a vigil at his bedside for 21 days. When he died, unmarried and childless at age 77, his will named her executor of his $50 million estate.

Suddenly Kirby—described in Wright's obituary as "his longtime personal secretary and friend"—became one of the most powerful wheeler-dealers in the state, negotiating with U.S. Steel over land for condos on Sand Key and flying to Tallahassee to pressure the governor into buying

Weedon Island. People wondered how Wright's fortune had landed in the hands of this woman with the pageboy haircut who lived in a two-story log cabin with her sisters, kept a stable of horses not far from downtown St. Petersburg and drove a gold Cadillac, but she wasn't giving interviews.

The best clue lay far to the north, in Gilchrist County. In 1958, according to Davis and Barr, Wright had given Kirby the deed to Blue Springs and all the undeveloped land around it as a gift.

An engagement gift. From the groom-to-be to his fiancée. Yet the couple never walked down the aisle.

"Four or five times they were going to get married," Barr said. "But every time he got sick or something like that."

After a while, Davis said, "they just remained companions." This sort of arrangement was never openly discussed back then, though, so in public Kirby remained a mere employee.

Kirby relished visiting the springs, Davis said, and believed others should get the same opportunity. She built the diving dock and board-walk, then charged the public just a dime for admission. The place quickly became popular with swimmers, campers and canoeists.

In the 1950s, Blue Springs belonged to a St. Petersburg business mogul named Ed C. Wright—but he gave it to his longtime secretary, Ruth Kirby, as a token of their secret love. Photo courtesy of Florida State Parks.

In 1971, she persuaded her nephew, Barr and Davis's father, to sell his Tampa moving business and move his family to Blue Springs Park to run the place. The siblings, then teens, adapted well to the change. Their after-school chores now included cleaning the park's restrooms and picking up trash, but they could also ride dirt bikes through the woods for hours.

Since Kirby's death in 1989 at age 78, her family has labored to keep the springs looking the way Great-Aunt Ruth wanted them to, Davis said.

"It's hard in this day and age to keep it natural," she said. "It's a daily struggle to protect the water and the watershed."

Thanks to those efforts, said nature photographer John Moran, as other springs have declined, "the water here still has the power to shock you with its stunning hues of electric blue."

Shortly before Davis and Barr's parents died earlier this year, they urged their children to sell the springs and get what they could for it, rather than hang onto the family heirloom any longer.

"People say it must be cool running a spring, but the trick is to never let that spring run you—and I think it's doing that," Davis said.

She said state officials have expressed an interest in buying Blue Springs but, thanks to budget cuts, they may be unable to afford its operating expenses. Tolbert and other fans of the park fear it will be sold to some heartless asphalt addict, but Davis said that won't happen.

"We're picky about that," she said. "We'd love for somebody to come in and run this place as well as it's been run up until now." After all, she pointed out, "they don't make springs like this anymore."

Note: In June 2017, the Florida Cabinet voted to buy the spring and turn it into a state park.

50

MY FLORIDA BUCKET LIST

Tampa Bay Times, December 29, 2017

Florida singer Wayne Cochran recently died at age 78. He didn't get the outpouring of grief and glowing obituaries granted to two other singers with Florida roots, Tom Petty and Gregg Allman, who died this year. But anyone who ever saw Cochran perform—or even passed him on the street—will never forget him.

Cochran was a White guy who sang get-down funk and soul in a gravelly, urgent voice while wearing outrageous outfits and a foot-high pompadour. Although his performances influenced everyone from Elvis to the Blues Brothers, his *Miami Herald* obituary noted that his hairstyle "was arguably more famous than his songs."

In recent years, following the footsteps of Al Green and Little Richard, he abandoned rock 'n' roll and joined the ministry. His church services still centered on his riveting performances.

"I believe in the power of music," he said in an interview. "If you don't want to get ecstatic, don't come to this church. There ain't no tombstones sitting in there and if they are, we're gonna resurrect them. We have a good time. We boogie."

When news of his death got out, one of my friends expressed his regret at having never seen this wild man at work.

"I wanted to see him preach," my friend said. "Best not to procrastinate on your bucket list items, I suppose."

That mournful comment sparked my imagination. A Florida bucket list! What a great idea! Florida is chock-full of wonderful things to see and experience beyond the usual theme-park fakery. Why not make a list and try to hit as many as possible?

After all, we are the Most Interesting State in the Union, a place where every day brings a fresh dose of what-the-heck. We are the place where a possum broke into a liquor store and got drunk, where a dead shark turned

Wild man Wayne Cochran was as famous for his pompadour as for his frenzied singing style. GDM Productions publicity photo, 1969.

up in a Walmart parking lot and an alligator attacked an airplane—all things that happened just this year. You can never be bored with Florida.

I quickly drew up a list and started checking off the ones I had already taken care of. Splash in the Suwannee River? Check. Marvel at the Florida Caverns near Marianna? Check. Visit the former bordello credited with giving Yeehaw Junction its name? Check. (P.S. for my wife: Please note the word "former" in there.)

I've gone on a Big Cypress Preserve swamp walk with acclaimed photographer Clyde Butcher, and squeezed into the nation's smallest post office in Ochopee (there was just enough room for me and the stamps). I've ridden an airboat through the Everglades and taken the "ghost tour" through St. Augustine.

In recent weeks I knocked off a few more. On a trip to Lakeland, I visited the campus of Florida Southern College, which has the most structures designed by Frank Lloyd Wright in one place—an even dozen. While I enjoyed strolling around the campus viewing his distinctive handiwork, what was even more enjoyable was imagining the reactions of Polk County folks in the 1940s as Wright stalked around in his ever-present cape.

Heading to the Keys this month, I drove out of my way to see my first endangered Key deer. I did so after first visiting the National Key Deer Refuge office, which happened to be in a strip mall on Big Pine Key, next door to a pack-and-ship place and a martial arts academy.

But there are oh so very many more items on my list. I want to camp overnight in the Dry Tortugas, where the stars shine so brightly because they're unimpeded by any city's artificial illumination. I want to drive on the abandoned Disney runway that has special grooves that make your tires play "When You Wish Upon a Star" when you hit 45 mph. I want to wade through the Fakahatchee Strand and see a ghost orchid in bloom.

We are about to enter a new year, full of hopes and aspirations. Traditionally this is a time for making resolutions and figuring out how to live a better life. I encourage you to start your new year by making your own Florida bucket list.

After all, with all the hurricanes, sinkholes, lightning strikes and shark bites that happen in Florida, your chances of kicking that bucket tend to be higher here than anywhere else. But at least if that happens, you can ask Wayne Cochran to sing you a song.

Note: In August 2019 I finally got to see a ghost orchid. I'm still working on some other items.

51

UNCLE CARLYLE KNEW THE WAY

St. Petersburg Times, December 9, 2001

I should've known something wasn't right as soon I saw the neatly trimmed lawn around the little whitewashed church and its modest cemetery. But I stopped the car, full of hope. Then I checked one of the headstones. Only 10 years in the ground.

Wrong cemetery.

So I pulled out my cell phone and called Uncle Carlyle, wondering if I could get service this many miles off Interstate 10. The phone rang for a while and I let it. I didn't have anything better to do, sitting on the edge of an anonymous dirt road in the middle of the North Florida woods. Besides, I figured Uncle Carlyle might take a while to hobble to the phone.

Carlyle Stewart was actually my great-uncle, my grandmother's brother. Twenty years ago, I used to see him bicycling around Pensacola, a trim, white-haired man with crinkles around his eyes from smiling so much. He usually had a striped racing cap perched on his head at a sporty angle, as if bumping along the old brick streets qualified as a leg on the Tour de France.

Over the years, whenever I came home to Pensacola for a visit, I would look him up. I might show up on his porch on a rainy afternoon, and he would invite me in, pull out his scrapbooks and spend an hour or so telling tales about our family history.

Carlyle's hobby was bicycling, but his passion was genealogy. He and my Aunt Maggie used to traipse all over the South, digging through records in tiny courthouses or slogging through weed-choked churchyards. They were determined to track the whole clan, back to the first Stewart who came over from Scotland to start a new life in the Colonies.

When Maggie got sick, Carlyle would leave her in the car with the motor running, maybe leave the heater on if the weather was cold, while he wandered around all those lonesome graveyards. After she died, he persuaded his daughter, Pat, to take Maggie's place as his companion in search of the long-ago Stewarts.

A couple of years back, on one of my visits to Carlyle, he told me about what he called "the Stewart family cemetery," where the first Stewart to settle in Florida had been buried more than a century ago. The minute I heard the story, I knew I had to see the place for myself.

The cemetery didn't have a name, Carlyle said. It was just a little place in Okaloosa County near the Yellow River, off the Hog and Hominy Road. I jotted down the directions, and the next time I was up in the Panhandle I cleared out a little time to go find the old family graves myself.

But now, looking at this Norman Rockwell version of a churchyard, I realized I had made a wrong turn somewhere and needed Carlyle to set me straight. He picked up the phone on the 14th ring. Cancer will slow anyone down, and his had messed him up to the point where he had been forced to park his bike.

We chatted a bit and then I told him where I was. He knew exactly which wrong turn I had taken and quickly told me how to get back on the right track. A few miles and a couple of turns later, I was jouncing along a washboard path cut through a pine plantation, where the spindly trees had been planted so close together that they eclipsed the afternoon sun. Beneath the boughs was a twilight so deep I turned on my headlights.

Then, suddenly, I broke into a sunny glade. In front of me was a rusted iron gate half off its hinges, and beyond that a few ragged rows of marble slabs. Any church that might have once stood alongside the graveyard was long gone, and clearly no caretaker had visited in years.

When I got out of the car, for some reason I took care not to slam the door. Somewhere nearby, a woodpecker tap-tap-tapped on a tree trunk. The only other sound came from my footsteps crunching through the underbrush.

A superstitious soul would have looked around for the wandering spirits of the blacksmiths and millwrights from Carlyle's scrapbook. But the only ghost I saw was a pale gibbous moon peeping shyly out of the blue sky. It reminded me I did not have much time left before sundown would bring the kind of total darkness you get out in the country.

So I set to work, picking my way around elaborate spider webs, checking the inscriptions on cracked headstones. One marked the grave of a Revolutionary War private. One was for a small child. Several were inscribed, "Gone, but not forgotten." The weeds told a different story.

The briefest inscriptions were done in a connect-the-dots style, clearly the work of a very determined person etching a loved one's name on the marble with just a hammer and a nail.

I thought about the perseverance it took to make a few lasting marks on a blank stone. Then I thought about the time and effort it must have taken Carlyle to track this place down. I pictured him here, peering closely at each stone, looking for the ones that said Stewart and pulling out his camera to snap photos for his scrapbooks.

Then I pictured Maggie—determined to accompany Carlyle no matter how ill she felt—sitting alone in their car, the life leaking out of her while the man she loved communed with his long-dead relatives.

At last I found the family graves Carlyle had told me about. Then, as the late afternoon shadows stretched across the uneven ground, I got into the car and headed back toward civilization. Along the way, I stopped by the Yellow River and wondered how this amber trickle had attracted those hardheaded, red-haired Stewarts so many years ago.

Logging trucks zipped by me, leaving the tangy smell of sticky pine tar lingering in their wake, and after a while I cranked up the car and followed them toward the main highway.

When I got home, I sent Carlyle a note to thank him for helping me find the old cemetery. I told him I hoped to take my son there someday, to teach him about our family history. But now I'm not sure I can do that. Carlyle died last month, and I don't know how I can find my way without him.

ACKNOWLEDGMENTS

This book you hold in your hands has only my name on it, but it's the work of dozens of others. I had help from lots of terrific editors in my 30 years at the *Times*—among them, Roy LeBlanc, John Cutter, Teresa Burney, Kim Kleman, Richard Bockman, Susan Taylor Martin, Charlotte Sutton, Tom Scherberger, Jamal Thalji and Bill Varian. I also owe a tremendous debt to scores of sharp-eyed copy desk folks who saved my butt from errors on a regular basis, not to mention ace news researcher Caryn Baird for digging out facts I needed and providing them with a winning smile. I'd also like to thank Diane Rado, my editor at the *Florida Phoenix,* Dwyer Murphy of *Crime Reads,* Dan Kos of *Slate,* and Pam Daniel and Susan Burns of *Sarasota* magazine. I am deeply indebted to John Martin for his help wrangling photos, and to my attorney Alison Steele for going above and beyond the call of duty to help me get permissions for everything. A major muchas gracias goes to Meredith Babb at the University Press of Florida for believing in this project, despite several delays. As always, though, my greatest thanks go to my wife, Sherry, forever my first reader as well as the love of my life, and to my kids, who are the reason I keep writing (otherwise how would we pay the grocery bills?).

CRAIG PITTMAN is a native Floridian and an award-winning journalist. He spent 30 years at the *Tampa Bay Times* and now writes a weekly column on environmental issues for the *Florida Phoenix*. He is the author of six books, including the *New York Times* bestseller *Oh, Florida! How America's Weirdest State Influences the Rest of the Country,* which won a gold medal from the Florida Book Awards. He is also cohost of the podcast "Welcome to Florida." In 2020, the Florida Heritage Book Festival named him a Florida Literary Legend. He lives in St. Petersburg with his wife and children.